Globalization, Southeastern Europe, and the World Economy

This book explores the key economic issues facing Southeastern Europe and Bosnia and Herzegovina, within the context of the serious challenges that the global economy has faced in recent years. It combines rigorous analysis of the issues faced by the region with a constructive approach to identifying solutions for a positive future trajectory.

The book starts by exploring the economic challenges facing the world economy both before and during the global economic crisis. The second part of the volume focuses on Southeastern Europe, and especially on the Western Balkans, assessing the best ways of achieving a positive economic future for small open economies in the region. The final part of the volume examines the economic challenges in Bosnia and Herzegovina.

One of Čaušević's main findings is his proposal for the creation of a European Union Guarantee Fund for the Western Balkans, which would guarantee long-maturity bond issues by the countries of the region, denominated in national currencies. These bond issues would be called Euro-Balkan bonds and they could be classified as financial assets with a lower degree of risk. The revenues realized would be used exclusively to finance capital projects, preferably at the cross-border level. Thus, one of the key problems facing small open economies which are not yet members of larger associations and therefore lack the backing of a supranational institution could be solved and systemic risk could be reduced, stimulating economic growth and employment.

Čaušević had also foreseen the need for a return to Keynes's thought before the crisis broke out. In his conclusion on the need for reform of the international financial system (in 2006), he stated that private institutions/entities would not be able to replace the international and national authorities in providing key financial resources for sustainable development.

Fikret Čaušević is Professor of Economics and International Finance at the Faculty of Economics, University of Sarajevo, Bosnia and Herzegovina.

Routledge studies in the European economy

1 **Growth and Crisis in the Spanish Economy, 1940–1993**
   Sima Lieberman

2 **Work and Employment in Europe**
   A new convergence?
   Edited by Peter Cressey and Bryn Jones

3 **Trans-European Telecommunication Networks**
   The challenges for industrial policy
   Colin Turner

4 **European Union – European Industrial Relations?**
   Global challenges, national developments and transnational dynamics
   Edited by Wolfgang E. Lecher and Hans-Wolfgang Platzer

5 **Governance, Industry and Labour Markets in Britain and France**
   The modernizing state in the mid-twentieth century
   Edited by Noel Whiteside and Robert Salais

6 **Labour Market Efficiency in the European Union**
   Employment protection and fixed-term contracts
   Klaus Schömann, Ralf Rogowski and Thomas Kruppe

7 **The Enlargement of the European Union**
   Issues and strategies
   Edited by Victoria Curzon-Price, Alice Landau and Richard Whitman

8 **European Trade Unions**
   Change and response
   Edited by Mike Rigby, Roger Smith and Teresa Lawlor

9 **Fiscal Federalism in the European Union**
   Edited by Amedeo Fossati and Giorgio Panella

10 **European Telecommunications Liberalisation**
   Edited by Kjell A. Eliassen and Marit Sjøvaag

11 **Integration and Transition in Europe**
   The economic geography of interaction
   Edited by George Petrakos, Gunther Maier and Grzegorz Gorzelak

12 **SMEs and European Integration**
   Internationalisation strategies
   Birgit Hegge

13 **Fiscal Federalism and European Economic Integration**
Edited by Mark Baimbridge and Philip Whyman

14 **Financial Markets in Central and Eastern Europe**
Stability and efficiency
Edited by Morten Balling, Frank Lierman and Andy Mullineux

15 **Russian Path Dependence**
Stefan Hedlund

16 **The Impact of European Integration on Regional Structural Change and Cohesion**
Edited by Christiane Krieger-Boden, Edgar Morgenroth and George Petrakos

17 **Macroeconomic Policy in the European Monetary Union**
From the old to the new stability and growth pact
Edited by Francesco Farina and Roberto Tamborini

18 **Economic Policy Proposals for Germany and Europe**
Edited by Ronald Schettkat and Jochem Langkau

19 **Competitiveness of New Europe**
Papers from the second Lancut economic forum
Edited by Jan Winiecki

20 **Deregulation and the Airline Business in Europe**
Sean Barrett

21 **Beyond Market Access for Economic Development**
EU–Africa relations in transition
Edited by Gerrit Faber and Jan Orbie

22 **International Trade, Consumer Interests and Reform of the Common Agricultural Policy**
Edited by Susan Mary Senior Nello and Pierpaolo Pierani

23 **Economic Governance in the EU**
Willem Molle

24 **Financial Integration in the European Union**
Edited by Roman Matoušek and Daniel Stavárek

25 **Europe and the Mediterranean Economy**
Edited by Joan Costa-Font

26 **The Political Economy of the European Social Model**
Philip S. Whyman, Mark J. Baimbridge and Andrew Mullen

27 **Gender and the European Labour Market**
Edited by Francesca Bettio, Janneke Plantenga and Mark Smith

28 **The Economic Crisis and Governance in the European Union**
A critical assessment
Edited by Javier Bilbao-Ubillos

29 **Competitiveness in the European Economy**
Edited by Stefan Collignon and Piero Esposito

30 **The Contradictions of Austerity**
The socio-economic costs of the neoliberal Baltic model
Edited by Jeffrey Sommers and Charles Woolfson

31 **The New Economic Governance in the Euro-Area**
Armin Steinbach

32 **The Economics of Urban Property Markets**
An institutional economics analysis
Paschalis Arvanitidis

33 **South-East Europe in Evolution**
Edited by Hardy Hanappi

34 **Designing a European Fiscal Union**
Lessons from the experience of fiscal federations
Edited by Carlo Cottarelli and Martine Guerguil

35 **Globalization, Southeastern Europe, and the World Economy**
Fikret Čaušević

Globalization, Southeastern Europe, and the World Economy

Fikret Čaušević

Taylor & Francis Group
LONDON AND NEW YORK

First published 2015 by Routledge

2 Park Square, Milton Park, Abingdon, Oxfordshire OX14 4RN
52 Vanderbilt Avenue, New York, NY 10017

Routledge is an imprint of the Taylor & Francis Group, an informa business

First issued in paperback 2020

Copyright © 2015 Fikret Čaušević

The right of Fikret Čaušević to be identified as author of this work has been asserted by him in accordance with the Copyright, Designs and Patent Act 1988.

All rights reserved. No part of this book may be reprinted or reproduced or utilised in any form or by any electronic, mechanical, or other means, now known or hereafter invented, including photocopying and recording, or in any information storage or retrieval system, without permission in writing from the publishers.

Notice:
Product or corporate names may be trademarks or registered trademarks, and are used only for identification and explanation without intent to infringe.

British Library Cataloguing in Publication Data
A catalogue record for this book is available from the British Library

Library of Congress Cataloging in Publication Data
A catalog record for this book has been requested.

ISBN: 978-1-138-83058-5 (hbk)
ISBN: 978-0-367-66897-6 (pbk)

Typeset in Times New Roman
by Wearset Ltd, Boldon, Tyne and Wear

Contents

List of figures	ix
List of tables	x
Foreword	xiii
PETER SANFEY	
Foreword	xv
MAX WATSON	

Introduction   1

PART I
Economic challenges in the world economy before and during the global financial and economic crisis   15

1. The international financial system during the great recession and its implications for a micro-state open economy in the Western Balkans   17

2. Financial liberalization, economic growth, and the need for reform of the global financial system   33

3. The international financial architecture and the global financial crisis: its causes, birth, and impact on small open economies – the case of Bosnia and Herzegovina   49

4. Market fundamentalism, religious fundamentalism, and economic growth   73

PART II
Economic challenges in Southeastern Europe and the Western Balkans: lessons learned in the first decade of the twenty-first century 83

5 What type of fiscal policy is needed to foster the economic development of the Western Balkans? 85

6 Fiscal policies in the European Union, the United States, and the Western Balkans in the age of global crisis: controlled fiscal expansion for a New Deal for the Western Balkans 91

7 Financial constraints on economic growth in Southeastern Europe 102

PART III
Economic challenges in post-Dayton Bosnia and Herzegovina 133

8 Macroeconomic management in Bosnia and Herzegovina on the road to EU accession: 1996–2006 135

9 Bosnia and Herzegovina's trade policy and competitiveness, 1996–2008: a policy brief 157

10 Economic perspectives on Bosnia and Herzegovina in the period of global crisis 166

Index 180

Figures

1.1	Notional value of OTC traded contracts in financial derivatives	24
3.1	The United States' and Japan's share in world GDP	50
3.2	Brazil, Russia, India, and China's share in world GDP	51
7.1	Change in ranking and GNI per capita of the Western Balkan countries, 2008–2012	108
7.2	Change in GDP per capita in SEE countries, 2001–2010	109
7.3	Current account balances of SEE countries, 2004–2010	110
7.4	Credit activity in Albania and FYR Macedonia, 2005–2010	116
7.5	Credit activity in Bosnia and Herzegovina, and Montenegro, 2005–2010	117
8.1	Change in the level of relative economic positions of the Former Yugoslav republics in relation to their economic position in 1991	138
8.2	Employment and unemployment in Bosnia and Herzegovina, 2000–2006	148
10.1	Percentage change in credit activity and assets, and nominal GDP growth rates (year-on-year): Bosnia and Herzegovina, 2005–2011	168
10.2	Foreign assets, foreign liabilities, and net foreign liabilities of commercial banks in Bosnia and Herzegovina, 2008–2011	169
10.3	Deposits of commercial banks in Bosnia and Herzegovina, 2008–2011	170
10.4	Change in total deposits and net foreign liabilities of commercial banks in Bosnia and Herzegovina	170
10.5	Exports, imports and trade balance of Bosnia and Herzegovina	171

Tables

1.1	World foreign exchange reserves	18
1.2	The foreign exchange reserves of developed and developing countries	19
1.3	The US Federal Reserve System balance sheet	20
1.4	Total assets of the euro system	21
1.5	Total assets of the five largest banks in France, Germany, and Italy	22
1.6	Total foreign claims of international banks, 2000–2012	25
1.7	Ten largest banks in the world, June 2012	26
1.8	Debts of certain Euro-zone and Western Balkan countries, September 2013	27
1.9	Lending by banks in Bosnia and Herzegovina	29
1.10	Debt and deposits of the governments of the Federation of Bosnia and Herzegovina and the Republika Srpska to the Bosnian banking sector	31
2.1	Market capitalization on major world capital markets	34
2.2	Change in the wealth coefficients of the fastest growing economies, 1990–2004	36
2.3	External equilibrium of the fastest growing economies, 1990–2004	37
2.4	Twenty fastest growing economies, 1990–1998–2004	38
2.5	Vulnerability indicators of transition countries	40
2.6	Gross domestic product: G-7 and world	42
2.7	Gross domestic product by region	44
2.8	External debt of developing countries	45
3.1	Changes in the importance of the major world economies, measured by the wealth coefficient	50
3.2	Changes in Brazil, Russia, India, and China's relative importance in the world economy, measured by the wealth coefficient	51
3.3	GDP for the G-7, G-4, and the world	52
3.4	Trade and current account balances of the G-7 in 2008	52
3.5	The current account balances and foreign exchange reserves of the fastest growing developing countries	53

3.6	Net savings in the United States, 1984–2007	55
3.7	The quota distribution at the International Monetary Fund in the first half of 2007	58
3.8	The notional value of derivative contracts on the over-the-counter market	65
3.9	Lending to businesses and households in Bosnia and Herzegovina	67
3.10	The balance and volume of trade in Bosnia and Herzegovina, 2000–2007	68
7.1	Ease of doing business and gross national income per capita	102
7.2	Doing business in FYR Macedonia	103
7.3	Doing business in Montenegro	103
7.4	Doing business in Croatia	104
7.5	Doing business in Albania	104
7.6	Doing business in Serbia	105
7.7	Doing business in Bosnia and Herzegovina	105
7.8	Doing business in Bulgaria	106
7.9	Doing business in Romania	106
7.10	Doing business in Greece	107
7.11	Doing business in Turkey	108
7.12	Competitiveness of SEE countries: ranking of Southeastern European countries in the *Global Competitiveness Report*	111
7.13	The most problematic factors for doing business in Albania, Bosnia and Herzegovina, and Croatia	112
7.14	The most problematic factors for doing business in Macedonia FYR, Montenegro, and Serbia	113
7.15	The most problematic factors for doing business in Bulgaria and Romania	114
7.16	The most problematic factors for doing business in Greece and Turkey	115
7.17	Credit to the private sector in Southeastern Europe	118
7.18	Current account balance, real GDP growth, and credit growth in SEE countries	120
7.19	The external debt to GDP ratio of Southeastern European countries	123
7.20	Percentage change in the level of indebtedness of SEE countries	124
7.21	Projected payments to the IMF based on existing use of resources and present holdings of SDRs	124
7.22	Foreign direct investment in SEE	126
8.1	Gross domestic product – Bosnia and Herzegovina, 1991–2006	137
8.2	Sectoral distribution of GDP in Bosnia and Herzegovina, 1999–2001	139
8.3	Sectoral distribution of GDP in Bosnia and Herzegovina, 2002–2004	141

Tables

8.4	Biggest exporters in Bosnia and Herzegovina, 1999–2004	142
8.5	Growth rates of the business sector in Bosnia and Herzegovina, 1999–2004	144
8.6	Ratio of the growth of banking sector assets and GDP growth	147
8.7	Breakdown of formal employment in Bosnia and Herzegovina	149
8.8	Breakdown of population, employment, and unemployment by canton and region, in accordance with ILO standards (including employment on informal labour markets), June 2005	150
8.9	Current account and trade balances of the SEE countries, 2004	152
8.10	Foreign debt of the SEE countries, 2004	152
8.11	Foreign debt and gross domestic product of the SEE countries, 1999 and 2004	153
10.1	Consolidated budget balances of Western Balkan countries	172
10.2	Total budget expenditures of Western Balkan countries	172
10.3	Fiscal balance of general government in Bosnia and Herzegovina	173
10.4	Projected payments to the IMF based on existing use of resources and present holdings of SDRs	174
10.5	State-owned capital in the four largest companies in the Federation of Bosnia and Herzegovina	175

Foreword

Peter Sanfey

Fikret Čaušević has established himself as one of Bosnia and Herzegovina's leading academic economists and thinkers, and this collection of papers is timely and welcome. I have known Fikret for some years and have come to value greatly his deep knowledge and understanding of the fundamental issues facing the Bosnian and regional economies, as well as his insights into the global economy and how it has evolved in recent years. All of these attributes are on display in the present volume, which combines an impressive breadth of facts with in-depth analysis that is hard to find elsewhere. The papers are all eminently readable, as well as being highly relevant in the difficult circumstances in which Bosnia and Herzegovina finds itself, as of early 2014.

The book is divided into three parts. The first part looks at the economic challenges facing the world economy both before and during the global economic crisis that shook the world in 2008–2009, the effects of which are still being felt today. The second part focuses on Southeastern Europe, and especially the Western Balkans. Lastly, the third part of the volume examines the economic challenges in Bosnia and Herzegovina. This structure of the book works well in my view, by taking the reader from the general to the more specific. Very often, Bosnia and Herzegovina is regarded as a special case, and indeed it is rather special in some important ways, but it is also part of the regional and global economies and it is important to see it in that context.

I believe the book has three main selling points. The first is the comprehensive attention Fikret pays to the Bosnian economy – its structure, problems, and potential. From many years of following Bosnia and Herzegovina and visiting the country, I know all too well how difficult it can be to get any kind of reliable and informed analysis of the way the country functions in the economic sphere. Even the most basic data can be hard to find. Very often, the lazy assumption is made abroad that, because the institutional structure of Bosnia is so complex and the data are questionable or non-existent, the economy must therefore be some kind of basket case. In fact, as Fikret shows quite clearly, the Bosnian economy is full of potential. Fikret's analysis of the industrial structure of Bosnia demonstrates the potential growth drivers in sectors such as wood processing, mining, agriculture, and tourism. The constraints to growth are well explained throughout the volume but some businesses and foreign investors have learned to cope with these and even thrive in difficult circumstances.

The second valuable feature of the volume is the detailed comparison that is drawn throughout with other Western Balkan countries. Bosnia and Herzegovina is a small, open economy and its economic fortunes are increasingly tied in with those of the neighbourhood. The legacy of the terrible war in 1992–1995 is still being felt, and Fikret reminds us of this with some of the statistics on war fatalities and war-related emigration. One legacy has been a level of intraregional trade and investment that is below what might be expected, given the close proximity of these different economies. But this is starting to change in a very positive way. Regional cooperation in the Western Balkans, which the international community tried to impose in a rather heavy-handed way 10–15 years ago, is actually emerging as a natural force and as a conscious choice of the countries themselves. This point was vividly illustrated on 24 February 2014, when all seven prime ministers of the region attended and spoke at an investor conference for the Western Balkans, in front of about 500 (mostly business) people, at the headquarters of the European Bank for Reconstruction and Development (EBRD) in London.

The third selling point is the strong focus on policy implications. The book contains clear and sensible recommendations, based on an analysis and understanding of the factors that are holding back the development of the Bosnian and regional economy. Perhaps the most interesting and controversial suggestion, outlined more than once in the volume, is for the introduction of 'Euro-Balkan bonds', namely, bonds that would be issued by governments in the Western Balkans but covered by a guarantee fund established by the European Union and perhaps international financial institutions such as the EBRD and the European Investment Bank. The proceeds of these bonds would be used for regional infrastructure projects that boost the region's competitiveness and growth prospects. In order to attract private finance, priority would be given to projects that have a public–private partnership element. Although this idea has not yet gained support from the international community, there are elements of this approach in current thinking about, and projects in, this region. Notably, the Western Balkan Investment Framework is now an important vehicle for coordinating international financial institutions (IFI) and bilateral assistance and investments and, to some extent, is working towards the achievement of the goals that Fikret identifies in this volume.

In conclusion, I hope that this volume reaches a wide audience, not only in Bosnia and Herzegovina but also elsewhere, because the messages contained within are important and deserve to be heard. Too often, the debate about this country and the wider Western Balkan region is couched in overly negative terms, creating a serious image problem for the region. Fikret has managed to combine rigorous analysis of the main issues with a constructive and even optimistic approach to identifying solutions and a better way ahead. The more people can follow this approach, the better the prospects for sustainable growth and a bright future – for Bosnia and Herzegovina and for its neighbours.

Dr Peter Sanfey
Deputy Director, Country Strategy and Policy
European Bank for Reconstruction and Development

Foreword

Max Watson

Who better than Fikret Čaušević to draw together the national, regional, and global story that is told in this book? The approach he adopts is both analytic and policy-oriented, befitting his dual role as an academic thinker and as a seasoned contributor to the work of the Central Bank of Bosnia and Herzegovina. This twin experience has led him to confront some of the key economic dilemmas our societies face – avoiding overreliance on purely theoretical models, whose limitations in handling real-world problems he has had to live with, as a policy thinker, day by day.

A very strong thematic unity thus links the essays presented here and makes this much more than a rich description of Bosnia and its economic environment. The unifying perspective is one that both accepts and questions the market system in which emerging and developing countries are seeking, today, to catch up with the living standards of advanced economies. One is tempted to think of the English novelist Charles Dickens, describing the world of the French Revolution, which also seemed so full of new promise yet so replete with hazards: 'It was the best of times, the worst of times.'

This said, the critique of today's economic system (or non-system) in Fikret Čaušević's work is devoid of nostalgia. The political history and economic context of Southeastern Europe discourages sentimentality in that regard. In a sense, his call is not to unwind economic liberalization but to go further – identifying its dilemmas with greater intellectual honesty and trying to develop syntheses that unlock the benefits of the marketplace without discarding the guiding hand of the state.

Perhaps the most succinct way of conveying this vision is to highlight three of the main themes that run through the essays and which have high relevance at the different levels – national, regional, and global – that are discussed.

- How can the international financial architecture better support national policy-makers as they struggle with these tasks? The liberalization of the past three decades has been associated with an expansion of debt-financed imbalances at the global and regional level, and these imbalances have proved vulnerable to delayed and sometimes savage reversals of risk-preferences among private portfolio-holders. Market discipline appears in need not of replacement but of modulating by global surveillance to mitigate these storms in which small economies are at risk of being buffeted.

- Pending a more stable financial architecture at the global level, how can members of economic regions – such as Europe, and in particular Southeastern Europe – better associate themselves to foster productive investment, thus laying (among other things) the infrastructure links that are crucial to build a more productive and better integrated economy? Can they share and thus mitigate the risk for investors in such investment?
- Amid financial markets that seem myopic and economic policies at the global level that have been failing to embed stability, what strategies can national policy-makers adopt in a small and open economy? More modernization, indeed more integration, is seen as essential to achieve economic catch-up. But integration entails automatically a greater interdependence and – in volatile times – vulnerability. There is a delicate challenge of assuring prudent macroeconomic policies yet crafting sufficient fiscal space for the state to be able to support more rapid restructuring and to foster the working population's technical expertise. Čaušević notes that Keynes, since 2008, has been rediscovered – but these are challenges that he only partly answered as they are posed in a world of ever-deeper integration, huge private portfolios, and totally free capital flows.

These issues are all highly pertinent in Southeastern Europe today. The past decade, with security problems stabilized, saw a period of quite strong growth that encouraged observers to consider that the region has at last embarked on a process of sustained catching-up with the living standards of the core EU states. But, as becomes clear in the chapters that follow, the global setting of very low interest rates and risk premia during much of that decade, in a regional context of lagging structural reforms, led to a pattern of economic growth that was not to prove sustainable. It relied too heavily on mortgage and other household spending, financed by cross-border loan flows. It was thus triply vulnerable to the global recession that followed – seeking to reorient growth patterns in a sluggish global economy, fighting the headwinds of euro area deleveraging, and wrestling with overstretched domestic balance sheets. In a hazardous global environment, structural and fiscal weaknesses at the level of national policies had heightened the region's vulnerability. Efforts are now underway to achieve a more outward-looking growth model, and these can by strongly enhanced, if regional economic cooperation in Southeastern Europe moves to a new and higher level.

Such themes, at the stage of policy development in the region today, are best conceived as questions that can only be partially answered. And indeed this book is not a compendium of easy answers. Specific policy suggestions are certainly made along the way – for example, cooperative solutions to improving investment financing. But these answers, stimulating though they are, are not the point of the book. Nor is the impressive wealth of information about the wider context in which Bosnia's policy-makers have to shape a better future. Rather, the role of this volume is to leave the reader more critical; more aware of linkages (both intellectual and real); and ultimately more ambitious for what economics can deliver in today's world.

Max Watson
Visiting Fellow at Southeastern European Studies at Oxford (SEESOX),
St Antony's College, University of Oxford

Introduction

This book contains a collection of selected texts written between 2003 and 2013 on problems emerging in the world of global finance, the changing relations of economic power due to financial liberalization and deregulation since the 1980s, the global economic crisis of 2008, the greatest financial and economic shock to date, as well as on the impact of transition on the countries of Southeastern Europe and the Western Balkans.[1] The book is in three parts. In the first part, there are four texts presenting an analysis of economic challenges at the global level, starting from the impact of financial liberalization on the effectiveness of economic policy during the final two decades of the last century and working our way through the problems and challenges facing reform of the international financial system during the period both before and after the global financial crisis of 2008, up to the present day. The second part of the book focuses on the results of transition in the countries of Southeastern Europe and the Western Balkans during the last two decades and some possible paths towards economic and financial integration in the region. The third part of the book comprises three texts dealing with the challenges of transition as experienced by Bosnia and Herzegovina, as a small, open, post-conflict country in transition.

In contrast to the final two decades of the twentieth century, in which the G-7 countries' share in world GDP increased from approximately 55 per cent in 1980 to 62.5 per cent in 2000,[2] during the first 13 years of the twenty-first century, it was, according to the International Monetary Fund, the developing countries that boosted their foreign exchange reserves from $718 billion to $7,856 billion, some 994 per cent. Over the same period, the developed countries only increased their foreign exchange reserves from $1,213 billion to $3,817 billion, or 214 per cent.[3] Consequently, during the first five years of this century, developing countries had greater foreign exchange reserves than developed countries for the first time since World War II. This difference grew over the next eight years to form a ratio of two to one in favour of the developing countries. According to World Bank data, the share in world GDP of the four large economies popularly known as the BRIC countries (Brazil, Russia, India, and China) rose over the first 12 years of this century from 8 per cent to 19.8 per cent.[4] The US and Japan's share in world GDP declined, over the same period, from 45.2 per cent to 30.6 per cent, while that of the G-7 overall fell from the already mentioned 62.5 per cent to 47.5 per cent.[5]

The first essay in the book presents an analysis of changes in monetary and fiscal policy in the most developed countries and, more particularly, changes in the monetary policy of the United States and the Euro-zone countries in response to the global financial crisis of 2008. Financial expansion in the US from 2002 to 2007 had reduced the rate of unemployment to close to the level of the last two years (1999–2000) of the Clinton administration. Under his administration and, particularly, in his second mandate, economic and employment growth were driven by changes in the productivity of the telecommunications sector, media, and new technologies, combined with a financial bubble in the shares of companies in those sectors. Under the Bush administration, by contrast, employment growth was primarily based on the property sector and associated financial assets developed during that period, which played a major role in creating the financial bubble on the over-the-counter (OTC) markets. There was a spectacular rise in trading in OTC market financial derivatives as a direct consequence of market deregulation, thanks to repeal of the Glass–Steagall Act (1999) and passage of the Commodity Futures Modernization Act (2000), which reduced the supervisory role of the US Securities and Exchange Commission (SEC) very significantly, compared to the final two decades of the twentieth century. As a consequence of passage of this law and the almost complete deregulation of the OTC markets, the notional value of OTC contracts grew from $98.5 trillion to $668 trillion in just the first seven and a half years of this century (2000–June 2008).[6]

The second essay, on the theme of financial deregulation and liberalization's impact on economic sovereignty and the effectiveness of economic policy in a world of globally integrated capital flows, was originally published as the conclusion to my book *Economic Sovereignty and Global Capital Flows*,[7] referenced at a number of places in the various papers collected in this volume and which reviewed the experiences of 124 countries around the world between 1980 and 2004. The theoretical debate on the effects of financial liberalization was initiated by the works of Ronald McKinnon and Edward Shaw.[8] This pair of authors published, independently of each other, works whose basic hypothesis was that economies in which there is financial repression or where the state imposes ceilings on the interest rate on savings and deposits and exercises control over to what industries and under what conditions the banking sector will extend credit necessarily face problems of insufficient savings, declining investment, and declining employment. In other words, both authors came to the conclusion that measures of financial deregulation and liberalization, removing the ceiling on interest rates on savings and deposits, were required to allow savings growth in the economy (through higher interest rates and a higher return on savings) and, so, higher levels of investment, as the fundamental precondition for economic growth and for attaining or maintaining full employment.

At the beginning of the 1980s, or more precisely from 1980 to 1986, the Reagan administration lifted all caps on interest rates at all deposit institutions in the US financial sector. The most important measures were taken in 1982. In Great Britain, Margaret Thatcher's government implemented the famous Big

Bang reforms in the City of London (1986), removing all restrictions on the free setting of interest rates, as well as any restrictions on fees for brokerages and dealer services, restoring London to its status as the main global centre of international finance.[9] During the 1970s, in the United States, the Chicago Board Options Exchange (CBOE) had introduced certain financial innovations (options, futures, and options on futures), while it was the World Bank itself that introduced swap contracts. These financial innovations became dominant, as the market in them grew strongly during the 1980s and 1990s, while in the first eight years of this century there was huge growth in trade in derivatives contracts, as a result of the almost complete deregulation of these markets, culminating in the passage of the Dodd–Frank Act (2010). In other words, financial liberalization opened up room for internationally active global financial institutions to expand their operations to practically every continent and, at the beginning of this century, to apply risk management models based on their own internal ratings.

Under McKinnon and Shaw's theses, financial liberalization should have led to a significant growth in savings in the financially most liberal and most sophisticated environments. Between 1982 and 2013, however, the two financially most sophisticated and most liberal economies, the United States and Great Britain, became importers of capital. Both economies managed, through the implementation of key measures of financial liberalization, to attract savings not only from residents, but also in large numbers from abroad. Net savings, measured as a percentage of GDP, in the United States, during the period in question, were negative, moving from an average of about –2.2 per cent of GDP in the 1980s, through to –3 per cent in the 1990s, and reaching –6.2 per cent of GDP in 2007.[10] Analysing the structure of the global financial system, Joseph Stiglitz pointed out that one of its fundamental paradoxes had to do with international capital flows. Thus, according to him, money had not been moving from the most developed countries towards developing and poor countries but the opposite:

> The global financial system is not working well, and it is especially not working well for developing countries. Money is flowing uphill, from the poor to the rich. The richest country in the world, the United States, seemingly cannot live within its means, borrowing $2 billion a day from poorer countries.[11]

These trends raised questions regarding the sustainability of the US dollar as the main world reserve currency, given that the economy whose currency fulfils that role should be cutting rather than increasing its external debt, or at least maintaining it at a level which is sustainable in the mid-to-longer term. The issue of the sustainability of the rising US trade deficit over the first seven years of this century and the consequent growth of US foreign debt was intensively discussed between 2003 and 2007. I present one of the approaches to analysing the sustainability of the US deficit, based on the work of Michael Mussa and Yoshitomi, in the third essay in this book. This text was written in November and

4 Introduction

December of 2008 and presents an analysis of the possible impact on small open economies of changes in the world of global finance during the pre-crisis period and in the initial phase of the global financial crisis.

The effects of the financial liberalization and globalization were intensively discussed in a large number of academic articles, published over the last decade of the twentieth and the first decade of the twenty-first century. Maurice Obstfeld and Alan Taylor[12] published a study in April 2002 of the effects of financial globalization. They had previously presented their conclusions at a conference in May 2001. Comparing the effects of the first (1870–1914) and second financial globalization (1970–2000), the authors concluded that global financial flows during the period of the first globalization had been away from developed towards developing countries, while in the 1970 to 2000 period the opposite had been the case, with more than three quarters of financial resources flowing from rich to rich:

> Globalized capital markets are back, but with a difference: capital transactions seem to be mostly a rich-rich affair, a process of 'diversification finance' rather than 'development finance'. The creditor-debtor country pairs involved are more rich-rich than rich-poor, and today's foreign investment in the poorest developing countries lags far behind the levels attained at the start of the last century.[13]

On the other hand, Kose, Prasad, Rogoff, and Wei have shown that financial globalization does not diminish the development opportunities of developing countries: 'there is little systematic evidence to support widely cited claims that financial globalization by itself leads to deeper and more costly developing country growth crises'.[14] Nonetheless, their fundamental conclusion is that the effects of financial globalization must be analysed within the new context where institutional stability and approaches to reform play a greater role. In one of the most detailed analyses of the impact of financial globalization on economic growth, William Cline notes:

> The general trend toward greater growth contributions associated with general increases in financial openness ... suggest that it is important to global growth to preserve the degree of financial globalization that has been achieved, despite likely new fears and doubts raised by the financial crisis of 2007–09.[15]

One of the most important issues regarding the place and the role of the state in the economy arises out of the predominant theoretical construction of the new classical economists, or rather the advocates of the rational expectations hypothesis and the real business cycle theorists. For them, economic policy measures can have no significant impact on the direction of the business cycle, because, given rational behaviour on the part of market actors and public access to all the information required to assess the government's economic policy and the business policies of companies, liberalized markets are inherently capable of maintaining equilibrium, which is to say employment at the level of full employment. On such views, there is no room for government involvement in macroeconomic management.

These theoretical propositions were, however, significantly out of step with events on financial markets in the late 1980s and 1990s, as well as in the first decade of the current century. In October 1987, the Dow Jones Industrial Average on the New York Stock Exchange fell 22.6 per cent in just one day. This was the largest fall since the Great Depression. Even though the fall was temporary in character and caused no major disturbance to either the US or the global economy, financial shocks would not be an exception in the years to follow. In October 1989, a period of steeply rising property and share prices ended in Japan. After this period, there followed 'a great implosion' in property and securities prices in the country, which was the basic cause behind the great stagnation of the 1990s. The next major shock came with the Mexican crisis in 1994, which was followed by an even greater financial crisis in the countries of Southeast Asia in 1997 and 1998. In the second half of 1998, a new financial shock hit Russia, whose markets for government bonds were host to a number of financial investors, including the best-known hedge funds of the day.

The story of the de facto bankruptcy of the Long Term Capital Management (LTCM) hedge fund was particularly instructive. The fund was partly owned by Myron Scholes and its portfolio management strategy was based on his famous formula for determining the prices of financial options. Only a year earlier (1997), Scholes had won the Nobel prize for economics. In an interview he gave after the de facto bankruptcy of LTCM, he admitted that he had not himself been in a position to predict how financial globalization would affect the growth of global systemic risk and that such events would likely lead to more frequent crises of a sort that he had not built into his models.[16] Two more disasters took place before the onset of the global financial crisis in 2008: the first was in Brazil in 1999, the second the implosion of the financial bubble in share prices in the US (the dot-com bubble), starting in the second half of 2000. These increasingly frequent episodes of financial crisis went against the basic tenet that financial liberalization would lead to increased efficiency and better functioning national and global financial markets, and so to a broadening of the field of choice for investing financial assets and therefore more successful risk management, by restructuring the portfolios of the globally most important private financial institutions.

The results of the above-mentioned study into the sample of 124 countries worldwide covering the period from 1980 to 2000 showed that three of the fastest growing economies in the world over that period (South Korea, China, Ireland) applied different combinations when it came to their economic policy and that South Korea and China had attained very high rates of growth at times when both countries retained elements of financial repression, including control over short-term capital flows. In addition to such control, throughout the period in question and since (that is up to and including the point at which the present was being written in June 2014), China has retained majority ownership over its banking sector. That is, the group of the ten largest banks in the country includes banks in which the state has majority or even 100 per cent ownership. Nonetheless, the key factors in the sharp rise of China's export capabilities were unrelated to its relative closure to financial flows. Rather, they were due to a 'phased' opening up to capital flows through export-oriented foreign direct investment.

The example of Ireland, the third fastest growing economy in the world between 1980 and 2000, shows that more developed small open economies, which are members of major economic integration (in this case, the EU), pursuing integration on the basis of financial liberalization with regard to both short and long-term capital flows can attain very fast growth, but the resulting absence of control over speculation can lead to banking sector crisis and a need for recapitalization of banks. Moreover, the main player in any such recapitalization, as the public debt crisis in the EU has shown, will be the state itself. Irish public debt grew, for precisely these reasons, between 2007 and 2013, from 25 per cent to 124 per cent of GDP.[17]

In the conclusions to the second essay in this book, I present my own view of the prospects for developing global finances and global institutions for managing them:

> The processes of financial liberalization and globalization raise the fundamental issue of future development: If John Maynard Keynes' fundamental revolution in economics, the introduction of economic policy as targeted intervention by the relevant government bodies to influence the direction of the business cycle, arose out of a need to prevent growing unemployment, a sharp drop in demand, and the phenomenon of widespread poverty, who are the main agents of economic development at the national and supra-national levels who will prevent the continued differentiation and increasing gap between the developed and the underdeveloped nations?[18]

In attempting to answer this fundamental question, my conclusion was that:

> Transferring some part of government spending to corporate budgets reduces the profit potential of the companies and would be on a collision course with the nature of the corporate form of business organization and the growing importance and role of financial markets in managing business cycles.... The role of the international institutions will therefore remain irreplaceable, alongside that of strengthening government institutional capacity to stimulate development and reduce the major disparities in the world.[19]

The events that followed the publication of my book in 2006 have confirmed these conclusions. During the period of global financial crisis from 2008 to 2009, there was a steep fall in the business cycle in the major world economies that could not be dealt with except through major financial assistance packages which the governments of those countries and the major global financial institutions secured. The crisis in public debt and major problems recapitalizing the largest banks in the European Union, and, more particularly, Euro-zone countries, were dealt with by coordinated intervention on the part of national governments and through the establishment of joint mechanisms to save the financial system, like the European Stabilization Mechanism (ESM), and its antecedent, the European Financial Stability Facility (EFSF). Add to this rapid intervention by the IMF, with an increase in its credit lines from SDR250 billion to SDR750 billion[20] and an increase of SDR182.7 billion in SDR distributed during 2009, it becomes clearer that the global crisis could not have been settled without the intervention of national governments, in cooperation with the international financial institutions. US public debt rose by $6,240 billion between 2008 and 2013,[21] while the Fed assets grew from $992 billion in mid-September 2008 to approximately $4,160 billion[22] in the first quarter of 2014. This series of actions confirmed that the global crisis could not be settled without organized and coordinated action on the part of the governments of the major world economies. From a theoretical perspective, these interventions represented a return to the original teachings of John Maynard Keynes, as contained in *The General Theory of Employment, Interest and Money*, at once that author's most important work and the most important work in economic science of the last century.

The fourth chapter in this collection is a text presented at a conference on Unity and Plurality in Europe, organized by International Forum Bosnia in Mostar in August 2008. The text provides an analysis of certain important problems regarding economic policy-making, and policy-making more generally, under conditions where market fundamentalism, on the one hand, faces off against religious fundamentalism, on the other. Taking as my starting point the views of George Soros, as presented in his book on *The Crisis of Global Capitalism*,[23] namely that market fundamentalism is a major threat to the future of open societies, I develop an analysis of how economic, political, social, and religious factors interact and of their impact on the sustainability of economic growth. In his book, Soros pointed out that rapidly implemented deregulation of world financial markets without appropriate institutions for the management of the world economy at the international level became a major threat to the sustainability of the world economy. Soros even claims that the current global capitalist system is a deformation of the open society. According to his view, the problem could be corrected for or avoided more successfully if the principles of the open society were better understood. Similar views are presented in the books *Globalization and Its Discontents*[24] and *Making Globalization Work*[25] by one of the most prominent economists in the world – Joseph Stiglitz. In his two books, Stiglitz stresses that economic globalization has outpaced political globalization and that this represents a major problem for the coordination and management of the world we live in. I conclude this chapter by looking at the approach proposed by Neil Fligstein in his *The Architecture of Markets – An Economic Sociology of Twenty-First Century Capitalist Societies*.[26] Analysing the market structure of the most important world economies in the final two decades of the previous century, drawing on the analysis of the real importance of governments, companies, trade unions, legal systems, and cultural traditions in the world's most important economies, Fligstein concludes that both neoliberal and the neo-Marxist approaches of looking at globalization are mistaken and do not correspond to reality.

The second and third parts of the book contain texts about Southeastern Europe, the Western Balkans, and Bosnia and Herzegovina. The economic challenges facing the countries of Southeastern Europe and the Western Balkans are presented in three texts, the first and second of which (Chapters 5 and 6) are dedicated to reviewing the fiscal standing of those countries, while the third (Chapter 7) was previously published as a chapter in *Defining a New Reform Agenda – Paths to Sustainable Convergence in South East Europe*.[27] The Western Balkan region, not including Albania, is essentially made up of the countries of the former Yugoslavia. The wars in the former Yugoslavia, between 1992 and 2000, the longest and most severe of which was in Bosnia and Herzegovina, produced a severe level of destruction. The losses in terms of human capital include, according to various sources, anything from 150,000 to 200,000 dead, and some 350,000 disabled veterans and civilians. The number of refugees in countries around the world reached nearly 1.5 million, while lost GDP was approximately equal to twice the GDP of the former Yugoslavia in 1990: its GDP in that year was $55 billion. The destruction of physical capital in Bosnia and Herzegovina alone has been estimated by the Chamber of Commerce at $35–$40 billion (1996 US$). While the region has received significant assistance from abroad, its main loss, that of human capital, can never be compensated for. Funds for civilian and military victims of the war (the war disabled) are financed out of the national budgets of the Western Balkan countries (excluding Albania), and the countries with the largest fiscal burden of this type are Bosnia and Herzegovina and Croatia.

And so it was that the countries of the Western Balkans (with the exception of Albania) began transition under considerably less favourable conditions than other regions with countries in transition (Central Europe, Eastern Europe, the Commonwealth of Independent States). On the other hand, again with the exception of Albania, the countries of the Western Balkans were constituent parts of the former Yugoslavia, whose economy had been mixed – developed at least in part on market principles since the 1950s, and particularly between 1965 and 1990. Many companies from the former Yugoslavia had, during the 1970s and 1980s, experienced a certain degree of success in Western European and US markets, while the transfer of technical knowledge based on joint ventures of the former Yugoslav companies with German, Austrian, Italian, and even in certain cases US companies had been a key source of development for domestic capacity in companies from the area of the former Yugoslavia in the car, metal processing, chemicals and pharmaceuticals, and wood processing industries. This knowledge attained during the pre-war period represented, in combination with the process of privatization in transition, a basic factor in attracting foreign direct investors to the countries of the former Yugoslavia. Nonetheless, some of the key problems affecting the countries of the Western Balkans during the first decade of the current century were related to the interruption of previously existing common production chains based on clusters, or on the breaking up of the markets, and the domination of political and economic elites created during and immediately after the wars that took place across the former Yugoslavia.

Although the region of the Western Balkans, again with the exception of Albania, thus found itself in a very difficult starting position for transition, the market expertise attained in the pre-war period and an associated capacity for rapid learning and for adopting market and technological knowledge allowed the region to implement financial liberalization relatively quickly (all the countries of the Western Balkans had current account convertibility by 2002), including banking sector privatization and liberalization of the foreign direct investment regime, so that their banking sectors were soon under the majority control of foreign banks (Western European banks from Austria, Italy, France, Slovenia, and Germany). Such a train of developments facilitated a sharp expansion in credit between 2004 and 2008, producing dynamic economic growth and reduced unemployment, but also a marked rise in external debt, particularly for Croatia and Montenegro. In the fifth and sixth chapters, entitled respectively 'What type of fiscal policy is needed to foster the economic development of the Western Balkans?' and 'Fiscal policies in the European Union, the United States, and the Western Balkans in the age of global crisis: controlled fiscal expansion for a New Deal for the Western Balkans', I present my own proposals on how to develop economic and financial linkages across the region.

My proposal for developing capital markets by issuing bonds I call Euro-Balkan bonds is based, in theoretical terms, on Markowitz's portfolio theory and the capital market theory developed by Treynor, Sharpe, and Lintner, on the one hand, and on Keynes' recommendations as set out in *The General Theory*, which, as already noted, have been widely used in the major world economies as a key instrument for managing exit from the global crisis of 2008. The analysis of the fiscal balance of the Western Balkan countries in the pre-crisis period of 2002 to 2008 presented in these papers reveals that, in spite of their significant handicap when embarking upon transition, as a result of the aforementioned higher fiscal spending due to wartime losses, the countries of the region in fact showed greater fiscal discipline than the countries of the Southern Euro-zone or indeed those of Central Europe. On the other hand, the relatively low budget deficits and public debts during that period were facilitated by the expansion of domestic demand and economic growth based on that expansion, the key source being the sharp rise in bank lending. The subsequent sharp fall in lending between 2009 and 2012 was the key reason for the decline in economic activity and fiscal capacity, producing recession in 2009 in all the countries of the Western Balkans, again excepting Albania. Indeed, despite the fact that in 2013 Croatia was the first country in the Western Balkans to become a member of the EU, the country had in the five years previous (2009–2013) been in recession. Thus, the decline in lending was a key reason for falling domestic demand, economic stagnation, and the fall in fiscal revenues, with fiscal expenditures not falling by the same rate at the same time. Consequently, access to financing became the dominant problem for business in the countries of Southeastern Europe, as argued in the seventh chapter, 'Financial constraints on economic development in Southeastern Europe'.

It was under these circumstances that I developed my proposal, first presented at a conference in Dijon in May 2010 and then reworked as a text published in Oxford. The fundamental thesis was that, since the small open economies of the Western Balkans had very limited scope for action based on monetary policy (as, under the Mundell–Fleming model, monetary policy, and indeed exchange rate policy, represented for them passive elements of economic policy), their only way out of economic crisis lay in fiscal policy, as in essence the only active economic policy instrument available to them. Stimulating economic growth during a period of crisis through expansionary fiscal policy, directed at financing capital projects, in the form of public–private partnerships investing in infrastructure or investment in developing business clusters at the cross-border level, presupposes a growth in public debt, based on bond issues to finance spending on cross-border projects in the Western Balkans. Insofar as quality, risk, and security of investment in government bonds under the current constellation of international finance depends on the institutional and political stability of the issuers, small open economies that are not members of international associations (like the European Union) face the problem of high risk associated with their bonds, particularly if denominated in national currencies, with accordingly high interest rates (high costs of repaying public debt) and low prices for these assets.

In order to deal with this problem, I proposed, using the example of the countries of the Western Balkans, the creation of a European Union Guarantee Fund for the Western Balkans, which would guarantee long-maturity bond issues by the countries of the region, denominated in national currencies. These bond issues would be called Euro-Balkan bonds and, as they would be guaranteed by the European Union, they could be classified as financial assets with a lower degree of risk and accordingly lower interest rates and higher prices. The revenues realized would be used exclusively to finance capital projects (infrastructural development projects) preferably at the cross-border level. Thus, one of the key problems facing small open economies which are not yet members of larger associations and therefore lack the backing of a supranational institution could be solved and systemic risk reduced, stimulating economic growth and employment and reducing the pressures leading to labour migration away from the poorer European countries towards Western Europe.

The EU Guarantee Fund would, in return, have the right to a golden share in public companies, in particular electricity and telecommunications. This would reduce the pressure for quick privatization at a time of crisis, when asset prices are generally falling, and would facilitate a higher level of cooperative governance in public companies. Moreover, the EU Guarantee Fund would have the right to a guarantee/equity swap regarding public company shares, as well as oversight of public finances. The key argument in favour of this proposal is, accordingly, that, through joint and coordinated action by the EU and the governments of Western Balkan countries to finance development projects creating jobs and connecting the region, the costs of public financing would be reduced, thanks to the European Union's guarantee schemes, while the prospects for a successful and rapid exit from economic crisis would be increased. The proposal would entail integration of the existing stock exchanges of Western Balkan countries, within a single electronic platform, perhaps to be called the Western Balkans Stock Exchange, which would allow transaction costs to be reduced and commercial bank and institutional investor portfolios to be structured more successfully across the region.

The final three chapters of the book (Chapters 8, 9, and 10) are dedicated to the analysis of the economic problems, achievements, potentials, and European prospects of Bosnia and Herzegovina. The initial position of the Bosnian economy was particularly unfavourable, due to war damage, even compared to those of the other countries of the former Yugoslavia, never mind the other countries in transition. During the war in Bosnia and Herzegovina, at least 102,622 people were killed,[28] while a further 260,000 ended up as disabled civilians or veterans as a direct result of the war. Lost GDP over the period from 1992 to 1995 was around US$30 billion in 1990 dollars,[29] while damage to business assets, hospitals, schools, universities, cultural institutions, roads and railways, and housing has been estimated at anywhere between $35 and $40 billion. According to Donald Hayes, one of the representatives of the international community in Bosnia and Herzegovina, around $14 billion in aid was invested in the country in the post-war period up to 2005. Nonetheless, it is pretty clear that the war losses outlined above, both in human and in physical capital, significantly outweighed even such levels of assistance. No state in Europe has suffered anything comparable to what Bosnia and Herzegovina underwent in terms of the intensity or degree of destruction, at least since World War II, and this data should not be ignored, at least by anybody attempting an objective, scholarly, or scientific perspective in comparing the post-war position and achievements of Bosnia and Herzegovina with those of its neighbouring countries and other countries in transition. Regardless of whether we take as our starting point the Swan-Solow model of growth or one of the models of endogenous growth, labour and capital are the two very important factors of economic growth.[30] The sharp and sudden loss of one or the other necessarily places a country in a disadvantaged position compared to its trading partners, which have not suffered such losses. This is all the more so for a country like Bosnia and Herzegovina, which has suffered the sharp and sudden loss of both.

Despite the deeply prejudicial and mistaken understanding of Bosnia and Herzegovina as economically the worst performing country in Southeastern Europe, actual economic results do not place the country as 'worst in class'. Bosnia's external debt at the end of 2013 was just 62 per cent of GDP. This compares to external debts for the other countries of the former Yugoslavia, in per cent of GDP, for the same year of: Slovenia 121 per cent,[31] Montenegro 113 per cent,[32] Croatia 107 per cent,[33] Serbia 83 per cent,[34] Macedonia 67 per cent,[35] and Kosovo 27 per cent.[36] Bosnia's public debt was 46 per cent of GDP, while the public debts of the other countries of the former Yugoslavia (as percentage of GDP) were: Croatia 66 per cent, Serbia 61 per cent, Slovenia 59 per cent, Montenegro 52 per cent, Macedonia 33 per cent, and Kosovo 9 per cent.[37]

Although the unemployment rate in Bosnia and Herzegovina was high in December 2013 (27.5 per cent by ILO standards), it was close to those of Spain and Greece (or indeed Serbia and Macedonia). But neither Spain nor Greece had suffered the ravages of a major war and both were EU members.[38] Moreover, while Bosnia's debt to the IMF was just 215 per cent of its quota,[39] at the time of writing, Greece's was approximately 1,954 per cent of its quota and its public debt as high as 175 per cent of GDP (nearly four times Bosnia's). Or consider that the debt of the Republic of Ireland at the IMF is 1,548 per cent, that country's quota[40] and its public debt rose from 24 per cent of GDP in 2008 to 124 per cent of GDP in 2013. It may well seem, then, that access to the resources required to support economic recovery and indeed the interpretation given of an economy's condition and efficiency differ greatly, depending not least on specific aspects of geopolitical context and relationship to integrative trends (the EU), aspects that do no favours to the countries of the Western Balkans or to Bosnia and Herzegovina more particularly.

Within this international context (and not least the conditions and constitution imposed under the Dayton Agreement), the political economy of transition in Bosnia and Herzegovina remains directly dependent on its institutional and ethnic structure and is particularly marked by the dominant role played by the entities and the main ethnic groups. I have presented my analysis of the problems arising from the entity and ethnic basis of economic transition in the country and, more particularly, of privatization, as one of the most important elements of this, in a chapter of a book recently published by Longo Editore.[41] Here I would like to single out one of the most important elements of the process of transition, one which is all too often neglected in analysis of what has happened and what is happening in the countries in transition, including Bosnia and Herzegovina. The key factor of the process of transition is the legal institutional arrangements which define the legal framework and the rights of the major agents of that process of transition as derived from that framework. In Bosnia and Herzegovina, the key actors in the process of transition have been the entity structures, which effectively means the entrenched elites of the three constitutive peoples (ethnic groups) who make up the majority population of the country.

Along with a reduction in social differences and the elimination of disintegrative tendencies both in the region and, more particularly, in Bosnia and Herzegovina, the nation-formation process in the Western Balkan region will necessarily entail accelerated action to promote its integration with the European Union and/or give it special status, involving direct and close cooperation with the European Union and resolution of security issues, within the context of Euro-Atlantic integration (i.e. NATO and the Western European Union). The chronic lack of institutional capacity, and the low level of confidence in the institutions of the small open economies of the Western Balkans, will be dealt with only by creating a series of regional guarantee schemes under the 'umbrella' of the key players in international policy.

Introduction 13

Notes

1 For the reproduced chapters, readers should take note that any time/date references (e.g. 'this year'/'last year') relate to the date of the original publication.
2 Data taken from various issues of the World Bank's *World Development Indicators* (1999, 2002, and 2003).
3 Data on the foreign exchange reserves of both developed and developing countries are available on the IMF website, www.imf.org/external/np/sta/cofer/eng/cofer.pdf.
4 Data on the BRIC countries' share in world GDP for 2000 and 2012 calculated on the basis of: World Bank Statistics for GDP at http://data.worldbank.org/indicator/NY.GDP.MKTP.CD.
5 World Bank data on GDP can be accessed at http://data.worldbank.org/indicator/NY.GDP.MKTP.CD?order=wbapi_data_value_2000%20wbapi_data_value&sort=asc.
6 See the Bank for International Settlements' website: www.bis.org/statistics/derstats.htm.
7 Fikret Čaušević, *Economic Sovereignty and Global Capital Flows*, International Forum Bosnia, Sarajevo, 2006.
8 Ronald McKinnon, *Money and Capital in Economic Development*, Brookings Institution, Washington, 1973; Edward Shaw, *Financial Deepening in Economic Development*, Oxford University Press, New York, 1973.
9 Jonathan Guthrie, 'Big Bang Gave London Top Tier Status', *Financial Times*, 8 April 2013, www.ft.com/intl/cms/s/0/bd6ec894-a074-11e2-a6e1-00144feabdc0.html#axzz36CljfboQ.
10 Data on savings and investment in per cent of GDP are available in statistical Annexes of the *World Economic Outlook* (WEO) issued by the IMF. Data presented in this text can be found in the WEOs for 2005, 2007, 2009, 2010, and 2013 (the October issues).
11 Joseph Stiglitz, *Making Globalization Work*, W.W. Norton & Company, New York, 2006, p. 245.
12 Maurice Obstfeld, Alan Taylor, 'Globalization and Capital Markets', *National Bureau of Economic Research*, NBER Working Paper 8846, April 2002.
13 Maurice Obstfeld, Alan Taylor, op. cit.
14 A.M. Kose, E. Prasad, K. Rogoff, and S.J. Wei, 'Financial Globalization: A Reappraisal', *IMF Working Paper*, 2006.
15 W.R. Cline, *Financial Globalization, Economic Growth, and the Crisis of 2007–09*, Peterson Institute for International Economics, Washington, 2010, p. 215.
16 An excellent interpretation of the LTCM debacle is presented in: Roger Lowenstein, *When Genius Failed – The Rise and Fall of Long Term Capital Management*, Fourth Estate, London, 2001.
17 See data at: http://epp.eurostat.ec.europa.eu/tgm/table.do?tab=table&plugin=1&language=en&pcode=teina225.
18 Fikret Čaušević, *Economic Sovereignty and Global Capital Flows*, International Forum Bosnia, Sarajevo, 2006, p. 208. Selected parts from the above source written on pages 183–194 and 201–209 are included in the second chapter of this book under the title 'Financial liberalization, economic growth, and the need for reform of the global financial system'.
19 Fikret Čaušević, op. cit. p. 209.
20 The 2009 April package of G-20 and the IMF.
21 See: Board of Governors of the Federal Reserve, *Financial Account of the United States – Flow of Funds, Balance Sheets, and Integrated Macroeconomic Accounts*, September 2013.
22 Available at: www.federalreserve.gov/monetarypolicy/files/quarterly_balance_sheet_developments_report_201403.pdf.
23 George Soros, *The Crisis of Global Capitalism: Open Society Endangered*, PublicAffairs, New York, 1998.

14   Introduction

24 Joseph E. Stiglitz, *Globalization and Its Discontents*, W.W. Norton & Company, New York, 2002.
25 Joseph E. Stiglitz, *Making Globalization Work*, W.W. Norton & Company, New York, 2006.
26 Neil Fligstein, *The Architecture of Markets – An Economic Sociology of Twenty-First Century Capitalist Societies*, Princeton University Press, Princeton and Oxford, 2001.
27 Othon Anastasakis, Peter Sanfey, Max Watson, *Defining a New Reform Agenda – Paths to Sustainable Convergence in South East Europe*, SEESOX, St Antony's College, University of Oxford, 2013.
28 Smail Čekić, *Research of Genocide Victims, With a Special Emphasis on Bosnia and Herzegovina – Problems and Issues in Scientific Theory, Methods and Methodology*; Institut za istraživanje zločina protiv čovječnosti i međunarodnog prava Univerziteta u Sarajevu, Sarajevo, 2009, pp. 88–89. The minimum number for those killed during the war in Bosnia and Herzegovina given in the aforementioned text (102,622) is from one of the sources cited in Čekić's book, namely Ewa Tabeau-J. Bijak, 'War-Related Deaths in the 1992–1995 Armed Conflict in Bosnia and Herzegovina: A Critique of Previous Estimates and Recent Results', *European Journal of Population* 21 (2–3): 187–215, 2005; while Čekić also cites an estimate of 200,000 people killed in Bosnia and Herzegovina, from: Rony Blum, Gregory H. Stanton, Shira Sagi, Elihu D. Richter, '"Ethnic Cleansing" Bleaches the Atrocities of Genocide', *European Journal of Public Health* 18 (2): 204–209, 2008.
29 According to the Statistical Almanac of BiH 1992, the value of Bosnia and Herzegovina's GDP as part of the SFRY in 1990, converted using the average official US dollar/Yugoslav dinar rate of the day, was US$10.7 billion. Annual production during the war years (1992–1995) was estimated by the World Bank as close to US$1.2 billion. See: The European Commission and the World Bank, 'Bosnia and Herzegovina – 1996–1998 Lessons and Accomplishments – Review of the Priority Reconstruction Program and Looking Ahead Towards Sustainable Economic Development', Report prepared for the May 1999 Donors Conference, May 1999, p. 47.
30 One of the best textbooks on economic growth is written by Barro and Sala-i-Martin: See: Robert Barro, Xavier Sala-i-Martin, *Economic Growth*, The MIT Press, Cambridge, Massachusetts; London, England, 2001 (third imprint). See Chapters I to V.
31 Available at: www.imf.org/external/np/sec/pr/2014/pr1413.htm.
32 Available at: www.intellinews.com/montenegro-1017/imf-lifts-montenegro-s-2013-gdp-growth-forecast-to-1-5-from-1-2-table-14982/.
33 Available at: www.moodys.com/research/Moodys-changes-outlook-on-Croatias-Ba1-government-bond-rating-to--PR_295208.
34 National Bank of Serbia, 'Analysis of Republic of Serbia's Debt', June 2013, available at: www.nbs.rs/internet/english/90/dug/debt_II_2013.pdf.
35 Available at: http://tr.ebrd.com/tr13/en/country-assessments/1/fyr-macedonia#main-macroeconomic-indicators.
36 Available at: www.intellinews.com/kosovo-1311/kosovo-s-gross-external-debt-up-to-26-7-of-gdp-at-end-march-2013-10066/.
37 See: www.cia.gov/library/publications/the-world-factbook/rankorder/2186rank.html.
38 Data on Greek debt, as of 31 May 2014, available at: www.imf.org/external/np/fin/tad/exfin2.aspx?memberKey1=360&date1key=2014-07-02.
39 Data on Bosnian debt, as of 31 May 2014, available at: www.imf.org/external/np/fin/tad/exfin2.aspx?memberKey1=75&date1key=2014-07-02.
40 Data on Irish debt, as of 31 May 2014, available at: www.imf.org/external/np/fin/tad/exfin2.aspx?memberKey1=470&date1key=2014-07-02.
41 Fikret Čaušević, 'Bosnia and Herzegovina's Economy since the Dayton Agreement', in: Ola Listhaug, Sabrina Ramet (Eds) *Bosnia and Herzegovina Since Dayton: Civic and Uncivic Values*, Longo Editore, Ravenna, 2013, available at: http://digital.casalini.it/10.1400/212369.

Part I
Economic challenges in the world economy before and during the global financial and economic crisis

Part 1

Economic challenges in the world economy before and during the global financial and economic crisis

1 The international financial system during the great recession and its implications for a micro-state open economy in the Western Balkans[1]

The global financial system and the role of the US dollar

Since the establishment of the International Monetary Fund (IMF) in July 1944, the US dollar has preserved its status as the most important reserve and dominant invoicing currency in the world. The first period of the international financial system, known as Bretton Woods I, immediately followed World War II, ending in August 1971, when the then US president, Richard Nixon, suspended the convertibility of the dollar into gold. In March 1973, he officially declared a shift to a free floating exchange rate regime, in force ever since. In the period since World War II, the two greatest challenges to the dollar's position as leading reserve currency have been (i) the inflationary pressures and the built-in inflation expectations of the second half of the 1970s and (ii) the introduction of the euro as the single Euro-zone currency in January 1999. The first manifested as a rapid loss of confidence in the sustainability of the dollar due to inflationary expectations between 1973 and 1980 and was resolved by the appointment of Paul Volcker as Chair of the Federal Reserve System (the Fed) and his decisive and credible pursuit of a restrictive monetary policy (monetary targeting), cutting inflation and eliminating inflationary expectations. Thanks to this policy and to a sharp reduction in the monetary base between 1980 and 1982, both nominal and real interest rates increased sharply and inflation was kept under control.

The second challenge to the dollar's supremacy emerged after the introduction of a single Euro-zone currency – the euro. Over the first 24 months after introduction, the artificially determined exchange rate against the dollar reduced sharply (from 1.176 to 0.855). In other words, over this period the euro lost 37.5 per cent in value against the dollar. Between January 2001 and July 2008, however, the euro recovered by some 85.7 percentage points, reaching its highest value against the dollar in the second week of July 2008, with an average exchange rate of 1.588.[2] The financial crisis deepened as major problems arose following the de facto bankruptcy of five major investment banks in the United States on 15 September 2008 (starting with Lehman Brothers). The Fed was forced to undertake measures of monetary expansion of a sort not seen since World War II. In just two weeks, between 17 September and 1 October 2008, the Fed increased its balance sheet from $992 billion to $1,502 billion. This extraordinary expansionary monetary policy was also reflected in the institution cutting its main monetary policy tool – the federal funds rate – from 3.75 per cent in December 2007 to a target rate between zero and 0.25 per cent on 9 December 2008. Although the European Central Bank (ECB) kept its main monetary policy instrument – the main refinancing operation rate – at much higher levels than the Fed's (on 10 December 2008, the ECB rate was 2.5 per cent),[3] the euro lost nearly a third in value against the dollar between July 2008 and July 2010.

These changes directly affected the currency composition of world foreign exchange reserves. According to the data in Table 1.1, the euro's share in allocated foreign exchange reserves increased from 18.3 per cent in 2000 to 26.5 per cent in 2008.[4] The Euro-zone sovereign debt crisis and lack of decisiveness on the part of the ECB and the Euro-zone member countries' ministries of finance between 2009 and 2011 caused a loss of faith in the euro, however, with a subsequent decrease in its importance in the currency composition of world foreign exchange reserves. Thus, while the dollar's share in world foreign exchange reserves decreased over the first nine years of the euro's existence (from 71.1 per cent to 61.8 per cent), the decisive monetary policy measures taken by the Fed during the period of the financial crisis (2008–2010) gave the dollar a minor boost at the expense of the euro. Prolonged problems regarding labour markets in both the USA and the Euro-zone member countries, however, coupled with the public debt ceiling problem in the US between 2010 and February 2013, caused 'a run to gold' by certain major central banks in the developing world, reducing the importance of both major currencies in structuring world foreign exchange reserves. This 'gold bubble', however, ended in the middle of March 2013, causing huge losses to the developing countries' central banks – in particular, the People's Bank of China.

The redistribution of total foreign exchange reserves between the advanced and developing countries reflects a major change in the balance of economic and

Table 1.1 World foreign exchange reserves (in US$ billions)

Year	Total	Allocated	Allocated in US$	Allocated in EUR
2000	1,937	1,516	1,078 (71.1%)	278 (18.3%)
2004	3,749	2,649	1,746 (65.9%)	658 (24.8%)
2008	6,713	4,213	2,698 (64.0%)	1,117 (26.5%)
2010	9,263	5,161	3,192 (61.8%)	1,343 (26.0%)
Third quarter 2013	11,434	6,191	3,804 (61.4%)	1,496 (24.2%)

Source: The Bank for International Settlements (www.imf.org/external/np/sta/cofer/eng/cofer.pdf) – accessed on 10 January 2014.

financial power between West and East, which took place during the first 13 years of the current century, after the most populous developing countries had opened up during the final two decades of the preceding one.

Table 1.2 shows that developing countries have increased their foreign exchange reserves more than tenfold over the last 13 years, while the advanced countries have only tripled theirs. In other words, developing countries' foreign exchange reserves increased by 968 per cent and advanced countries' reserves by 209 per cent. More importantly, the total amount of foreign exchange reserves now held by developing countries greatly exceeds the amount held by advanced ones. In 2000, the ratio of foreign exchange reserves between the advanced and developing countries was 1.7:1, in favour of the advanced countries. Twelve years later, it had been reversed to approximately 1:2 in favour of the developing ones. This distribution reflects the increasing importance of the BRIC countries in world trade and finance, on the one hand, and certain potential problems associated with dollar volatility and changing prices for US government securities, in which the BRIC countries have held a significant proportion of their foreign exchange reserves for the past seven years, on the other.

Returns (yields) on US government securities (T-bills, notes, and bonds) are linked to and strongly influenced by the Fed's monetary policy. In other words, the return on foreign exchange reserves held by the BRIC countries and six Southeast Asian newly industrialized countries in dollar-denominated securities (US government securities) is directly determined by the Fed's monetary policy. The Fed's extremely expansionary monetary policy between September and December 2008 meant the federal funds rate had been cut effectively to zero by mid December 2008.[5] From 17 September 2008 to the end of December 2008, the Fed's balance sheet increased 124 per cent (see Table 1.3).

The Fed has continued to conduct an extremely expansionary monetary policy (introducing the measures known as quantitative easing or QE1, QE2, and QE3), keeping the federal funds rate unchanged (a de facto zero level). As a consequence, returns on US securities are at the lowest level in three decades. The yield on three-month T-bills plunged from 4.64 per cent in 2007 to 1.59 per cent

Table 1.2 The foreign exchange reserves of developed and developing countries (in US$ billions)

Year	Total amount	Advanced countries	Developing countries
2000	1,936	1,217	718
2003	3,025	1,767	1,258
2005	4,320	2,078	2,241
2007	6,704	2,432	4,272
2009	8,164	2,779	5,385
2011	10,203	3,398	6,804
September 2013	11,434	3,763	7,670

Source: The Bank for International Settlements (www.imf.org/external/np/sta/cofer/eng/cofer.pdf) – accessed on 10 January 2014.

Table 1.3 The US Federal Reserve System balance sheet

The balance sheet as of:	Assets in US$ billions
31 December 2007	922
17 September 2008	995
1 October 2008	1,504
31 December 2008	2,239
31 December 2010	2,420
31 December 2012	2,907
31 December 2013	4,067

Source: The Federal Reserve (www.federalreserve.gov/monetarypolicy/bst_recenttrends_accessible.htm) – accessed on 13 January 2014.

in 2008 and just 0.07 per cent on average between 2009 and 2013.[6] Insofar as the BRIC and Southeast Asian countries have tended to hold most of their allocated foreign-exchange reserves in dollars (i.e. in US Treasury bills), they have faced a significant increase in the opportunity costs of holding those reserves in dollar-denominated financial assets. On average, the group of developing countries has held around $1,480 billion (yearly) in short-term US securities. Comparing yields on the same amount held in US Treasury bills in 2007 (4.64 per cent) and between 2009 and 2013 (average yield of 0.07 per cent) reveals a huge disparity: a yield of $68.67 billion (in 2007) compared to just $1.04 billion (the average return earned between 2009 and 2013). The opportunity cost of holding foreign-exchange reserves in US Treasury securities has, therefore, sharply increased and could be estimated (as a very rough measure) as the difference between the return in 2007 and the average annual return during the crisis period. In other words, it comes to approximately $320 billion over the last five years.

The role of the euro and the sovereign debt crisis in the Euro-zone countries

The first half of 2012 was marked in the Euro-zone countries by major problems caused by high levels of public debt. For some countries from the southern Euro-zone, public debt was twice, or more, the level set in the Stability and Growth Pact (in Italy and Greece, for example). One of the main threats to sustainability of the euro as a single European currency and for financial stability in Euro-zone countries was the decision by the European banking authorities to require large banks to increase their capital to assets ratio from 6 to 9 per cent by the end of June 2012.[7]

The ECB has since implemented a set of unconventional measures to stabilize and strengthen the banking industry in Euro-zone countries. Under the leadership of its newly appointed president, Mario Draghi, the ECB pursued an expansionary monetary policy, based on long-term refinancing operations (loans to banks with maturity of three years), instead of on short-term loans (main refinancing operations based on loans to banks and maturity of up to three months, as extensively used for the crisis). A second measure was to introduce outright market purchase – the purchase of government bonds issued by southern Euro-zone member countries. This measure was intended to stabilize the market for sovereign debt in the Euro-zone and to reduce the required rate of return on government bonds issued by Euro-zone member countries in serious difficulties with public finances.

The data presented in Table 1.4 reveal major changes in the monetary policy pursued by the ECB over the period between 2010 and 2013. During the first seven years of the century, the ECB used main refinancing operations (MRO) as its major monetary policy instrument, but over the past six years and especially between 2010 and 2013, its main policy tools have been LTRO and OMP – long-term refinancing operations and outright market purchase. The percentage accounted for by LTRO increased from around 7 per cent in 2007 to almost one third by the beginning of 2013. Over the same period, the percentage accounted for by government bonds issued by Euro-zone governments and held by the ECB went up from 7.5 per cent to almost 20 per cent. In just five months, between September 2012 and the end of February 2013, the ECB decided to purchase government bonds to the tune of €257 billion (€99 billion in Italian government bonds, €41.6 billion in Spanish government bonds, and €31.5 billion in Greek government bonds). While all this data about the ECB's monetary measures and changes in policy tools may at first sight seem unrelated to the financial situation in Bosnia and Herzegovina, these decisive measures have contributed to stabilization of the euro and the Euro-zone banking industry and thus had an important knock-on impact on financial stability in Bosnia and Herzegovina, as well as in

Table 1.4 Total assets of the euro system (in € billions)

Assets	January 2010	January 2013
Gold and claims in gold	266.9	438.7
Claims on non-residents (outside the Euro-zone) in foreign currencies	193.8	253.9
Claims on residents in foreign currencies	28.3	31.2
Claims on non-residents in euros	18.1	22.0
Loans to credit institutions in euros	726.3	1,156.2
• *of which main refinancing operations (MROs)*	*64.0*	*125.3*
• *of which long-term refinancing operations (LTROs)*	*662.2*	*1,030.9*
Other claims on credit institutions from Euro-zone countries in euros	26.7	131.3
Debt securities issued by Euro-zone member countries in euros	331.2	582.8
Government debt in euros	36.2	30.0
Other assets	250.2	282.7
Total assets	**1,877.7**	**2,928.8**

Source: European Central Bank (www.ecb.int/press/pr/wfs/2012/html/fs120306.en.html).

the other countries of the Western Balkans and Southeastern Europe, insofar as the financial systems of all the countries in the region are highly dependent on those of Western Europe. The banking industry in Bosnia and Herzegovina and the other Western Balkan countries is, after all, largely based on foreign investors or banks from Western Europe.

The role of Euro-zone residents' securities in ECB assets also grew sharply during the period of the crisis. In January 2007, this item accounted for 7.5 per cent of ECB assets, but by January 2013 it had increased to approximately 20 per cent. Again, these data about changes to ECB operating procedures and the structure of assets in the euro system may appear somewhat irrelevant to analysis of the economic and financial situation in Bosnia and Herzegovina. Insofar as Bosnia's currency, the Convertible Mark, is pegged to the euro and Euro-zone banks own nearly 90 per cent of the banking sector in the country, however, any changes to ECB operating procedures or measures to soften financial shocks due to the sovereign debt crisis or to changes in the structure of the portfolios of the main Euro-zone banks, including those of Euro-zone mother banks with daughter banks in Bosnia and Herzegovina (and in all other Western Balkan countries), have necessarily had an important impact on the potential for credit expansion in recent years, including the current one.

The major significance of the commercial banks and the financial groups that own them for the financial system and, indeed, the overall stability and status of the Euro-zone economy is clearly indicated by the extraordinarily high concentration of assets within five major banks in each of three key Euro-zone countries: Germany, France, and Italy. This is confirmed by data from their respective central banks regarding bank assets, which make clear that the assets of the five largest banks in France are equivalent to 3.3 times the country's GDP,[8] while the assets of the five largest banks in Germany are equivalent to 1.64 of that country's GDP,[9] and the assets of the five largest banks in Italy are equivalent to 1.35 of that country's GDP.[10] The data in question are for 2011 and 2012.

The data in Table 1.5 make clear why the French, German, and Italian governments are so sensitive to any changes in the quality of the assets of their banks. It was precisely because their own government securities comprise so significant a part of their largest banks' assets and because changes in those securities' value would significantly affect the banks' profitability and capital adequacy that the European Central Bank took the unconventional measures

Table 1.5 Total assets of the five largest banks in France, Germany, and Italy

Country	Assets of five largest banks as of 30 June 2012 (€ billions)	Assets of five largest banks as percentage of GDP
France	6,756	333.2
Germany	4,230	164.6
Italy	2,120	135.4

Source: The Deutsche Bundesbank, Banque de France, Banca d'Italia.

outlined above to mitigate major financial shocks and any losses the banks might have suffered, which would have had to be covered by their respective national governments, which have already, to a very significant degree, violated the fiscal rules set out in the Pact for Stability and Growth in the European Union.

Problems with the regulation of international banking and derivatives markets

Three key issues lie at the heart of the global financial crisis: first, financial deregulation, which allowed an enormous and uncontrolled growth in transactions through derivative instruments on the over-the-counter markets; second, a relaxation of oversight over globally active banks, with adoption of the Basle II regulations, allowing banks to set their own capital needs on the basis of their internal risk management models; and third, an enormous expansion in international lending both between the major banks and between the banks and their clients. These problems were created nearly two decades before the appearance of the global financial crisis and remain key unresolved issues. They represent major challenges and threats to maintaining international financial stability and so international peace and stability.

The first factor to lead to major problems in the international financial system was the unregulated over-the-counter market in financial derivatives, which became one of the main sources for the formation of fictive liquidity, as well as a very important mechanism by which major private financial transactors evaded the direct impact of national regulators and central banks' measures. Data from the Bank for International Settlements[11] provide the best indicators of the increase in these markets' role and importance between 2000 and 2008. The value of contracts traded on the over-the-counter markets grew from approximately $98.5 trillion in 2000 to approximately $668 trillion by the end of June 2008. Given that over the same period the world GDP increased from $31.5 trillion to $54.5 trillion, it follows that the ratio of the value of contracts traded on over-the-counter markets to world GDP grew from 3:1 to 11:1.

While Figure 1.1 shows that the value of contracts traded on the over-the-counter (OTC) markets has not increased since 2008, it remains very high, representing some US$637 trillion by the end of 2012, or a ratio to world GDP of approximately 8.8:1. The disproportion between these contracts' value and world GDP was thus still three times greater than in 2000. The lack of regulation of over-the-counter markets prompted American president Barack Obama to lobby for new laws to regulate them. This led to passage of the Dodd–Frank Act, which Obama signed in July 2010. The American Congress had, however, already passed the Commodity Futures Modernization Act in 2000, which disqualified the American Securities Exchange Commission (SEC), the main regulatory body for capital markets, from overseeing key data related to trade on OTC markets, and particularly trade in swap contracts, which accounts for approximately 70 per cent of all trades on OTC markets.

Passage of the Commodity Futures Modernization Act therefore directly influenced the enormous expansion of trade in derivatives shown in Figure 1.1,

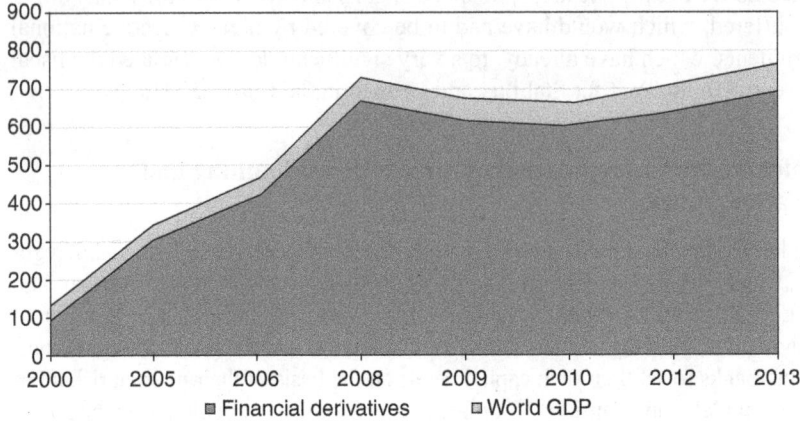

Figure 1.1 Notional value of OTC traded contracts in financial derivatives (in US$ trillions).

almost all of which took place outside of the control or oversight of national or even international regulatory bodies. The Dodd–Frank Wall Street Reform and Consumer Protection Act did create a legal basis for monitoring trades in derivatives, including an obligation to clear contracts through a third party – the CCP (central counterparty). This was because clearance of OTC derivative contracts is done by calling margins for the total value of contracts and it would, according to the estimate of Stephen O'Connor, the Chairman of the International Association for Swap and Derivative Contracts, require a sum of close to $10.2 trillion[12] just to make a deposit for the initial margins to secure sufficient liquidity for effective clearance of these contracts. Alternative estimates suggest a sum of as much as $22 trillion might be needed. As we are dealing with such enormous sums, the central question for those active on the OTC market becomes how to ensure adequate collateral and what might serve as adequate collateral and allow clearance of OTC contracts by providing sufficient liquidity on the market. This, along with the so-called financial trilemma, is one of the key issues facing the international financial system and determining its future. The financial trilemma arises from the impossibility of satisfying simultaneously the three following goals: financial stability, the development of international banking, and national systems of supervision and oversight of banking operations.[13]

The second major problem for the sustainability of the international banking system arose, in large part, from poor or inappropriate application of the Basle II rules in the countries that are home to the largest commercial banks and financial groupings. Applying the internal rules for determining the degree of risk associated with various forms and lines of business created the illusion that major banks could focus their financial leverage very intensively, in the hope that systemic risk would remain unaffected.

The expansion of lending activities, whether between banks or to clients, that took place between 2002 and 2008 was unprecedented in post-war history. According to the data of the Bank for International Settlements, the average growth in lending by internationally active banks measured as a ratio of lending to GDP was 4 per cent between 1985 and 2002, while from 2002 to 2008 it was twice as high – approximately 8 per cent per annum.[14] Table 1.6 presents the data on geographical distribution, or rather on channelling the funds of internationally active banks by region, as well as the total amounts so placed. Total lending by internationally active banks, nearly three-quarters of which comprised approved loans, two-fifths of which was in turn bank-to-bank lending, tripled between 2000 and 2008. According to the data from Table 1.6, lending by internationally active banks increased at a much slower rate between 2006 and 2012. Nonetheless, even if this increase in lending was slower in the second six years than in the first six years of this century, by far the greatest percentage of that increase still related to lending between the same banks.

One problem that surfaced after the adoption of the new regulatory standards known as Basle III related to the requirement that internationally active banks significantly increase their liquid reserves and capital bases, causing significant pressure on financial markets around the world, but particularly in Europe, where some of the largest world banks hail from. It is clear from Table 1.7 that six out

Table 1.6 Total foreign claims of international banks, 2000–2012

Claims on the region:	Total foreign claims (US$ billions)	European banks (in %)	Japanese banks (in %)	US banks (in %)	Other banks (in %)
All countries:					
2000	9,018	73.8	12.9	8.2	5.1
2006	23,072	80.0	8.1	5.8	6.1
Q2 2012	33,359	74.9	8.9	9.7	6.5
Developed countries:					
2000	6,997	75.8	12.6	6.7	5.0
2006	18,455	82.1	7.5	4.4	6.0
Q2 2012	24,648	76.3	8.7	8.6	6.4
Off-shore centres:					
2000	779	59.6	25.1	9.1	6.2
2006	1,756	66.1	19.5	7.3	7.1
Q2 2012	4,260	60.5	19.0	12.8	7.7
Developing countries:					
2000	1,180	70.0	7.5	17.4	5.1
2006	2,804	75.0	4.8	13.9	6.3
Q2 2012	3,760	75.2	5.0	13.5	6.3

Source: The Bank for International Settlements.

Table 1.7 Ten largest banks in the world, June 2012

Bank	Assets – in US$ billions
1. Deutsche Bank	2,800
2. HSBC	2,556
3. BNP Paribas	2,543
4. Industrial and Commercial Bank of China	2,456
5. Mitsubishi UFJ Financial Group	2,448
6. Credit Agricole	2,432
7. Barclays Group	2,417
8. Royal Bank of Scotland	2,330
9. JPMorgan Chase	2,266
10. Bank of America	2,129

Source: Global Finance (www.gfmag.com/tools/best-banks/11986-worlds-50-biggest-banks-2012.html#axzz2fAKjgaNV).

of the ten largest banks in the world last year were European, as were the three largest. The total assets of the six leading European banks last year amounted to US$15.078 trillion – an amount roughly equal to American GDP for the year or 45.2 per cent of the value of all lending by internationally active banks.

Financial (in)stability in Bosnia and Herzegovina

From the onset of the global financial crisis, the Bosnian authorities were unwilling to coordinate economic policy in an appropriate way or create a sound basis for fighting the crisis – that is, for anti-cyclical action. A series of statements by the Bosnian ministers of finance (at the state and entity levels), as well as by senior officials in the indirect taxation authority, regarding a surplus of revenue collected from indirect taxes during 2008, created an illusion of fiscal sustainability and that the consequences of the global financial crisis could be avoided in Bosnia and Herzegovina and the Western Balkans more generally. A number of irresponsible statements and projections by certain of the more significant global or European financial institutions to the effect that Bosnia and Herzegovina and the region had enjoyed real rates of economic growth of between 3 and 3.2 per cent during 2009 simply added fat to the fire.

This increase in revenues from indirect taxation was directly due to the global financial cycle outlined above and the enormous expansion of lending involved by internationally active banks, certain of the more important of which are active in the region and in Bosnia and Herzegovina itself. This expansion in lending by European financial markets directly facilitated access to favourable loans drawn down by the daughter banks from their mother institutions in Western Europe. The consequent expansion of lending activities in Bosnia and Herzegovina and in the region between 2004 and 2008 was a major factor in the growth in purchasing power, investment activity, and so of fiscal capacity of Bosnia and Herzegovina and of the other countries in the region. The average annual increase in lending to companies and to the public in Bosnia and Herzegovina between 2005 and 2008 was 1.6 billion KM.[15] In 2008 itself, loans to businesses and to households (aggregated) grew approximately 2.7 billion KM, record growth for the first eight years of the century. One direct consequence of this expansion in credit was the increase in fiscal capacity and income based on indirect taxation. There was, therefore, no 'surplus' of revenues collected on this basis and therefore no grounds for concluding fiscal equilibrium could be maintained as lending activity was declining.

The following year (2009), the global financial crisis transferred to the region, and Bosnia and Herzegovina. Unlike 2008, when there had been an increase in lending and so in the purchasing power of households and companies of some 2.7 billion KM, in 2009 overall loans fell by approximately 700 million KM, followed by purchasing power and employment and the income of the effectively employed, as the structure of spending in the business sector adapted to the emerging circumstances. The planned significant growth in fiscal spending, combined with a marked reduction in fiscal revenues, produced serious fiscal problems, whose consequences remain visible and will continue to be so for years to come. One consequence of the fiscal imbalance in Bosnia and Herzegovina, Serbia, Macedonia, and half the countries of the Euro-zone itself is an urgent need for standby arrangements or extended facility arrangements with the IMF.

The data from Table 1.8 suggest that Bosnia's debt to the IMF, measured as a percentage of its quota at the IMF, is significantly lower than those of Greece, Ireland, Portugal, and Romania. These data indicate the existence of a double or even triple standard in international financial circles when ranking various countries by degree of fiscal burden and problems arising on various bases, particularly bearing in mind that Bosnia and Herzegovina is the only European country since World War II to have experienced such a reduction in population (of more than half a million over four years, as a result of the physical liquidation or displacement of the population between 1992 and 1995). Moreover, Bosnia and Herzegovina is the only country in Europe to have seen the number of persons with disabilities (both civil and military) multiply, to the extent that spending on this basis is always one of the largest items in the entity budgets.

Table 1.8 Debts of certain Euro-zone and Western Balkan countries, September 2013

	IMF quota in millions of special drawing rights (SDR)	IMF loans as percentage of quota
Greece	1,101.80	2,192
Ireland	1,257.60	1,448
Portugal	1,029.70	1,913
Romania	1,030.20	646
Bosnia and Herzegovina	169.10	237
Macedonia	68.90	286
Serbia	467.70	177

Source: The International Monetary Fund (www.imf.org/external/country/index.htm) – accessed on 16 September 2013.

On the other hand, the significantly lower debt to quota ratio than other countries does not mean Bosnia and Herzegovina and the engineers of its economic policy, or indeed its of-age inhabitants and voters, should be amnestied from mistakes they made, whose consequences they must bear themselves and for which they must search together for the best possible or at any rate least bad solutions. The problem of indebtedness comes into sharper focus if one takes into account the very modest lending activity of the Bosnian banking sector, owned as it is by mother banks from Western Europe. Table 1.9 shows changes in lending activities to the three main sectors: businesses, households, and government. According to this data, commercial banks have largely abstained from lending to businesses or to households, considering it safest to place funds with the entity governments. An expansion of lending to the entities was, under current circumstances, a logical move, but over the mid-to-long term, banks will have to change this policy, particularly with regard to lending to businesses, since continued stagnation and/or very modest growth will result in considerable illiquidity, under circumstances where the Central Bank of Bosnia and Herzegovina is forbidden to intervene on money or capital markets.

In the 2013 *Global Competitiveness Report*, Bosnia and Herzegovina ranked 87 out of a total of 148 countries,[16] one rank better than the year before, when there were 144 countries in the report. Bosnia's ranking with regard to the factors affecting improved efficiency of the overall economy was lowest for the development of financial markets (113th place). The country ranked next lowest with regard to the efficiency of goods markets (104), followed by market size (96), and finally efficiency of the labour market (88). Interviews with managers indicated that they view access to financing, political instability, and the tax rate as the three main obstacles to improving the business climate and business results. For most of them, access to financing has been the main problem they have faced in developing their business since 2010. This is why it has remained a, or even *the*, fundamental problem throughout the period of the crisis, alongside the key political problems which generate constant business instability and the negative image of the country as unstable and an insufficiently secure destination for investment.

These results regarding the ranking of the most problematic factors for conducting or developing business in Bosnia and Herzegovina are hardly surprising, given that most companies rely on the banking sector to finance their operations, that is to say on the lending cycle, in part as a consequence of international flows of capital and in part because of the underdeveloped and atomised condition of money and capital markets in Bosnia and Herzegovina. It is the narrow and shallow nature of the financial system that has these companies oriented principally towards commercial banks for financing current resources, as well as some part of investment in fixed assets. This has a direct impact on their reduced flexibility in bridging cyclical fluctuations in minimum cash-flow required for current liquidity. The very underdeveloped money market in Bosnia and Herzegovina does not allow companies to issue their own short-term securities/bonds in order to bridge shortfalls in their liquid resources, generated through stagnant

Table 1.9 Lending by banks in Bosnia and Herzegovina (in millions of KM)

Year	Commercial loans	Change in %	Personal loans	Change in %	Loans to government	Change in %
2010	7,715	–	6,423	–	466	–
2011	7,936	2.9	6,769	5.4	905	94.2
March 2012	8,053	1.5	6,759	–0.2	945	4.4
June 2012	8,143	1.1	6,884	1.8	1,042	10.3
September 2012	8,225	1.0	6,884	0.0	1,168	12.1
December 2012	8,263	0.5	6,873	–0.2	1,236	5.8
July 2013	8,302	0.5	6,996	+1.8	1,255	1.5

Source: Central Bank of Bosnia and Herzegovina (www.cbbh.ba/index.php?id=33&lang=bs&sub=mon&table=konsolidovani_bilans_komercijalnih_banaka_bihh) – accessed on 16 September 2013.

trends on the credit markets. The introduction of VAT into the Bosnian tax system (January 2006) brought with it additional costs in financing current funding. The problem was not so prominent during 2006, 2007, and 2008, when expanding bank lending allowed companies to bridge their liquidity difficulties by taking out new loans. Over the past four years, however, the average in new loans approved to businesses has been just 200 million KM, in contrast to new lending to companies of 1.6 billion KM in 2008 alone. This is a very major difference and illustrates in the clearest fashion possible why managers considered this the priority issue for sustainability of the real sector.

The problem of real sector illiquidity requires urgent measures as early as the current quarter and no later than the first half of next year.[17] Expectations of a potential significant increase in lending in the Euro-zone leading to more lending in the region and in Bosnia and Herzegovina in particular are not, from this perspective, founded on any real bases. The rather optimistic speech by José Manuel Barroso (first week of September 2013) elicited critical and rather negative reactions in the European Parliament regarding its insufficient grounding in reality. Meanwhile, significant warning signals regarding a potential second wave of financial crisis are coming from financial professionals in the United States and the European Union, or rather the Euro-zone. Such a train of events would result in further stagnation of lending in Bosnia and Herzegovina and, should any of the systemically important banks in Bosnia prove incapable of maintaining their position on the market, could even result in a reduction in lending. Under such circumstances, it will not be possible to deal with the problem of marked illiquidity except through the creation of financial institutions in the ownership of the state, or possibly entities, whose purpose will be to manage these shocks. One problem arising from such potential requirements is that the governments of both entities have loaded themselves heavily with debt on the domestic market. This is particularly true of the Republika Srpska (RS), whose debt to the banking sector (the RS government debt) is 138 per cent greater than that of the federal (FBiH) government (see Table 1.10).

These financial problems and the need to deal with them come at a very inopportune time, when the political situation is both very unstable and insecure, due in part to the need for constitutional reform and in part to the upcoming elections and the resultant unclear division of responsibilities and absence of any institutional focus of initiative on proposals for institutional arrangements to combat illiquidity. What is without doubt is the fact that the Federation of Bosnia and Herzegovina has a very significant share in or is the owner of more than 4.5 billion KM in four infrastructural companies with indisputably significant development potential, regardless of the problems facing the management of those companies. By contrast, the government in the RS no longer has any major ownership rights in companies with good development prospects that might generate positive cash flows or profit growth. Nonetheless, the RS government's 65 per cent share in MJP Elektroprivreda a.d. RS (the RS Public Electricity Company) does offer the entity some scope for using the potential in that sector or partial privatization to begin at least gradually to deal with the problem of the

Table 1.10 Debt and deposits of the governments of the Federation of Bosnia and Herzegovina and the Republika Srpska to the Bosnian banking sector (in millions of KM)

Year	Republika Srpska		Federation of Bosnia and Herzegovina	
	Debt	Deposits	Debt	Deposits
2007	93	1748	35	587
2008	185	1337	81	413
2009	271	883	86	515
2010	314	470	152	652
2011	625	355	280	600
2012	824	328	413	520
July 2013	883	316	373	454

Source: Central Bank of Bosnia and Herzegovina (www.cbbh.ba/index.php?id=33&lang=bs&sub=mon&table=konsolidovani_bilans_komercijalnih_banaka_bihh) – accessed 16 September 2013.

buildup of debt. In addition to this very significant and attractive property owned by the entity governments, one should not, in this context of tackling the burning problem of financial sustainability, neglect the very considerable property belonging to the state of Bosnia and Herzegovina, which could serve as a guarantee for an initial issue of government securities, as the least risky form of financial asset under international financial and banking standards. Such a securities issue could in turn serve to set basic reference interest rates denominated in the local currency.

Notes

1 This text was presented at the annual conference of the Association of Accountants of the Federation of Bosnia and Herzegovina, held in Neum, Bosnia and Herzegovina. Translated by Desmond Maurer, M.Sc.
2 See: www.investing.com/currencies/eur-usd-historical-data.
3 The ECB's main refinancing operation rates are available on the ECB's website: www.ecb.europa.eu/stats/monetary/rates/html/index.en.html.
4 The currency composition of foreign exchange reserves (COFER) is available on the IMF's website: www.imf.org/external/np/sta/cofer/eng/cofer.pdf.
5 See: www.newyorkfed.org/markets/omo/dmm/historical/fedfunds/index.cfm.
6 See: http://pages.stern.nyu.edu/~adamodar/New_Home_Page/datafile/histretSP.html.
7 See: www.advisorone.com/2011/11/09/eurozone-banks-boost-capital-by-redefining-risk.
8 See: www.relbanks.com/europe/france.
9 See: www.german-way.com/travel-and-tourism/banks-money/top-german-banks/.
10 See: www.relbanks.com/europe/italy.
11 For data on total market value of contracts traded on over-the-counter markets, see the Bank for International Settlements' webpage: www.bis.org/statistics/derstats.htm.
12 Jane Cooper, 'Collateral: The Hunt Is On', *The Banker*, March 2013, p. 17.
13 On the financial trilemma, see Dirk Schoenmaker, 'How to Save International Banking', *The Banker*, August 2013, p. 8.

14 See the Bank for International Settlements, *Long Term Issues in International Banking*, a report submitted by a study group established by the Committee on the Global Financial System, CGFS Papers, No. 41, July 2010, pp. 6–7.
15 Data on lending by banks and the consolidated balance sheet for commercial banks may be found on the Central Bank of Bosnia and Herzegovina webpage: www.cbbh.ba.
16 See World Economic Forum, *The Global Competitiveness Report 2013–14*, Geneva, Switzerland, 2013. The report is available at: http://reports.weforum.org/the-global-competitiveness-report-2013-2014/.
17 Editor's note: This refers to the situation in September 2013, when the text was presented at the annual conference of the Association of Accountants of the Federation of Bosnia and Herzegovina, held in Neum, in Bosnia and Herzegovina.

References

The data for this paper were drawn from the various institutional webpages cited in the endnotes.

Cooper, Jane, 'Collateral: The Hunt Is On', *The Banker*, March 2013.

Schoenmaker, Dirk, 'How to Save International Banking', *The Banker*, August 2013.

The Bank for International Settlements, *Long Term Issues in International Banking*, CGFS Papers, No. 41, July 2010.

The World Economic Forum, *The Global Competitiveness Report 2013–14*, Geneva, Switzerland, 2013.

2 Financial liberalization, economic growth, and the need for reform of the global financial system[1]

The results of financial liberalization and its impact on economic growth and the efficiency of economic policies in the developed and developing countries: 1980–2004

In the late 1980s and 1990s, financial liberalization caused the role of American financial markets to increase. The importance of Japanese financial markets, however, declined significantly during the final decade of the twentieth century. One of the largest financial bubbles of the century, pushed by 'wash sale' transactions and inflated property values used as collateral for loans on the Japanese financial markets, finally burst in 1989–1990. Transactions shifted from Japanese to other, particularly US, financial markets. Between 1990 and 2002, the role of US financial markets grew and their share in total world market capitalization rose from 32.6 per cent to 50.1 per cent. The behaviour of financial investors between 2000 and 2002, after the US (the telecommunications, media, and technology sector, or TMT) financial bubble burst, is particularly interesting in this context. US financial assets within financial portfolios increased their share in world market capitalization from 46.9 per cent to 50.1 per cent between 2000 and 2002. Changes in Fed interest rate policy in 2002–2003, recovering Japanese financial markets, more competitive euro-denominated fixed yield assets, and increased attractiveness of investment in Chinese and Russian financial markets between 2003 and 2005 all affected the restructuring of international financial investors' portfolios, causing the US financial markets' share in world market capitalization to fall from 50.1 per cent in 2002 to 42 per cent in 2005 (see Table 2.1).

An excellent analysis of financial market development in 18 highly developed countries, published in the *World Economic Outlook* (September 2006), argues that financial markets are deeper and financial assets therefore play a greater role in household wealth in the US, UK, Canada, and Australia, so that the banking sector has less influence on capital costs than in the developed countries of Continental Europe and Japan. The financial cycle, or the impact of financial assets and derivatives on the formation of final demand and the financing of innovative projects, is much more important in the US, UK, Canada, and Australia.[2] These conclusions are fully in line with our analysis of economic performance using the wealth coefficient.[3]

Table 2.1 Market capitalization on major world capital markets

	1990		1998		2002		2005	
	$ billion	%	$ billion	%	$ billion	%	$ billion	%
1. USA	3,059.4	32.6	11,308.8	48.0	13,810.4	50.1	16,323.7	42.0
2. Japan	2,917.7	31.0	2,216.7	9.4	2,251.8	8.2	3,678.3	9.5
3. UK	848.9	9.0	1,996.2	8.5	2,217.3	8.0	2,815.9	7.2
4. France	314.4	3.3	674.4	2.9	1,174.4	4.3	1,857.2	4.8
5. Germany	355.1	3.8	825.2	3.5	1,071.7	3.9	1,194.5	3.1
6. Canada	241.9	2.6	567.6	2.4	700.8	2.5	1,177.5	3.0
7. Spain	111.4	1.2	290.4	1.2	468.2	1.7	940.7	2.4
8. Hong Kong	83.4	0.9	413.3	1.8	506.1	1.8	861.5	2.2
9. Switzerland	160.0	1.7	575.3	2.4	521.2	1.9	825.8	2.1
10. Italy	148.8	1.6	344.7	1.5	527.4	1.9	789.6	2.0
11. China	2.1	0.0	231.3	1.0	463.1	1.7	780.8	2.0
13. Australia	108.9	1.2	696.7	3.0	374.3	1.4	776.4	2.0
12. Netherlands	119.8	1.3	468.7	2.0	458.2	1.7	622.3	1.6
14. Sweden	97.9	1.0	272.7	1.2	232.6	0.8	376.8	1.0
15. Finland	22.7	0.2	73.3	0.3	190.5	0.7	183.8	0.5
WORLD	9,399.7	100.0	23,540.7	100.0	27,561.7	100.0	38,904.4	100.0

Sources: The World Bank, *World Development Indicators*, for 1999, 2000, 2002, and 2003; chapters on stock markets in 1999 and 2000 and in 2002, 2003, and 2006 (Chapters 5.2 and 5.4, respectively).

Between 1998 and 2004, the world of international economic relations saw the first supra-national currency introduced into circulation, the bursting of the bubble in financial asset prices in the telecommunications, media, and technology sector, first on US markets and then on other major markets, terrorist attacks on the US, and the American and then world recessions in 2001–2002, followed by recovery in 2003 and 2004. The Maastricht Treaty conditions for the introduction of a single currency for 11 EU member countries (later joined by a twelfth) were met and the euro was introduced into cashless transactions on 1 January 1999. After 2002, the national currencies of the 12 Euro-zone countries were withdrawn and the euro became the only means for both cash and cashless payment. Introduction of the euro meant the US dollar faced serious competition on world financial markets for the first time. The artificial initial EUR/US$ exchange rate of 1.176 fell over the first three years to 0.85.

The bursting of the US financial market bubble during the first eight months of 2001 and the sharp fall in prices of US$-denominated financial assets after the 9/11 terrorist attack brought about important changes in American fiscal and monetary policies. The Fed management, anxious to prevent deepening of the recession and massive job losses, due to a drop in the investment cycle, decided to switch from a restrictive to an expansionary monetary policy, so that interest rates on federal funds fell from 6.25 per cent to just 1 per cent between mid-2001 and the first quarter of 2003. This cut in US interest rates made fixed yield financial assets in Euro-zone countries more attractive, as the ECB did not cut its rate below 2 per cent even when the Fed rate was at 1 per cent.

The euro's decline against the dollar halted in May 2002 and the euro began gradually to strengthen. In November 2002, the currencies were at parity on the markets (€1 = US$1), but the euro's rise continued. In 1999, for the first time in 30 years, the US had a budget surplus. It continued to have one for the following two years. After the 9/11 attacks, the US government prioritized the war on terror, which entailed great increases in government spending. The US again began to experience major budget deficits between 2002 and 2005. High budget deficits, which had also been characteristic of the Reagan period, went along with steeply rising trade and current account deficits.

The fastest growing economies in 1990–2004

Analysis of the relative performance of 126 countries between 1990 and 2004 shows that the countries whose relative economic position improved most were Vietnam, the Lebanon, China, Poland, Albania, Ireland, Hungary, the Czech Republic, Guatemala, and Nicaragua (see Table 2.2). With the exception of the Lebanon and Guatemala, these economies improved their relative economic position in both sub-periods, namely 1990–1998 and 1998–2004. The average wealth coefficient for the 20 richest countries rose 8.9 per cent during the 1998–2004 period, reflecting the continued widening of the gap between the richest and the poorest countries. This widening gap is well illustrated by the difference between the average wealth coefficient of the five richest and five

Table 2.2 Change in the wealth coefficients of the fastest growing economies, 1990–2004

Country	Change of Cw in % 2004/1998	Change of Cw in % 1998/1990	Change of Cw in % 2004/1990
1. Vietnam	+15.07	+204.17	+250.00
2. Lebanon	–11.72	+284.09	+239.09
3. China	+44.65	+112.00	+206.67
4. Poland	+16.29	+126.08	+162.90
5. Albania	+97.96	+23.27	+144.03
6. Ireland	+51.97	+39.67	+112.26
7. Hungary	+58.08	+26.43	+99.87
8. Czech Republic	+44.55	+37.25	+98.41
9. Guatemala	–3.88	+89.01	+81.68
10. Nicaragua	+50.00	+19.44	+79.17
11. Slovak Republic	+52.33	+9.82	+67.28
12. Slovenia	+25.80	+31.06	+64.88
13. Kuwait	+25.89	+30.95	+64.86
14. Chile	–17.49	+95.70	+61.47
15. South Korea	+53.53	+0.71	+53.63
16. El Salvador	–10.80	+71.55	+53.02
17. Mauritius	+5.20	+43.13	+50.57
18. Trinidad and Tobago	+50.00	0.00	+50.00
19. Costa Rica	+5.58	+37.50	+45.18
20. Greece	+21.02	+18.59	+43.52

Source: The author's calculations using World Bank data.

poorest countries in our sample. Over the six years in question, the difference grew from 249:1 to 343:1. Germany paid the greatest price during the first six years of the introduction of a single Euro-zone currency, with its relative position deteriorating by 4 per cent, in contrast to Italy and France, whose positions improved 7.6 per cent and 4.9 per cent, respectively. Amongst highly developed countries, the ones with the highest rates of growth between 1998 and 2004 were Iceland, Ireland, Spain, Norway, Australia, Luxembourg, Canada, and Great Britain. Rich countries that experienced major decline in their relative position, based on the wealth coefficient, included Hong Kong, Singapore, and Japan.

Of the 20 economies (1990–2004) shown in Table 2.3, China and Ireland enjoyed the best economic performance. Despite the fact that China's foreign debt rose by a factor of 4.5, the country is the only one in the group to have foreign reserves several times its foreign debt. China's total foreign reserves at the end of 2004 were 2.5 times its foreign debt. During 2005 and the first nine months of 2006, China's foreign reserves rose an additional US$300 billion (to total US$946 billion). For the entire period, the country had both trade and current account surpluses. From 1998 to 2004, the current account surplus rose by a factor of 5.7, while between 2004 and September 2006 it went up from US$68.7 to US$161 billion. According to the World Economic Forum's *Global Competitiveness Report* for 2006, the five economies with the highest rates of

Table 2.3 External equilibrium of the fastest growing economies, 1990–2004 (in US$ billions)

Country	Current account balance		Foreign debt		Foreign exchange reserves	
	1990	2004	1990	2004	1990	2004
1. Vietnam	–	–0.60	23.27	17.83	–	7.04
2. Lebanon	+0.12	–	1.78	22.18	4.21	15.77
3. China	+12.00	+68.66	55.30	248.93	34.48	622.95
4. Poland	+3.07	–10.36	49.36	99.19	4.67	36.78
5. Albania	–0.12	–0.41	0.35	1.67	–	1.37
6. Ireland	–0.36	–1.43	–	–	5.36	2.91
7. Hungary	+0.38	–8.82	21.20	70.57	1.19	15.96
8. Czech Republic	–	–5.57	6.38	45.30	–	28.45
9. Guatemala	–0.21	–1.19	3.08	5.53	0.36	3.52
10. Nicaragua	–0.31	–0.78	10.75	5.15	0.17	0.67
11. Slovak Republic	–	–0.28	–	23.70	2.00	14.91
12. Slovenia	+0.98	–0.67	–	20.95	0.11	10.19
13. Kuwait	+3.89	+18.88	–	–	2.93	9.35
14. Chile	–0.49	+1.39	19.23	44.06	6.78	16.00
15. South Korea	–2.00	+27.61	34.97	–	14.92	199.20
16. El Salvador	–0.15	–0.61	2.15	7.25	0.60	1.94
17. Mauritius	–0.12	+0.12	0.98	2.30	0.76	1.63
18. Trinidad and Tobago	+0.46	+0.08	2.51	2.93	0.51	3.20
19. Costa Rica	–0.42	–0.97	3.76	–	0.53	1.92
20. Greece	–3.53	–11.23	–	–	4.72	2.71

Sources: The World Bank, European Bank for Reconstruction and Development, and the World Trade Organization.

saving in 2005 were Kuwait, Qatar, Algeria, China, and Singapore.[4] The savings rate in China in 2005 was 47.6 per cent of GDP. With regard to McKinnon and Shaw's basic premises regarding interest rate deregulation and the introduction of real positive interest rates as a necessary condition of savings and investment growth, it is worth noting that World Bank and IMF data show that average real interest rates in China fell from 3.5 per cent in 1990 to a *negative* real interest rate of (–1.2 per cent) in 2004.[5] In other words, precisely when China's rate of savings growth was among the highest in the world, real interest rates were negative. Similarly, according to the World Bank data, average real interest rates in Kuwait, the country with the highest rate of savings (59 per cent of GDP in 2005), fell from 10.3 per cent in 1990 to –14.3 per cent in 2004.[6] Over the same period, the average real interest rate in Ireland fell from 12.1 per cent to –0.9 per cent.

The grounds on which Central European countries (Poland, Hungary, the Czech Republic, and the Slovak Republic) have pursued economic prosperity and better economic standing have characteristically been large amounts of foreign direct investment, letting the current account deficit expand significantly (except the Slovak Republic), a sharp rise in foreign debt, rising foreign currency reserves, and access to EU funds for restructuring. The actual levels of foreign direct investment have varied significantly. Cumulative flows between 1989 and 2004, in US$ *per capita*, were highest for the Czech Republic ($4,080) and Hungary ($3,693). Per capita FDI flows to Poland were somewhat lower ($1,502). Real interest rates in all four countries grew between 1990 and 2004: in Poland from −0.4 per cent to 4.5 per cent, in Hungary from 2.5 per cent to 7.9 per cent, in the Czech Republic from −3.6 per cent to 2.9 per cent, and in the Slovak Republic from −11.0 per cent to 4.3 per cent. The rise in real interest rates in these countries was a consequence of financial liberalization, implemented during the 1990s and early years of this century in preparation for EU membership.

Analysis of the period after introduction of the euro to 2004, based on a comparison of the wealth coefficients for 1998 and 2004, shows twelve European, seven Asian, and one Central American country to have made most progress in improving their relative standing. The 20 fastest growing economies during this six-year period included 13 transition countries. Comparing the 20 fastest growing economies for 1990–2004 and the group from 1998–2004 shows only five countries in both groups: Ireland, Albania, Hungary, the Slovak Republic, and the Republic of Korea (see Table 2.4).

Of the 13 transition countries included among the 1998–2004 fastest-growing 20, only five experienced growth relative not just to 1998 but also to 1990

Table 2.4 Twenty fastest growing economies, 1990–1998–2004

Country	Change of Cw in % 2004/1990	Country	Change of Cw in % 2004/1998
1. Vietnam	+250.00	1. Turkmenistan	+100.00
2. Lebanon	+239.09	2. Albania	+97.96
3. China	+206.67	3. Indonesia	+92.63
4. Poland	+162.90	4. Yemen	+83.02
5. Albania	+144.03	5. Estonia	+80.00
6. Ireland	+112.26	6. Lithuania	+73.59
7. Hungary	+99.87	7. Latvia	+70.76
8. Czech Republic	+98.41	8. Iceland	+67.95
9. Guatemala	+81.68	9. Russian Federation	+60.98
10. Nicaragua	+79.17	10. Macedonia, FYR	+58.11
11. Slovak Republic	+67.28	11. Hungary	+58.08
12. Slovenia	+64.88	12. Armenia	+55.96
13. Kuwait	+64.86	13. Azerbaijan	+55.77
14. Chile	+61.47	14. Bosnia and Herzegovina	+54.95
15. Korea, Republic of	+53.63	15. Bulgaria	+54.75
16. El Salvador	+53.02	16. Korea, Republic of	+53.53
17. Mauritius	+50.57	17. Slovak Republic	+52.33
18. Trinidad and Tobago	+50.00	18. Ireland	+51.97
19. Costa Rica	+45.18	19. Mongolia	+51.47
20. Greece	+43.52	20. Trinidad and Tobago	+50.00

Source: The author's calculations using World Bank data.

(Albania, Hungary, Slovak Republic, Estonia, and Lithuania). Six had in contrast seen major drops in economic activity and relative standing between 1990 and 1998: Bosnia and Herzegovina (–65.5 per cent), Armenia (–63.9 per cent), the Russian Federation (–58.8 per cent), the FYR of Macedonia (–52.1 per cent), Latvia (–52 per cent), and Bulgaria (–45.1 per cent). This meant that GDP growth enjoyed in 1998–2004 was not enough to restore them to their 1990 position. In 2004, the wealth coefficients for these countries were the following fractions of what they had been in 1990: Bosnia and Herzegovina (53.5 per cent), Armenia (56.3 per cent), the Russian Federation (66.3 per cent), FYR of Macedonia (77.8 per cent), Latvia (82 per cent), and Bulgaria (84.9 per cent).

Analysis of the sources of GDP growth and the relative standing of the 20 fastest growing economies during 1998–2004 shows that improvements in the Russian Federation and South Korea over this period had the most solid basis. The Russian Federation under Vladimir Putin saw high rates of economic growth thanks to rational economic management and rising energy prices on world markets. After the crash of the Rouble and the fixed exchange rate regime, following very poor fiscal discipline due to institutional instability under the Yeltsin presidency, the Russian Federation converted to a managed float and fiscal discipline improved considerably, producing major growth in the current account surplus. According to EBRD data,[7] the Russian government's debt fell from 90 per cent of GDP in 1999 to just 18 per cent in 2005 and the 1999 budget deficit of 4 per cent of GDP changed to an 8 per cent surplus in 2005. In spite of its major foreign debt, the Russian Federation succeeded during the six years in question in increasing foreign currency reserves by a factor of 15.4, ensuring a high ratio of reserves to foreign debt (62.7 per cent).

After the great financial crisis of 1997/1998, South Korea converted from a system of fixed to floating exchange rates. The country maintained a positive current account balance and practically tripled foreign currency reserves by 2004, in comparison to the year of the crisis. Korea's foreign currency reserves in 2004 were enough to cover the entire external debt. The country's wealth coefficient in 1998 was nearly the same as in 1990. Thanks to the recovery programme, however, over the previous six years the country had attained a high rate of growth under stable conditions. Similarly, comparing the coefficients for 1980 and 2004, a gap of 24 years, South Korea had attained the highest level of wealth coefficient growth (+228.4 per cent).

Fast-growing transitional economies have over the last six years been characterized by economic growth based on faster growth of imports than exports and consequently widening trade and current account deficits and steeply rising foreign debt (excluding Turkmenistan, Albania, Bosnia and Herzegovina, and Armenia). All countries in transition, except Turkmenistan and Belarus, have taken steps to liberalize the current account and fully deregulate interest rates. Real interest rates, however, differ significantly between the fastest growing transition countries. During 2004, the lowest real interest rate among the 20 fastest growing economies of 1998–2004 was to be found in the Russian Federation (–5.6 per cent). Therefore, the country which achieved economic growth on the most stable basis, with an increase in the net savings rate of more than 15 per cent of GDP, also had a negative real interest rate. Real interest rates in 2004 were 0.3 per cent in Latvia, 2.4 per cent in Lithuania, and 2.5 per cent in Estonia.

The EBRD-published vulnerability indicators for transition economies (see Table 2.5) suggest that Poland, Slovenia, and the Russian Federation are the only countries in transition not threatened by liquidity or solvency risk, whether in public finances or in international economic relations. In all three, the state plays a strong role in directly or indirectly influencing financial flows. Despite the fact that capital account liberalization and interest rate deregulation have been carried out, state-owned commercial banks have continued to have very real influence over the formation of real interest rates and targeted loan-making to prepare companies for integration with European markets. This is particularly true of the Russian Federation and Slovenia (1992–2002).

The countries most affected by declining relative economic standing between 1998 and 2004 were South American: Argentina, Brazil, Paraguay, and Uruguay. The only South American country to improve its position over these six years was Ecuador. Argentina paid a high price for the combination of enormous debt and inability to engage more intensively with international trade through export-oriented investment. In 2004, Argentina's foreign debt was 159 per cent of GNI and 510 per cent of the value of exported goods and services and income.[8] High domestic demand, generated by high levels of debt, is a sure way towards deeper economic and social crisis.

Table 2.5 Vulnerability indicators of transition countries

	Central Europe and Baltic states	Southeastern Europe	Commonwealth of Independent States
Public sector			
Liquidity	Czech Republic, Hungary	Albania	Belarus, Kyrgyz Republic, Tajikistan, Turkmenistan
Solvency	Hungary	Bosnia and Herzegovina, FYR Macedonia, Serbia and Montenegro	Armenia, Georgia, Kyrgyz Republic, Moldova, Tajikistan
External sector			
Liquidity	Estonia, Hungary, Latvia, Lithuania	Albania, Bosnia and Herzegovina, Serbia and Montenegro	Kyrgyz Republic
Solvency	–	Croatia, Serbia and Montenegro	Armenia, Georgia, Kyrgyz Republic, Moldova, Tajikistan
Exchange regime and domestic monetary conditions	Latvia	–	Belarus, Moldova, Tajikistan, Uzbekistan

Source: EBRD, *Transition Report 2005*, p. 38.

Financial liberalization, problems of the world financial architecture, and the scope for reform

In most countries that liberalized their financial markets to any considerable degree, deposit interest rates rose sharply, in order to attract a wider customer base, which, logically enough, entailed higher interest rates on loans. The rate of interest on short-term loans also grew sharply, increasing the cost of short-term sources of finance in most developing countries undergoing liberalization. The rise in these costs led directly to higher liquidity risk and systemic risk, destabilizing the markets. Foreign banks can contribute to stabilization of conditions on the money market, by participating in the privatization of state-owned banks or by establishing affiliated banks, which then face the limits of the local market as regards the possibility for increasing market potential. By definition, both domestic and foreign banks are in the game for profit, but foreign banks, with their insurance and reinsurance networks, are in a better position to attain their goal. Under conditions of financial deregulation, capital inflows represent the most important source of potential stabilization of the real sector in capital importing countries.

Foreign direct investors, however, ground their investment in developing countries on an economic imperative: save on costs. This saving is sought in a lower cost of labour of much the same quality as is available in the home country, in lower financing costs, and in a lower fiscal burden. Given that labour costs under conditions of open and globalized world markets are lower in countries with high concentrations of population, less densely populated countries are less competitive on these grounds for foreign direct investment. Moreover, foreign direct investors are loath to invest in countries whose infrastructure is underdeveloped and where the state's institutional capacity to maintain stability and rule of law is insufficiently developed. Tax competition between developing countries is very intense, so that there is increasingly little difference between their tax systems, on the one hand, and an increasing requirement that they cover government expenditures by receipts, on the other.

Tax competition, for which read the introduction of tax incentives for foreign direct investors, reduces the tax base by the amount of the exemption from profit tax, as well as by customs and tax on imported materials required to produce goods for export. On the other hand, these tax exemptions should stimulate foreign direct investors to invest, which should contribute to higher employment. More employment means more real demand and increases the tax base, through greater purchasing power, with more income from tax levied on consumption. Since taxes levied on consumption are the main source of budgetary revenue for developing countries and they are paid by all consumers, this form of fiscal arrangement results in an unfair distribution of the fiscal burden and accelerates the development of social differences, undermining one of the basic principles of taxation outlined already in Smith's *Wealth of Nations*, the principle of generality and fairness.

Underdeveloped and inefficient government structures, particularly characteristic of countries in transition and the new states that have appeared over the past

15 years, inspire very low levels of confidence in the institutions of the system and insufficiently stable political, economic, and social conditions. It is an additional problem that most such countries are under-populated and have insufficiently competitive labour markets to ensure productivity growth at a sufficiently attractive price for foreign investors. AT Kearney provide data which illustrate the attractiveness of countries for foreign direct investment. Countries are ranked by attractiveness to interested foreign investors from the most developed countries. The most attractive destinations over the past ten years were the US, the UK, and China. In spite of China's political system, the country still appears as one of the most attractive destinations for major world companies because of the cultural environment, the low price of labour, and the satisfactory level of skills required for mass production of various kinds. In contrast to China, the countries of Southeast Asia, and to some extent South America and Central Europe, investment in other world regions was insufficient to prevent backsliding or to render those regions potentially attractive. Table 2.6 shows that the G-7 countries increased their share of world GDP between 1980 and 2004 by 2.9 per cent.

The logic of sustainable development in the global context of the twenty-first century must be based on reducing differences between levels of development, which means increasing the share of developing countries and undeveloped countries in world GDP. The then World Bank president, James Wolfensohn, explaining the overall approach of the World Bank, stressed:

> What is new is the commitment to integration of effort, essential in today's global economy where overseas aid is declining significantly. It is also a commitment to expanded partnership, transparency, and accountability under the leadership of the government. What is new is that the international financial architecture must reflect the interdependence of macroeconomic and financial, with structural and social and human concerns. I personally

Table 2.6 Gross domestic product: G-7 and world (in US$ billions)

Country	1980	2004
United States	2,709.0	11,667.5
Japan	1,059.2	4,623.4
Germany	850.0	2,714.4
United Kingdom	537.4	2,140.9
France	664.6	2,002.6
Italy	449.9	1,672.3
Canada	266.0	979.8
TOTAL G-7	6,536.1	25,800.9
TOTAL WORLD	10,960.2	41,290.4
SHARE G-7	59.6%	62.5%

Source: The World Bank, *World Development Indicators 2000*, Washington DC, 2003, pp. 190–192, www.worldbank.org – publications and data for 2004.

believe that unless we adopt this approach on a comprehensive, transparent, and accountable basis, we will fail in the global challenge of equitable sustainable development and poverty alleviation. We will fail to build a sustainable international architecture for the coming millennium.[9]

Globalization of world financial markets and the growing importance of institutional investors in developed country markets,[10] and the corresponding growth in importance of institutional investors in developing countries, under conditions of social insurance reform, will presuppose a much wider basis for choice and structuring portfolios than is currently the case. It is characteristic of the current structure of financial markets that institutional investors dominate business sector financing in the US, the UK, and Canada. Networks of institutional investors are not as yet sufficiently developed in the remaining four of the G-7 for them to dominate the financial markets and, more particularly, the market in shares and company bonds.

On the other hand, calls for reform of the social insurance systems in countries in transition and underdeveloped countries are coming from the international financial institutions, particularly the International Monetary Fund. Their aim is to cut the fiscal burden, as a way to depress the price of labour and open up room for new private social insurance institutions. The initial process of founding and developing private pension insurance systems in less developed countries will face difficulties in maintaining an acceptable (minimal) standard of living for the existing caseload of pensioners as well as ensuring pension funds have appropriately structured portfolios with sufficient yield.

The appearance of domestic private institutional investors may boost demand for local stocks and bonds. Whether or not economic growth can be speeded up will depend in part at least on the successful implementation of social insurance reform and the scope for creating portfolios for future private pension funds. This general rule, however, encounters real problems with the structuring of portfolios in countries with low rates of growth, where medium to large companies have insufficient resources to generate positive cash-flow or profit potential to attract portfolio investors. For precisely these reasons, a change is needed in investment thinking with regard to developing countries, i.e. financial resources must be allocated to them under favourable terms.

Development financing is possible in developing countries on the basis of foreign direct investments, long-term loans, and portfolio investments. Because of the damage that can be done in regions where portfolio investors invest major resources, it would be useful to adopt international standards for portfolio investing that do not put at risk the sustainability of economic growth in capital importing countries. Such criteria would have to be binding on all countries, regions, and investors. Foreign direct investment depends on infrastructure and the institutional structure of the countries being invested in. Since economic policy in developing countries has no means of actively influencing the business cycle under arrangements designed to maintain open capital accounts, there is a need for joint (regional) development financing. Regional financing would entail either control of capital flows, which contravenes the principles of free movement of capital and convertibility of the capital account, or the creation of consortium-style investment groups, to be founded by major international private financial groups that can issue derivative instruments to cover the risk of operating in certain regions. International financial organizations, whose primary mandate is to finance reconstruction and development, like the IBRD, EBRD, IADB, and IDB, could participate.

The main task of these regional financial investment groups would be to support the development of capital markets, in particular markets in company stocks and bonds from the region and denominated in the regional currency. Every region would in this case have to have its own currency, whose exchange rate would correspond to the average level of productivity in the region, so as to avoid the rigidity of pegging the exchange rate to the exchange rates of the most developed countries. The regional currencies would have to be insured against undesirable oscillations by currency swaps – which arrangements would be undertaken by the regional consortia of financial groups, in cooperation with the central banks of the regions. These arrangements would allow a higher percentage of accumulated capital to be retained in insufficiently developed regions, stimulating the development of stock markets as a means of sharing risk, covered by arrangements on derivative markets, and widening the financing base for the real sector with lower capital cost than primary exploitation of debt instruments as sources of financing in development to date. From Table 2.7, it is clear that such regional investment consortia of investment companies are needed most in regions where GDP between 1980 and 2004 grew at best 93 per cent and in some cases as little as 34 per cent, i.e. in the Middle East, Central African, and Sub-Saharan African regions.

Table 2.7 Gross domestic product by region (in US$ billions)

Country category	1980	2004	2004/1980
Low-income countries (excluding China and India)	451.8	1,239.2	2.74
Middle-income countries	2,322.8	7,156.8	3.08
• Lower-middle income countries	1,158.5	4,165.3	3.40
• Upper-middle income countries	1,164.3	2,991.5	2.57
Low and middle-income countries together	3,134.1	8,395.2	2.68
• East Asia and Pacific	503.6	2,650.9	5.26
• Europe and Central Asia	–	1,769.7	–
• Latin America and Caribbean	787.9	2,022.0	2.57
• Middle East and North Africa	409.9	547.5	1.34
• South Asia	237.3	880.2	3.71
• Sub-Saharan Africa	271.8	523.3	1.93
High-income countries	7,936.1	32,900.1	4.15
WORLD	10,960.2	41,290.4	3.77

Source: The World Bank, *World Development Indicators 2000*, Washington DC, 2000, p. 188 (data for 1980); www.worldbank.org – publications and data for 2004.

Considering it a priority to create such groups in the poorest regions does not imply that they would be any less significant in regions which have achieved higher rates of growth. In principle, all regions where the rate of GDP growth was lower than the rate in developed countries will, in the first three decades of the twenty-first century, have to grow faster than developed countries. Table 2.8 shows that basing development on debt instruments of financing provides no grounds for supposing that under such circumstances the basic economic goal of the twenty-first century can be attained, namely long-term growth on a sustainable basis without major business cycle crises.[11]

The regional central banks would have discretionary powers in order to communicate their intentions in a reliable, flexible, and swift manner to regional markets, providing indirect stimulus to the development of capital markets, as bases for growth in creditor confidence, and reducing systemic risk. Countries belonging to the region would be allowed to issue public debt, to assist in dealing with social problems and tensions through the provision of social security to the large number of socially vulnerable categories of the population. Public debt issue would be related to national GDP. Purchase of debt issued by the countries of the regions would be supported by both the regional central banks and by the regional investment consortia, significantly increasing the scope for stabilization of social and political conditions, the precondition for further development of investment. The markets in government securities would be under the control of the major financial groups, while the markets in goods and services would be in line with WTO provisions. In line with the theoretical and practical elaboration of the principle of the efficient functioning of central banks in deregulated environments, the presidents of the regional central banks would have to be conservative central bankers, whose conservatism would result from thorough understanding of the economic fundamentals of the region and extensive experience in finance, which would in turn give the individuals involved the credibility to inspire the confidence of the consortia of financial groups, which would support and foster development in the region through enlarged registration of securities in regional currency, secured by derivative financial contracts.

Table 2.8 External debt of developing countries (in US$ billions)

Region	1998	2001	2004
Africa	282.7	258.5	305.8
Central and Eastern Europe	269.8	316.0	553.8
Commonwealth of Independent States	222.8	194.4	281.0
Developing Asia	695.0	661.2	751.0
Middle East	290.9	306.4	347.4
Western Hemisphere	789.4	782.9	844.7
TOTAL	2,550.6	2,519.4	3,083.7

Source: International Monetary Fund, *World Economic Outlook*, September 2006, p. 238.

The fundamental characteristics of national autonomy and sovereignty from an economic point of view entail the following three minimum conditions:

- the existence of central monetary institutions with the discretionary power to change the quantity of money in circulation and influence the formation of short-term interest rates;
- the capacity to issue public debt, combined with flexibility in pursuing public spending policy, in line with the direction of the business cycle (the downside of the business cycle should be mitigated by increased budgetary spending, and vice versa); and
- the capacity to influence the exchange rate, so as to improve foreign trade in goods and services, as well as capital flows (inflows and outflows).

The process of financial liberalization increased the mobility of capital compared to the first two decades after World War II. Changes to IMF rules also had a direct impact on the ever decreasing room allowed the nation-state for the exercise of economic policy. The processes of financial liberalization and globalization raise the fundamental issue of future development: If the fundamental revolution of John Maynard Keynes in economics, the introduction of economic policy as targeted intervention by the relevant government bodies to influence the direction of the business cycle, arose out of the need to prevent growing unemployment, the sharp drop in demand, and the phenomenon of widespread poverty, who are the main agents of economic development at the national and supra-national levels who will prevent the continued differentiation and increasing gap between the developed and the underdeveloped nations? The trend for the gap between rich and poor to widen is evident not just on the global level, between regions, but also within politically sovereign states. The foundations on which the new economy is based are knowledge and the open market, so that the most vulnerable groups of the population are the least educated.

Given current business thinking and the fundamental strategic function of the private sector, based as it is on the principle of long-term sustainability of profit potential while maintaining positive cash flow, the private sector by definition is not the agent to take over part of the role of the economically sovereign state or its discretionary rights. Rules of the game imposed on the nation-state from outside have eaten away at economic sovereignty, suggesting that the world system has returned to the rules that were in place at the beginning of the twentieth century. Private corporations could take over part of the state's functions or cooperate with states in maintaining the stability of the system. This would entail shouldering some of the costs of maintaining ecological stability and of research and development that aims at raising the capacity of various regions to use efficiently the resources invested in them by foreign direct investment.

Transferring some part of state spending to corporate budgets reduces the profit potential of the companies and would be on a collision course with the nature of the corporate form of business organization and the growing importance and role of financial markets in managing business cycles. Namely, reducing the profit potential, as a result of increased costs caused by transferring some public expenditures to the company budget, would reduce the attractiveness of investing in shares, at least where there is an expectation of dividends, as the dividend is, in the final analysis, drawn on the net profit potential of the company. Such a change in business thinking and the mission and strategic function of companies could have a very progressive and developmental impact, particularly on regions and countries which have been sidelined by contemporary development (for example, Africa), but would in the end mean reaffirmation of the importance of the firm's goal function in line with Joan Robinson's theory of imperfect competition. The role of the international institutions would remain irreplaceable, however, alongside that of strengthening government institutional capacity to stimulate development and reduce the major disparities in the world.

Notes

1 This text was originally published as the third part of *Economic Sovereignty and Global Capital Flows* (pages 183–194 and 201–209), published by International Forum Bosnia, Sarajevo, in 2006, with whose kind permission it is reprinted here. Translated by Desmond Maurer, M.Sc.
2 IMF, *World Economic Outlook*, Chapter IV, September 2006.
3 The wealth coefficient is the ratio of a country's share in overall world GDP and its share in world population, as introduced by the author in Fikret Čaušević, *Economic Sovereignty and Global Capital Flows*, International Forum Bosnia, Sarajevo, 2006.
4 The World Economic Forum, *Global Competitiveness Report 2006–2007*, p. 445.
5 The World Bank, *World Development Indicators 2006*, Washington, 2006. (Section – 'Markets').
6 Ibid.
7 EBRD, *Transition Report Update*, London, May 2006, pp. 64–65.
8 The World Bank, *World Development Indicators 2006*, Washington, 2006.
9 James D. Wolfensohn, 'A Proposal for a Comprehensive Development Framework', *The World Bank Group*, 21 January 1999.
10 The main institutional investors are pension funds, insurance companies, mutual funds, and investment funds. The assets of institutional investors comprise mostly of the bonds and shares of companies from the business sector, and of government securities. The total assets of institutional investors in the USA in the second half of the 1990s were almost twice the US GDP.
11 See Joseph E. Stiglitz, *Making Globalization Work – the Next Steps to Global Justice*, W.W. Norton & Company, New York, 2006, Chapter 8.

References

Čaušević, Fikret, *Economic Sovereignty and Global Capital Flows*, International Forum Bosnia, Sarajevo, 2006.
EBRD, *Transition Report 2005*, London, 2005.
EBRD, *Transition Report Update*, London, May 2006.
IMF, *World Economic Outlook*, Washington, September 2006.
Stiglitz, Joseph, E., *Making Globalization Work – the Next Steps to Global Justice*, W.W. Norton & Company, New York, 2006.
The World Bank, *World Development Indicators 1999*, Washington, 1999.

The World Bank, *World Development Indicators 2000*, Washington, 2000.
The World Bank, *World Development Indicators 2002*, Washington, 2002.
The World Bank, *World Development Indicators 2003*, Washington, 2003.
The World Bank, *World Development Indicators 2006*, Washington, 2006.
The World Economic Forum, *Global Competitiveness Report 2006–2007*, Geneva, Switzerland, 2006.
Wolfensohn, James D., 'A Proposal for a Comprehensive Development Framework', *The World Bank Group*, 21 January 1999.

3 The international financial architecture and the global financial crisis

Its causes, birth, and impact on small open economies – the case of Bosnia and Herzegovina[1]

Changes in the international balance of economic power

The significance and roles of the two largest economies in the world, those of the United States of America and Japan, have undergone significant change over the past seven years, when measured in terms of gross domestic product (GDP). The data on the G-7 nations' share in the creation of world GDP indicate a major fall in Japan's importance:[2]

- The United States' share in world GDP declined from a record level of 30.6 per cent in 2000 to 25.4 per cent in 2007 (Figure 3.1). This reduction in the US's importance vis-à-vis the world economy may be expressed in percentage terms as a fall of 15.3 per cent in its wealth coefficient (Table 3.1).[3]
- Japan's share in world GDP went from 14.6 per cent in 2000 to just 8 per cent in 2007 (Figure 3.1). Japan's importance relative to the world economy has therefore reduced by some 40.4 per cent over the past seven years (Table 3.1).
- Unlike the two largest world economies, the remaining five G-7 nations have all seen their economic importance increase over the past seven years: Italy by some 17.8 per cent, Great Britain by 16.7 per cent, France by 16.2 per cent, Germany by 10.9 per cent, and Canada by 9.1 per cent.

The Big Four developing countries (the G-4 or BRIC, as they are known, are Brazil, Russia, India, and China) made very considerable progress during the first seven years of this century, both in terms of the absolute or nominal increase in GDP and in terms of their relative share in the world economy (see Figure 3.2 and Table 3.2). Taken together, these four countries' share in world GDP rose from 8 per cent in 2000 to 13 per cent in 2007. Russia made the greatest individual progress, improving its relative position by some 228 per cent. China's position improved by 68 per cent, India's by 48 per cent, and Brazil's by 19 per cent.

Table 3.3 presents the nominal GDP data for the G-7, G-4, and the world. These data show that in the first seven years of this century the G-7 saw its share

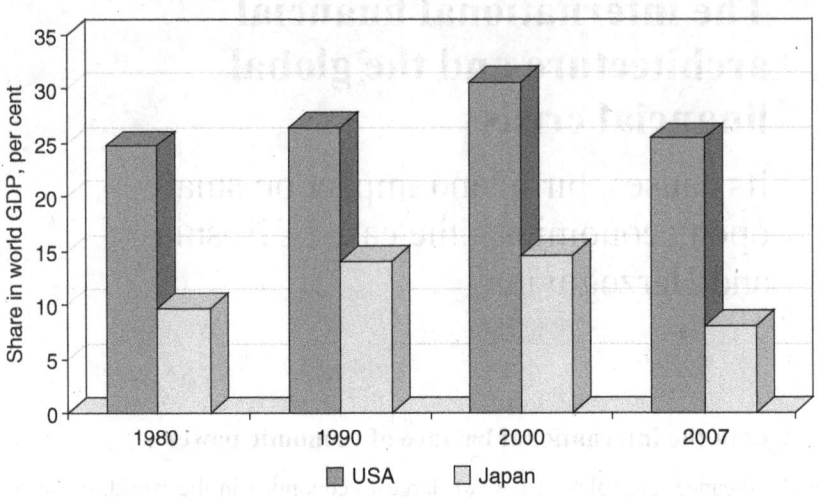

Figure 3.1 The United States' and Japan's share in world GDP (source: the author's calculations based on data published by the World Bank).

Table 3.1 Changes in the importance of the major world economies, measured by the wealth coefficient

Country	Wealth coefficient 2007	Wealth coefficient 2000	Change 2007/2000 (in %)
United States	5.572	6.580	−15.3
Japan	4.168	6.997	−40.4
Germany	4.877	4.396	+10.9
United Kingdom	5.438	4.658	+16,7
France	4.982	4.289	+16.2
Italy	4.318	3.666	+17.8
Canada	4.892	4.484	+9.1

Source: The author's calculations based on World Bank data.

in world GDP fall (by some 10 per cent). The overall share of the Big Eleven (G-7+G-4) also fell. The main reason the share of the remaining countries increased was higher income from exports enjoyed by oil and gas-producing countries. The share of the other, non-oil producing countries was down, representing a certain repression of the 'rest of the world' by the G-11 and the five major oil-exporting countries.

The change in the balance of power and direction of capital flows is made clear by the data on the Big Seven's trade and current account balances (see Table 3.4).

Table 3.4 shows that the aggregate current account deficit for the G-7 countries in early December 2008 recalculated at the annual level was $434 billion.

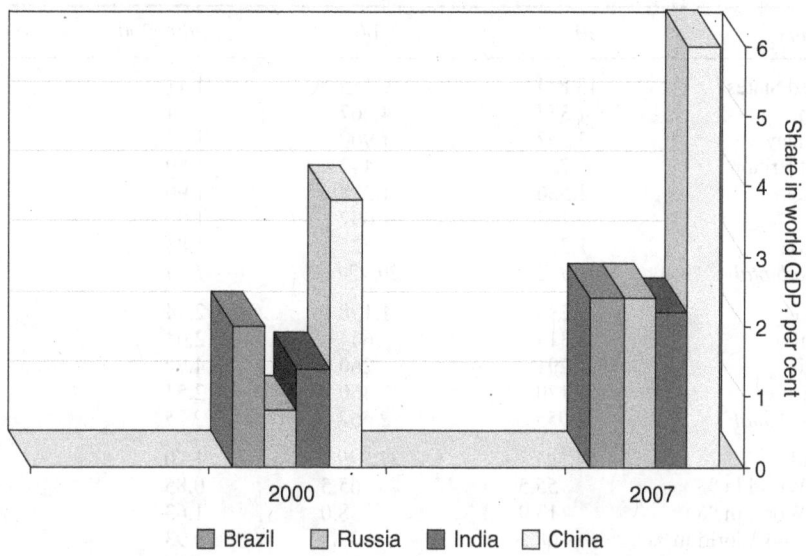

Figure 3.2 Brazil, Russia, India, and China's share in world GDP (source: the author's calculations based on data published by the World Bank).

Table 3.2 Changes in Brazil, Russia, India, and China's relative importance in the world economy, measured by the wealth coefficient

County	Wealth coefficient 2007	Wealth coefficient 2000	Change 2007/2000 (in %)
Brazil	0.834	0.704	+18.5
Russia	1.109	0.338	+228.1
India	0.127	0.086	+47.7
China	0.302	0.180	+67.8

Source: The author's calculations based on World Bank data.

These countries are therefore net importers of capital. The two largest debtors (importers of capital) amongst the G-7 are the United States and Great Britain. Great Britain, however, is not the second largest debtor in the developed part of the world. That honour belongs to Spain, whose current account deficit at the beginning of December 2008, in annual terms, was $166 billion (11.2 per cent of GDP).

On the other hand, the fast-growing Asian economies and Russia increased their current account surplus over the past seven years from $94 to $420 billion. Data are given in Table 3.5. Their aggregate current account surplus last year almost equals the sum of the G-7's aggregate current account deficit. Due largely

Table 3.3 GDP for the G-7, G-4, and the world (in US$ billions)

Country	2007	2000	2007/2000
United States	13,811	9,765	1.41
Japan	4,377	4,667	0.94
Germany	3,297	1,900	1.74
Great Britain	2,728	1,442	1.89
France	2,526	1,328	1.90
Italy	2,107	1,097	1.92
Canada	1,326	725	1.83
G-7 subtotal	30,172	20,924	1.44
China	3,280	1,198	2.74
Brazil	1,314	644	2.04
Russia	1,291	260	4.97
India	1,170	460	2.54
G-4 subtotal	7,055	2,562	2.75
World	54,347	31,949	1.70
G-7/World in %	55.5	65.5	0.85
G-4/World in %	13.0	8.0	1.63
G-7+G-4/World in %	68.5	73.5	0.93
Rest of world in %	31.5	26.5	1.19

Source: www.worldbank.org – data on GDP values; other data calculated by the author.

Table 3.4 Trade and current account balances of the G-7 in 2008 (in US$ billions)

Country	Balance of trade	Current account balance
United States	–851.1	–699.0
Japan	+64.8	+185.9
Germany	+288.4	+266.8
Great Britain	–185.5	–82.9
France	–80.7	–53.6
Italy	–17.0	–70.8
Canada	+52.6	+19.2

Source: The central banks of the relevant countries, the Bank for International Settlements; taken from *The Economist*, 6 December 2008.

to higher exports and the higher price of oil (in the case of Russia), which resulted in the current account surpluses, and to foreign direct investment flows, these countries' overall foreign exchange reserves have risen from $595 to $3,182 billion. Approximately two-thirds of these reserves are held in US$-denominated financial assets.

Table 3.5 The current account balances and foreign exchange reserves of the fastest growing developing countries

Country	Current account balance 2000	Current account balance 2007	Foreign reserves 2000	Foreign reserves 2007
China	+16	+250	160	1528
Hong Kong SAR	+10	+27	103	160
India	–6	–11	32	295
Singapore	+22	+39	77	168
South Korea	+13	+6	93	262
Taiwan	+8	+32	112	278
Russia	+31	+77	22	491

Source: The central banks of the relevant countries; the Bank for International Settlements.

Trends in international trade and the structure of the international financial system

Very important changes have taken place during the past 15 years in international economic relations and particularly in the international trade in goods. These changes have had a direct impact on the international movement of capital, which is to say on international debt. In the early 1990s (1993), the leading exporting countries were:[4]

- United States (12.6 per cent);
- Germany (10.3 per cent);
- Japan (9.9 per cent);
- the six fast-growing countries of Southeast Asia (9.7 per cent); and
- France (6.0 per cent).

The five main importers of goods the same year were:

- United States (15.9 per cent);
- the six fast-growing countries of Southeast Asia (10.3 per cent);
- Germany (9.0 per cent);
- Japan (6.4 per cent); and
- France (5.7 per cent).

With the rapid economic expansion of China and the countries of Southeast Asia, on the one hand, and the US economy's declining export record and the transfer of a significant part of US production to China and Southeast Asia, on the other, the US's relative weight in world trade or, more precisely, in world exports of goods has declined significantly. At the end of 2007, the five leading exporters were:

- Germany (9.7 per cent);
- the six fastest-growing countries of Southeast Asia (9.3 per cent);

- China (8.9 per cent);
- United States (8.5 per cent); and
- the countries of the Near East (5.6 per cent).

Over the 14 years in question, the US's role in world imports has not changed significantly. The US is still the leading importer, though its share in total imports is less than in 1993 (down 1.4 per cent). The five leading importers in 2007 were:

- United States (14.5 per cent);
- the six countries of Southeast Asia (8.7 per cent);
- Germany (7.6 per cent);
- China (6.8 per cent); and
- Japan (4.4 per cent).

The data show that Japan suffered the greatest decline in importance vis-à-vis world trade in goods. Its share in world exports fell 4.7 percentage points, while its share in world imports fell 2 percentage points. Japan's importance as a world exporter had reduced sufficiently that it was no longer to be found amongst the top five in 2007. On the other hand, China's contribution to world exports rose some 6.4 percentage points between 1993 and 2007, while its share in world imports was up 4.1 percentage points. When considering the sustainability of China's economic growth rate, one should pay particular attention to the absorption capacity (purchasing power) of her major markets. This is because Chinese economic growth has been very largely dependent on export-led growth. China's total exports of goods in 2007 amounted to $1,217 billion. The main recipients, looking regionally, were Asia (42.8 per cent), the United States (21.7 per cent), and Europe (21.7 per cent).

Given the importance of the United States' dollar for the international financial system, for which it remains the dominant reserve currency, any reduction in the US's role in world exports and any consequent increase in its trade and current account deficits may have far-reaching consequences for international financial stability and sustainability.

Although the US trade deficit reduced in 2007 as a percentage of GDP, its nominal value was essentially unchanged. Table 3.6 illustrates one of the major paradoxes of economic globalization over the past two decades. According to the theoretical position put forward by McKinnon and Shaw in 1973, countries with more developed and liberal financial systems should be major generators of savings and exporters of capital. What has actually happened during the past two decades is precisely the opposite. The United States, the country with the most sophisticated and deepest, which is to say the most liberal, financial market in the world has become a net importer of savings. Moreover, the net imports of savings, which remained at a relatively stable level from the mid-1980s to the end of the 1990s, increased significantly during the first seven years of this century, jeopardizing the American dollar's hegemony in international finance.

Table 3.6 Net savings in the United States, 1984–2007

Period	Savings (as % GDP)	Investment (as % GDP)	Net savings (as % GDP)
1984–1991	17.3	19.9	−2.6
1992–1999	16.4	19.0	−2.6
2000	18.0	20.8	−2.8
2003	13.4	18.5	−5.1
2006	14.1	20.6	−6.5
2007	14.0	19.7	−5.7

Source: International Monetary Fund, *World Economic Outlook*, September 2006; October 2008.

In this context, some clarification is required of the prospects for sustaining the United States' gaping trade deficit and its repercussions for international financial relations.

The sustainability of the US trade deficit

Bearing in mind the United States' major trade and current account deficits, analysis of the sustainability of international financial architecture and global financial system necessarily raises the question of how such global imbalances are to be sustained in future. The United States' trade deficit increased between 1997 and 2000 from $200 to $430 billion. Over the following seven years (2000–2007), it increased from $430 to $820 billion. The country's current account deficit increased over the same period from $160 to $795 billion. Over the past seven years, the United States has increased its trade deficit with China alone from $40 to $256 billion. China has become the third largest export market for products from the United States, but also the largest exporter to the American market.[5]

Given that over the 1992–2007 period (with the exception of 2007) the United States' trade and current account deficits have been steadily growing, so has the country's debt towards the rest of the world. Masaru Yoshitomi[6] has analysed the sustainability of the United States' trade deficit by calculating the amount of American debt that has to be carried in the portfolios of foreign financial investors. In drawing his conclusions, Yoshitomi relied on certain assumptions regarding future interest rate trends and risk premium on American liabilities, which is to say financial assets in the US possessed by the rest of the world, as well as the projected American GDP growth rate.

As his starting point for treating this global imbalance, Yoshitomi took the equation expressed by Michael Mussa in his 2004 work on 'Exchange Rate Adjustments Needed to Reduce Global Payments Imbalances'. The formula, which relates to long-term equilibrium in the value and quantity of net American liabilities relative to GDP, is as follows:

$$n^* = c/(g-r)$$

Where:

n* represents the long-term ratio of net foreign debt to GDP;
c represents the current account deficit as a percentage of GDP;
g represents the nominal growth rate of GDP; and
r represents the nominal rate of return on net foreign debt.

The last value, **r**, the nominal rate of return on the net external debt, is defined as the net yield from international investment expressed as a percentage of net foreign debt. The net yield from international investment is calculated in the following way:

(The yield on US residents gross foreign assets) *minus* (the yield on non-residents' gross US assets, i.e. non-residents' income from the gross US external debt).

Assuming that the US will continue to maintain a current account deficit in the region of 6 per cent of GDP and will enjoy an average nominal rate of growth of 5 per cent, but that foreign investors' rate of return on assets held in the US will be practically negligible (close to 0), as has been the case over the past two years, Yoshitomi concludes that the above equation entails a long-term ratio of net external debt to GDP of 120 per cent.

Yoshitomi further claims that, under the above assumptions, the US net external debt will reach a level of 64 per cent in ten years. This would be 19 per cent of the property or assets of all other investors in the world. This would not be alarming were foreign investors ready and willing to retain such a level of US assets in their portfolios. Yoshitomi bases his conclusion on the attractiveness of US financial markets to foreign investors due to innovation in the creation of financial instruments. This attractiveness based on the innovative nature of American markets did exist up to the first half of 2007. Since the mortgage crisis broke, however, with the subsequent major problems in maintaining leading US investment banks' liquidity, financial instruments based on financial innovation have become of rather more doubtful attractiveness to investors.

Foreign investors' rate of return on US financial assets (the net US external debt) between 2003 and 2005 was very low compared to the rate US residents abroad enjoyed (US assets abroad). This very low US rate of return was due to monetary measures taken by the Fed, which by mid-2003 had reduced the rate on federal funds to just 1 per cent. This was followed by an increase, but remained below the level for financial assets denominated in euro or British pounds. Consequently, while US net foreign liabilities had already reached the level of 29 per cent of GDP by 2004, net income from international investments was nonetheless modestly positive, to the US's benefit. Given these trends, the rate of return on net foreign liabilities was negative, facilitating the sustainability of America's external debt under the circumstances. The financial troubles which have afflicted nearly every significant financial market in the world produced sharp reductions in interest rates, particularly during the second half of 2008.

These developments require us to look at the figures again and review capital flows within the context of the global crisis, as well as the prospects for reforming the international financial architecture and the position of the International Monetary Fund.

The international financial architecture and the International Monetary Fund

The dynamic of change in the balance of economic power between the most developed countries of the world, namely the G-7, the four high-growth and high population countries (the BRIC or G-4), the six newly industrialized countries of Southeast Asia (Hong Kong, Singapore, Malaysia, Indonesia, Thailand, and the Philippines), and Mexico, as well as Turkey and the oil-exporting countries, over the past 15 years, and particularly during the first seven years of this century, has had the effect of increasing pressure on the management of the International Monetary Fund (IMF) by the fast-growing developing countries to redefine the voting rules and the distribution of voting rights in the institution.

One consequence of these demands was a decision made by the IMF management at its annual meeting in Singapore in September 2006 to pass a package of reforms that would last two years. Because of the great importance of the balance of power between the member countries in one of the most important financial institutions in the world, I will now go through the basic phases of reform as presented on the IMF webpage.[7]

The content of the reform package

The proposed and partially realized IMF reform package involves the following five measures:

1 An ad hoc increase of the quotas for China, Korea, Turkey, and Mexico;
2 A new formula for determining the quota, to be used in assessing the suitability of IMF member countries' current quotas;
3 A second ad hoc increase in the quota based on the new formula;
4 An increase in basic votes, with a view to ensuring that low-income countries can participate in voting, as well as increasing their weight in the voting mechanism based on the basic votes; and
5 Allocating adequate resources to the executive directors representing many countries at the IMF.

The ad hoc quota increase

This first step has already been carried out, resulting in increased payments by China, Korea, Turkey, and Mexico, totalling 3.8 billion in special drawing rights (SDR), equivalent to $5.66 billion. The resulting total value of the quota for all members of the IMF is 216.8 billion SDR, or $321.9 billion (see Table 3.7).

Economic challenges in the world economy

Table 3.7 The quota distribution at the International Monetary Fund in the first half of 2007

Country/region	Share – in %	Value – in billions of special drawing rights
United States	17.1	37,149
European Union	32.4	70,404
Asia	11.5	25,010
China	*3.7*	*8,090*
India	*1.9*	*4,158*
Korea	*1.3*	*2,927*
The Near East and Turkey	7.6	16,426
Turkey	*0.5*	*1,191*
Latin America	7.6	16,501
Mexico	*1.5*	*3,153*
Brazil	*1.4*	*3,036*
Africa	5.3	11,498
Canada	2.9	6,369
Russia	2.7	5,945
Switzerland	1.6	3,459
Australia	1.5	3,236
Other countries	9.8	21,317

Source: www.imf.org.

Note
This is the quota schedule for 21 May 2007.

New formulae for quota determination

The formulae for determining the IMF member country quotas have changed over time, to reflect the pattern of economic relations in the world. The first was the Bretton Woods formula, which originally comprised the following five elements for the determination of the quota: national income, official reserves, the value of imports, the fluctuation of exports, and the ratio of exports to current national income.

The multi-formula approach was introduced in the 1960s, when the Bretton Woods formula was supplemented by a further four new formulas. National income was replaced by the substitution of gross domestic product (GDP), while in external transactions services and transfers were added to goods. Greater weights were thus given to current account transactions and fluctuation. The next revision of the formula was carried out in 1982–1983, when the weight previously assigned to fluctuation was reduced and official reserves were reintroduced as a factor, while maintaining the basic structure of the formula unchanged.

The importance of the quota for IMF governance and decision-making is reflected in the following four elements:

1 It determines the amount each member country must contribute to IMF financial resources;

2   It determines each country's voting rights, in combination with basic voting rights;
3   It determines each country's ability to access IMF resources; and
4   It determines the value of the SDR allocation assigned to each member country.

A resolution by the IMF board of governors was adopted at the September 2006 Singapore meeting to change the formula and give greater weighting to country members' GDP and reward countries that are more open to international flows of goods, services, and capital. The new formula was not defined, as the goal was for the IMF members to reach consensus over the determination of the quota, and by the 2007 annual meeting, or, at the latest, by the 2008 spring meeting.

The second ad hoc increase in the quota

This step will be implemented once the new quota formula has been confirmed, as even after application some countries may be inadequately represented in decision-making and voting. The Board of Executive Directors will be able to propose a second ad hoc change to the quota to the Steering Board, to ensure under-represented countries obtain appropriate voting rights.

Changes to country members' basic votes

Changing the basic votes of the IMF country members is one of the basic aims of these reforms. Under the current system, each member of the IMF receives 250 basic votes, with an additional vote for every 100,000 special drawing rights allocated under the quota system. As the quota has been changed a number of times, the real weight of low-income countries in the IMF has reduced from 11 per cent to 2 per cent. The intention is to increase basic votes and at least double the low-income countries' share in the overall value of the quota, maintaining the same voting rights after the planned ad hoc changes.

The financial systems of the Big Seven[8]

The financial systems of the United States, Great Britain, and Canada are so-called arm's-length systems in which securities markets (shares and bonds) play a major role, while derivative instruments, like term contracts and options, are very important for financing the investment cycle and so the corporate sector. In these three G-7 countries, institutional investors (pension funds, insurance companies, mutual funds) are major players in forming the average cost of capital to the real sector. Institutional investors' assets are made up mostly of corporate securities (shares and bonds). Securities markets do not play anything like the same role in the countries of continental (Western) Europe, however, where investment cycle financing is based predominantly on bank-client relations. The structure of their financial systems makes these countries less vulnerable to major oscillations in securities' prices and their impact on the economic cycle. They are not, however, isolated from shocks coming from the US and British markets.

In line with the preceding paragraph, the basic characteristics of the financial systems of the United States, Great Britain, and Canada can be summed up as follows:

- Financial markets play a very significant role in the economies of these three countries, and in particular those of the US and the UK;
- Between 1995 and 2006, the market capitalization to GDP ratio averaged 140 per cent in Great Britain, 135 per cent in the United States, and 87 per cent in Canada;
- Capital markets' importance for economic development and the creation of investment finance sources derives from the effects of financial innovation;
- Historically speaking, one of the most important financial innovations was the founding of private pension funds and mutual companies (institutional investors);
- Institutional investors' assets reached some 165 per cent of GDP in Great Britain (including foreign assets) and 145 per cent of GDP in the United States.

Commercial banking in these three countries plays a very significant role in financing the supply of current and fixed resources, but still a less dominant one than in the countries of continental Europe, Japan, and the fast-growing economies. The basic characteristics of the position of commercial banking may be described as follows:

- Commercial banks' role in these countries' financial systems is significant, but less important than in continental Europe;
- Commercial banks increasingly derive their income from charges for banking services, including mediation in the sale of rights to purchase financial instruments;
- Money markets have a very important role in managing the liquidity of the system, because of the high level of public debt, particularly in the US.

Unlike the US, Great Britain, and Canada, the financial systems of Germany, France, Italy, and Japan display the following structural characteristics:

- Commercial banks play the dominant role in business financing in these countries;
- The role of the capital markets is significant, but considerably less than in the US, the United Kingdom, or Canada when it comes to financing investment;
- Average market capitalization in these countries between 1995 and 2006 ranged from 55 per cent in Germany to 40 per cent in Italy.

On the other hand, banking sector loans to the non-financial sector (companies from the non-financial sector, households, and government) over the past 12 years averaged from 38 per cent in Italy to 50 per cent in Germany, compared to just 15 per cent in the US.

In the US, the public is very active on financial markets, with close to 45 per cent of households in possession of some form of financial assets (securities). Overall, households account for some 25 per cent of all holdings of corporate shares in the US (in terms of value). In the countries of continental Europe, the public are considerably less inclined to invest in securities, with securities on average making up around 5 per cent of household wealth in Germany, France, and Italy. Public habits are similar in Japan.

A direct consequence of the structure of the G-7 countries' financial systems is the different positions taken by the central banks with regard to economic growth. Managing the monetary supply is considerably more complicated in countries where market capitalization represents a higher percentage of GDP. As a result, managing the dollar supply is more complicated than managing the supply of euro. On the other hand, the position of the US offers it more scope for influencing international capital flows.

Problems with inflationary trends during the first half of 2008

One of the basic characteristics of the economies of the fast-growing developing countries during the first half of 2008 was accelerated price growth. The rate at which prices grew during the first two quarters of the year was, in fact, the highest in ten years. The inflation rate in China during the first quarter of this year rose to 8.5 per cent from 3 per cent the previous year. In Russia, the inflation rate during the first three months of the year was 14 per cent per annum, compared to 8 per cent the previous year. In India, where it is focused on the wholesale price index, the annual inflation rate during the first half of the year averaged 7.8 per cent. This was the highest rate in this country for four years.[9]

The inflation rate in Brazil was up to 5 per cent during the first quarter of 2008, from 3 per cent for the same period the year before. The rise in prices was more marked in Chile – from 2.5 per cent in the previous year to 8.3 per cent during the first quarter of this year. The inflation rate was highest in Venezuela (29.3 per cent). In Argentina, the authorities manipulate the data on the real rate of inflation to show just 8.9 per cent, but *The Economist* reports Morgan Stanley experts' view that the real rate during the first half of the year (including food and fuel) was 23 per cent.

The Central Banks of Brazil, Indonesia, and Russia have all increased interest rates. Real interest rates are, however, negative in most fast-growing countries, with the exception of Brazil, Mexico, and South Korea. In Russia, the base rate of 6.5 per cent was almost 8 per cent lower than the rate of inflation. Negative real interest rates were a major feature of money markets in both China and Russia from 1998 to 2004, when the average negative real interest rate in Russia was −5.6 per cent and in China the rate fell from a positive level of 3 per cent in 1990 to a real negative rate of −1.2 per cent in 2004.[10]

The impact of food prices on the inflation rate depends on the pattern of household consumption, which is to say on the level of development, as this determines the role food costs play in the consumer price index. According to *The Economist*'s report on inflation in developing countries, food costs account on average for 15 per cent of the consumer price index in G-7 countries, while in fast-growing large developing countries they account for: 60 per cent in India, 42 per cent in Indonesia, 40 per cent in Russia, 36 per cent in Saudi Arabia, 32 per cent in China, and 21 per cent in Brazil.

Analyses of price trends in developing countries carried out by HSBC experts have drawn attention to the following key factors as contributing to the creation of inflationary pressure between 2005 and the first half of 2008:

- It is a problem for most fast-growing developing countries (FGDC) that they lack surplus fixed capacity which could be used to increase production, instead of increasing prices.
- For example, capacity utilization is at record levels in Brazil and India – the employment rate in Brazil is the lowest in 20 years.
- Lack of capacity is a consequence of insufficient investment in these countries.
- The narrow inflation rate, which excludes changes to food and fuel prices, is also rising – at 3.4 per cent in Asia, 6.2 per cent in Latin America, and 7.4 per cent in Eastern Europe.
- There is clear inflationary pressure in Argentina, Brazil, India, Russia, and the oil-exporting countries of the Near East.

The FGDC face specific problems related to their (in)ability to exercise effective control over the exchange rate or inflation, namely:

- The international movement of capital is very mobile and intense, so that countries which have fully liberalized (both long-term, but more particularly short-term) capital flows are prevented from conducting effective economic policy.
- If FGDC central banks want to maintain a fixed exchange rate while allowing capital inflows from abroad, they have to print local currency – which contributes to rising prices.
- One potential solution is the introduction of flexible exchange rates or revaluation of the local currency.
- One problem arising from the introduction of flexible exchange rates, or revaluation, is that those countries' currencies may be expected to grow in value.
- These expectations of further appreciation of FGDC currencies (especially China) affect major flows of capital from abroad and the increasing money supply on the domestic market.

One possible option for reducing inflationary pressures in FGDC, and particularly in China, from the perspective of the first half of 2008, would have been to suspend the practice of cutting the Fed rates in reaction to the financial crisis triggered by the property market crisis in the US. Halting the rise in interest rates, by increasing the Fed rate, would have resulted in capital flowing into the US and reduced pressure on the National Bank of China. Appreciation of the Chinese currency during 2007 and the first half of 2008 led, amongst other things, to a rise in the price of Chinese goods intended for the US market, which in turn increased inflationary pressures in the US. The deepening of recessionary trends in the US during the second half of 2008, however, affected decision-making regarding interest rates, bringing them near to zero for the first time in the history of the American Fed.

The turn from inflationary to deflationary trends during the second half of 2008

The inflationary pressures which were a major feature of the first half of 2008 peaked during the first half of July, when the price of oil reached $147 per barrel, the price of gold was between $950 and $975 an ounce, and the value of the US dollar reached its lowest level to date against the euro (US$1.60 for €1). The problems of illiquidity on inter-bank markets in the US and Western Europe translated into reduced liquidity in derivative transactions, particularly for term contracts, which play a crucial role in setting the price of all commodities (from grain, through metals, to fuels). The sharp reduction in demand for such goods, combined with insufficient liquidity on these markets, led to a major fall in the price of fuel (the barrel price of oil fell from $147 in July to $45 at the beginning of December), metals, and agricultural produce. Deflationary trends during the second half of the year, and particularly from October to early December, opened up room for the Fed, the European Central Bank, and the Bank of England to cut interest rates.

In addition to steadily cutting interest rates (from 5.25 per cent in June 2007 to the target range of between 0 per cent and 0.25 per cent, announced in December 2008),[11] the Fed took a very active approach to introducing new sources of liquidity. In early 2008, the TAF (temporary adjustment facility) was introduced – short-term loans with a maturity of 28 days, very low interest rates, and simplified procedures for approval. On the basis of these loans alone, the Fed was able to inject $950 billion into circulation during the first seven months of the year. In addition to this instrument, the Fed also determined on a CPFF, or 'commercial paper funding facility', with the direct authority to approve loans to the corporate sector. Similar measures were also taken by the two most important central banks in Europe: the European Central Bank and the Bank of England. The scale of the interventions made by the three most important central banks speaks to the seriousness and depth of the world financial crisis.

The financial crisis in the US and the spill-over to Europe

In an interview he gave to the journalist Judy Woodruff in May this year, George Soros cited data indicating that there is little prospect of a 'quick fix' for the current financial crisis.[12] Over the next two years, it is expected that 40 per cent of the total of six million loans made on the US mortgage market will be defaulted upon. This means nearly 2.4 million loans (this is the *number* of loans, not their value). A further approximately 2.6 million so-called 'adjustable-rate' loans will also most likely have to be written-off the balance sheets of the banks and associated financial institutions. With more than five million loans, with an estimated total value of more than $2 trillion, likely to be written off during the next two years, not even the Bush administration's action to save Freddie Mac and Fannie Mae and the major investment banks and insurance companies will be enough to bring the financial crisis to a quick halt.

The main responsibility for the situation lies with the management structures in the investment and commercial banks in the US, on the one hand, and the ineffective economic and foreign policy of the Bush administration, on the other. The management of the major investment banks was too oriented towards short-term profits (speculation on securities), while loans from commercial banks created additional liquidity (purchasing power), used for speculative activities. Similarly, between 2004 and 2007, the Fed was slow to decide on interest rate changes and desirable changes to financial sector regulation. George Bush's economic policy was largely oriented towards providing direct and indirect support to the enormous growth in the volume of property market transactions, which, alongside irrational fiscal policy, led to a growing budget deficit, increasing public debt, a reduction in the competitiveness of the US economy in producing for export, and a steady increase in the trade and current account deficits (with the exception of last year), leading to a weaker dollar and losses (expressed in terms of the opportunity cost of investing in low-yield US$-denominated financial assets) for most developing countries who hold their foreign exchange reserves largely in dollar deposits.

The markets in derivatives expanded sharply, creating the illusion of insuring against the risk of default, on the one hand, while at the same time contributing to the creation of fictive liquid power and inflating speculative financial balloons, on the other. Amongst the best indicators of the lack of fit between trends on financial markets and the real sector is what happened to the gross value of derivative contracts and the value of world gross domestic product over the past few years. The notional outstanding value of over-the-counter (OTC) derivatives included in the over-the-counter market increased in line with the following dynamic (Table 3.8):

According to the data in Table 3.3, world gross domestic product in the following years was:

- 2000 – $31,950 billion;
- 2007 – $54,350 billion.

Table 3.8 The notional value of derivative contracts on the over-the-counter market

Year	Notional amount in US$ billions
2000	95,199
2002	141,665
2004	248,288
2005	297,670
2006	415,183
2007	713,200

Source: Bank for International Settlements, Quarterly Reviews: September 2003, September 2005, December 2008.

This data clearly illustrate that world GDP accounted for 34 per cent of the nominal value of derivative contracts traded on the OTC market in 2000, but just 9 per cent in 2007. In other words, in 2000, the total nominal value of derivative contracts made on the OTC market was three times the value of world GDP, but seven years later it was 13 times.

Between 2003 and 2007, there was particularly intensive growth in derivative contracts in the area of 'credit default swaps' (CDS), which are a form of insurance against uncollectible liabilities. The leaders in the sale of such instruments were banks like Lehman Brothers, which then reinsured with the main insurance company AIG. The financial crisis that developed in the United States and Great Britain attained such dimensions because of the nature of these countries' financial systems, as explained above. It is still impossible to determine the final reach of the financial crisis because of the different systems for recording balance-sheet positions and the process of unbundling all balance-sheet positions based on borrowed resources and the use of very high degrees of leverage. European financial institutions which financed clients from Western Europe investing in the US property markets suffered significant losses and were forced to write off a certain percentage of uncollectible liabilities.

Hang Keynes – long live Keynes

January 2006 marked 70 years since the publication of Keynes' best-known work, *The General Theory of Employment, Interest and Money.* In June the same year, I spent some time in London at the London School of Economics and asked my colleagues whether the anniversary of the best-known work of twentieth-century economics had been marked in any way. The response was not in the affirmative. Very few universities marked this anniversary in Europe or elsewhere in the world. Two years ago (that is, in 2006) Keynes was still not particularly popular, as his teaching had been out of fashion for nearly three decades in most of the world's universities. On the other hand, the economic policy of the Bush administration, although formally and explicitly based on the philosophy of the free market, did not for most of the period Bush was in power function on that basis. The monetary and fiscal measures pursued in the US in the period following 11 September 2001 and up to mid-2003 were a classic application of Keynesian recommendations (with the exception of public works, which were missing).

That is to say, after 11 September 2001, the Bush administration approved a fiscal package which entailed new public borrowing, an increase in the national debt, and a return by the US to a period of budget deficits. The monetary policy was also classically Keynesian: in 13 consecutive sessions the FOMC[13] cut the federal funds rate from 6.25 per cent (the first half of 2000) to 1 per cent by mid-2003. The rate was kept at this level (1 per cent) for the following year (to mid-2004), since when it gradually rose to 5.25 per cent in the first half of 2007. Meanwhile, dealing with the recessionary dangers in the last quarter of 2001 and the first two quarters of 2002 was based on a classic combination of fiscal and monetary measures entirely in line with the recommendations of John Maynard Keynes.

George Bush's economic policy since the second half of 2007, and particularly during 2008, was an even more marked return to Keynesian recommendations. The major economic crisis, caused by the previous unrestrained investment in property and financial assets during the period from 2003 to 2006, entailed the accelerated reduction of interest rates, already mentioned above, from 5.25 per cent in the first half of 2007 to practically zero by the end of December, with a major expansion of the money supply and a highly expansionary fiscal policy, reflected in the approval of a fiscal package worth some $700 billion and an additional fiscal package expected under the new American administration to be led by Barack Obama, worth between $850 and $1,000 billion.

An even clearer and more interesting example of the return to Keynes and his recommendations for managing economic policy under conditions of recessionary trends comes from the first half of December 2008, promoted by what many economists would regard as the most rigid financial institutions in the world, when it comes to fiscal discipline. In a speech in Madrid, Dominique Strauss-Kahn, the managing director of the IMF, set forth a vision of how governments around the world should act to prevent the recession turning into a depression, with potentially very dangerous consequences for world peace. Kahn suggested the following measures:

- reinforcing and renewing the stability of the financial markets;
- an active and coordinated anti-cyclical fiscal policy; and
- support to maintain the liquidity of developing countries, to avoid sharp outflows of capital away from those countries.[14]

Kahn stressed clearly the urgent need for coordinated intervention by the governments of the leading countries of the world on their financial markets based on 3 Cs: clear, comprehensive, and cooperative.

The second urgent priority was support to aggregate demand. As Kahn himself said: during periods of global economic problems, the solution is normally of a fiscal nature. But this time, the IMF *did not recommend a restrictive* but an *actively expansionary fiscal policy* based on a combination of cutting taxes on consumption and personal income tax, while issuing new public debt with a view to financing useful public investment likely to have a major impact on the fiscal multiplier. As a good example of useful public investment, he cited Barack Obama's announced programme of public investment – a programme focused on the energy sector. These proposed measures are clear examples of the economic recommendations of John Maynard Keynes. Today, as never before in the past five decades, we have a very clear position taken by the most rigid global financial institutions that there is need for very swift reaction, deploying clearly expansionary fiscal policy measures and so following the classical Keynesian, or rather Keynes' own, recipe for exiting an economic crisis.

The financial and economic crisis in small open economies – the case of Bosnia and Herzegovina

The financial sector in Bosnia and Herzegovina has undergone liberalization in line with the recommendations of the World Bank, the IMF, and the European commission. Liberalization of the financial sector entailed the removal of any controls over interest rates in the hands of the entity governments or the Council of Ministers of Bosnia and Herzegovina, privatization of the banking sector, the free entry of foreign banks into the commercial banking sector, reform of the system of internal payments, the removal of all barriers to current account transactions, and the removal of the great majority of the barriers to long and short-term movement of capital. These measures, with the introduction of a single Bosnian currency and strengthening of the system of bank supervision in the direction of accepting the international (Basle) standards, resulted in flows of international capital into the Bosnian banking sector and its development on a stable basis. The banking sector has attained absolute dominance as the main source of financing business activities, as well as household spending.

The lending activities of banks in Bosnia and Herzegovina, since the arrival of the first major foreign banks in 2000, have, up until 2008, been characterized by more rapid growth in loans to households than in loans to businesses. It was only during the first ten months of 2008 that, for the first time in the past eight years, lending to businesses exceeded household loans (see Table 3.9).

Table 3.9 Lending to businesses and households in Bosnia and Herzegovina (millions of KM)

Year	Credit to businesses	Credit to households
2002	2,715	1,506
2003	3,038	2,038
2004	3,182	2,700
2005	3,956	3,538
2006	4,760	4,480
2007	5,839	5,754
October 2008	7,328	6,990

Source: The Central Bank of Bosnia and Herzegovina.

The net increase in individual purchasing power based on loans made between 2002 and the first nine months of this year was 5.5 billion KM. Over the same time period, loans to businesses totalled 4.6 billion KM. Alongside transfers from abroad, these ten billion KM were key channels for increasing purchasing power, investment activity, and effective demand in Bosnia and Herzegovina over the 2002–2008 period.

The gross domestic product of Bosnia and Herzegovina, based on the expenditure method, taken as an average for the past four years, displayed the following breakdown:[15]

- household consumption – 88 per cent;
- final government consumption – 21 per cent;
- gross investment – 22 per cent;
- net exports – 31 per cent.

Bosnia's total volume of trade saw an increase over the 2000–2007 period of 124 per cent, which is approximately 11 billion KM (see Table 3.10). As the trade deficit was considerably higher in 2007 than in 2006, the reduction in the deficit for 2006, compared to 2005, was principally a result of a major increase in imports during the last two quarters of 2005, as companies prepared for the introduction of VAT at the beginning of 2006. Consequently, the best indicator of the trade deficit is to take an average for the two years, which may be used as the comparative basis for the real increase in the trade deficit in 2007. Such comparison suggests that the trade deficit in 2007 was some 17 per cent up on the average for the previous two years. This increase was largely dictated by the rising price of fuel and of raw materials and inputs required for the production of steel, iron, and steel and iron products, as well as produce.

The five main export industries in Bosnia and Herzegovina over the past four years (2003–2007) have been in the following branches:[16]

Table 3.10 The balance and volume of trade in Bosnia and Herzegovina, 2000–2007 (millions of KM)

Year	Exports	Imports	Trade balance (exports – imports)	Volume of trade (exports + imports)
2000	2,265	6,583	–4,318	8,848
2001	2,256	7,331	–5,076	9,587
2002	2,089	8,048	–5,958	10,137
2003	2,323	8,319	–5,996	10,642
2004	2,819	9,306	–6,487	12,125
2005	3,783	11,179	–7,395	14,962
2006	5,164	11,389	–6,225	16,553
2007	5,937	13,899	–7,962	19,836

Source: The Central Bank of Bosnia and Herzegovina.

- The production of steel, iron, and related products: This branch's share in overall exports has risen by some seven points, to 14.1 per cent. The value has increased from 163 to 838 million KM.
- The production of machinery, equipment, and electrical devices: This branch's share in exports rose from 8.2 per cent to 12.9 per cent, while the value of those exports increased from 191 to 763 million KM.
- The generation of electrical energy and the production of products of mineral origin is the third most important exporting branch, with an increase in share from 9.5 per cent to 11 per cent and in value from 220 to 658 million KM.
- The production of aluminium and related products is the fourth branch of industry, having experienced a reduction in the relative importance of its exports, down from 13 per cent to 10.8 per cent. The total value for 2007 was 638 million KM.
- The fifth most important export industry is the production of timber and wood products, whose share in exports during 2007 was 8.9 per cent.

The companies that enjoyed the greatest increase in exports during the past five years and consequently account for most of the recent increase in exports from Bosnia and Herzegovina were:

- Arcelor Mittal Zenica;
- Aluminij Mostar;
- ASA Prevent Group;
- VW Vogošća Sarajevo;
- Elektroprivreda BiH;
- Elektroprivreda RS; and
- CIMOS TMD Gradačac.

Of these companies, only the generation and distribution of electrical energy will not experience an immediate negative impact from the recessionary trends in Western Europe and the rest of the world. Companies from the metal sector and the auto industry will be at direct risk of recessionary trends. Moreover, activities related to the production of timber, wood products, furniture, and prefabricated houses are linked to the investment cycle in construction and will be directly affected by the crisis. An additional complicating factor for the most important export industries in the economy here is that product prices in the metal sector have fallen sharply and we may consequently expect a fall in the total income of the leading export companies of the order of some 15 to 20 per cent. This reduction in their overall income will hamper these companies in adapting their cost structures during recession and will most likely be reflected in reduced demand for labour in the sector. The extent of this reduction in demand for labour will depend on orders from abroad. It is, however, realistic to expect that, over the coming year, between 2,000 and 2,500 of those currently employed in the metal sector alone may find themselves without regular employment (including the auto industry). In construction, in the absence of any major infrastructural projects, an additional 2,000 people may find themselves without temporary, part-time, or permanent employment. Increasing cost pressures and heightened competition in the banking sector may also lead to the loss of some 700 to 1,000 jobs.

In analysing gross domestic product and its constituent elements in Bosnia and Herzegovina, the following assumptions seem realistic:

- Household consumption: There is no realistic prospect that household consumption will grow in the coming year. The opposite is in fact likely. Over the coming year, we may expect reduced employment, for the reasons given above. Along with reduced employment, we may expect a reduction in net salaries, as companies cut costs, but also because of the increased tax burden following the introduction of income tax, which will affect companies where the average salary is above 700 KM. The number of personal loans made is unlikely to increase compared to last year. Overall, household consumption may even fall by as much as 10 per cent.
- Investment by the business sector and individuals. In the absence of strategic partnership agreements in the energy sector, there is no real basis for projecting any increase in investment in the business sector over the coming year. Individual investment in the construction of new buildings (houses) or the purchase of new apartments is also unlikely to increase. It is more realistic to expect a reduction in investment on these grounds.
- Government spending: Alongside a fall in the price of imported goods, in individual purchasing power, and in investment by companies, government spending on goods and services is also likely to be reduced, as revenues fall.
- Net exports: The value of exports by Bosnian and Herzegovinian companies may drop by between 20 and 30 per cent, for the reasons given above (a combination of falling orders and a significant reduction in export prices). The price of imports will also fall, but the net result could well be a deficit similar to that in the current year (2008).

The probability of these assumptions being realized in the coming year is 75:25, which is the same as to say that there is a considerable probability of stagnation or a fall in production in Bosnia and Herzegovina. Such negative, but by no means unrealistic, expectations may only be countered by the following two measures:

- signing contracts for the realization of major investment projects in the energy sector, which would mean a significant increase in industrial production in domestic companies associated with this complex; and
- issuing new public debt (state and entity bonds), the sale of which would create revenue which could then be invested in capital (infrastructure) projects.

Bosnia and Herzegovina does not have a wide range of choices, but there are realistic prospects for turning this crisis period into a new beginning of restructuring and investment in the renewal of technical expertise and major capital investment for the products for which real demand in Europe exists.

Notes

1. This text first appeared in *Forum Bosnae 49/09* on pages 95–125, after presentation at a public discussion in Sarajevo on 20 December 2008. It is reprinted here with the permission of the journal's publisher, International Forum Bosnia. Translated by Desmond Maurer, M.Sc.
2. GDP data for the countries in question and the world as a whole are taken from http://datacatalog.worldbank.org/.
3. The wealth coefficient is the ratio of a country's share in overall world GDP and its share in world population, as introduced by the author in Fikret Čaušević, *Economic Sovereignty and Global Capital Flows*, International Forum Bosnia, Sarajevo, 2006.
4. The data on these countries' share in world trade in goods are taken from the World Trade Organization's webpage: www.wto.org – International Trade Statistics 2008.
5. For more details on American and Chinese trade relations, see: Wayne M. Morrison, 'China–U.S. Trade Issues', Congressional Research Service, Foreign Affairs, Defense, and Trade Division, March 2008 (available at http://digitalcommons.ilr.cornell.edu/key_workplace/498/).
6. Masaru Yoshitomi, 'Global Imbalances and East Asian Monetary Cooperation', in: Duck-Koo Chung and Barry Eichengreen (Eds) *Toward an East Asian Exchange Rate Regime*, The Brookings Institution, Washington, 2007.
7. www.imf.org.
8. This part of the paper is based on the two following sources: International Monetary Fund, *World Economic Outlook – Financial Systems and Economic Cycles*, September 2006, Chapter IV: 'How Do Financial Systems Affect Economic Cycles?', authored by Fikret Čaušević; and Fikret Čaušević, *Economic Sovereignty and Global Capital Flows*, International Forum Bosnia, Sarajevo, 2006, Part II.
9. See *The Economist*, 'An Old Enemy Rears its Head', 24 May 2008, pp. 83–85.
10. See Fikret Čaušević, op. cit., pp. 188 and 192.
11. See Federal Reserve press release, 16 December 2008.
12. Judy Woodruff and George Soros, 'The Financial Crisis: An Interview with George Soros', *New York Review of Books* 55 (8), 15 May 2008.
13. The FOMC – Federal Open Market Committee – consists of 12 members and is the main decision-making body of the Federal Reserve System of the United States.
14. Dominique Strauss-Kahn, 'The IMF and Its Future', Speech at the Banco de España, Madrid, Spain, 15 December 2008. (www.imf.org/external/np/speeches/2008/121508.htm).
15. See the national accounts (expenditure) on the BiH Statistics Agency webpage: www.bhas.ba.
16. Data on Bosnia's trade may be found at the Central Bank of Bosnia and Herzegovina webpage: www.cbbh.ba.

References

The data for this paper were drawn from the various institutional webpages cited in the endnotes.

Čaušević, Fikret, *Economic Sovereignty and Global Capital Flows*, International Forum Bosnia, Sarajevo, 2006.

Chung, Duck-Koo and Barry Eichengreen (Eds) *Toward an East Asian Exchange Rate Regime*, The Brookings Institution, Washington, 2007.

Federal Reserve, press release, 16 December 2008.
International Monetary Fund, *Global Financial Statistics*, Washington, 2008.
International Monetary Fund, *World Economic Outlook*, Washington, 2008.
Morrison, Wayne M., 'China–U.S. Trade Issues', Congressional Research Service, Foreign Affairs, Defense, and Trade Division, March 2008.
Strauss-Kahn, Dominique, 'The IMF and Its Future', Speech at the Banco de España, Madrid, Spain, 15 December 2008.
The Economist, 'An Old Enemy Rears its Head', 24 May 2008, pp. 83–85.
The Economist, Special report: 'World Economy', 11 October 2008.
The International Monetary Fund, *World Economic Outlook – Financial Systems and Economic Cycles*, September 2006, Washington, Chapter IV: 'How Do Financial Systems Affect Economic Cycles?'.
Woodruff, Judy and George Soros, 'The Financial Crisis: An Interview with George Soros', *New York Review of Books* 55 (8), 15 May 2008.
Yoshitomi, Masaru, 'Global Imbalances and East Asian Monetary Cooperation', in Chung and Eichengreen, 2007.

4 Market fundamentalism, religious fundamentalism, and economic growth[1]

Major changes during the past three decades

In the worlds of economics and politics, the past three decades have been marked by the opening up of the two most populous countries in the world, China and India, to international trade and capital flows, by the religious revolution in Iran, the major struggle against inflation in the United States and the countries of Western Europe, the domination of the 1980s by Japan, followed by that country's stagnation, the tearing down of the Berlin Wall, the unification of Germany, the disintegration of the USSR and Yugoslavia, and the transformation of the former socialist countries into market economies, or rather the major socio-economic change in these countries and their shift from centrally planned towards market economies (this does not apply to the former Yugoslavia, whose system was based not on central planning but on self-management). These events have had an impact on how these former socialist countries, whose populations total approximately 300 million people, have joined the process of the international division of labour, specialization, trade in goods and services, and international capital flows. These major socio-economic changes have, on the one hand, acted to strengthen the advocates of free markets as the best regulators of economic relations, while, on the other hand, also strengthening the opponents of globalization, who ascribe to a wide range of ideological persuasions.

Economic globalization, which has encompassed almost half of the world population over nigh on three decades, was supported by the theory of limited political sovereignty, the essence of which is that internationally recognized countries cannot conduct entirely independent policy. Economic globalization has taken place, however, rather more quickly than political globalization. The lag in political globalization has resulted in a structure of international political institutions which is incapable of responding appropriately to all the challenges of economic globalization. One of the basic challenges of economic globalization is the redistribution of world wealth and its concentration in narrow social circles – the marked social stratification of the populations of the countries in transition, in the fast-growing economies of the Far East and of Southeastern and Southern Asia, and the increase of social inequality even in developed countries.

Between 1980 and 2005, the G-7's share in world GDP increased from 58.7 per cent to 62.5 per cent.[2] Over the same period, China's share rose from 1.8 per cent to 4.9 per cent. India presents an excellent example of the problems of the modern world. During the first seven years of the century, the Indian economy, viewed as a whole, was one of the ten fastest-growing. Regardless of this accelerated economic growth, however, some 600 million people in this country live on or below the UN defined poverty line. The number of the extremely poor in India (people who cannot afford even the most basic services because their resources are sufficient only for basic nutritional needs) is in and around 300 million. The population of India increased from 660 million in 1980 to 1.15 billion in 2007. Consequently, in spite of the fact that India has been one of the fastest-growing economies in the world during the past seven years, the country has not succeeded in dealing with the issues of infrastructural development, linking urban and rural areas, water supply, and heating. Over the past two decades, there has been a marked growth in poverty in most African countries, while in the countries of sub-Saharan Africa life expectancy has fallen to below 45 years (equivalent to average life expectancy in the countries of Western Europe some 170 years ago).[3]

The acceleration of economic growth in China, in the countries in transition, and Southern Asia and stronger linkage between the West and the East created an opportunity and provided arguments for the advocates of the decisive importance for economic growth of introducing market principles in the organization of the economy and society as a whole. There can be no doubt that the introduction of market principles of operation into economic relations have a positive impact on the promotion of the significance of individuality, creativity, and invention for economic growth in countries actively involved in international trade. One of the central problems of the intellectual basis for preaching the role and importance of the market in organizing social and economic relations derives from the fundamentally incorrect presentation of the meaning of markets themselves – what is commonly meant by the free action of the market in both developed and developing countries is actually a model of the unregulated market. Contemporary market structures are, for the most part, imperfect market structures, which result in the subordination of common interests to the interests of individuals or dominant economic groups. The contemporary term for this problem is market fundamentalism. On the other hand, resistance to the imposition of universal rules of the game based on market fundamentalism as the misguided intellectual basis for the process of economic globalization has manifested as religious fundamentalism, combined with ethnic separatism,[4] the apparent antithesis of market fundamentalism.

Market fundamentalism

In his book *The Force of Finance*, author Reuven Brenner[5] explains that the integration and development of financial markets are the main engine of United States economy and will ensure the primacy of this country through this century.

George Soros, by contrast, presents an analysis in his book *The Crisis of Global Capitalism*[6] of one of the greatest problems of global economic management during the last two decades of the twentieth century. Rapidly implemented deregulation of world financial markets without appropriate institutions for the management of the world economy at the international level created, in Soros' opinion, what is the leading threat to the sustainability of the world economy. Soros sees this threat in market fundamentalism. Market fundamentalism is, in fact, the term that Soros introduced to describe the advocates of the idea that the market forces of economic systems, and particularly those related to financial movements, are self-regulating. By its nature, market fundamentalism is an ideology whose roots in economic literature are already to be found in the work of Adam Smith. Adam Smith promoted the free operation of market forces, or the action of the 'invisible hand' of the market, in the *Wealth of Nations*, as a sui generis *spiritus movens* of the increase of the economic prosperity of nations. Moreover, in his earlier work, the *Theory of Moral Sentiments*, Adam Smith provided an analysis of the factors that cause individuals not to act exclusively in their own interests. Ekelund and Hebert present Smith's views on the organization of economic life and the role of the individual and his or her interests as follows:

> There are, according to Smith, two innate tendencies in human psychology. The first is that as human beings we are principally interested in things which are closest to us, and much less in what is remote (whether in time or space); we are all, therefore, important to ourselves ... the second characteristic, which in fact derives from the first, is the undeniable desire of each individual to improve *their* circumstances.... Expressing this in the narrow terms of our subject, human beings are led by personal interests, but this characteristic is not necessarily synonymous with selfishness. Smith's 'economic' man from the *Wealth of Nations* is no different from his 'moral' man from the *Theory of Moral Sentiments*. They are both beings of personal interest. In the *Theory of Moral Sentiments*, sympathy is a human attribute that moderates personal interest, while in the *Wealth of Nations* competition is the economic attribute that limits personal interest.[7]

Moreover, the 'me first rule' is one of the basic principles on which the development of modern financial theory and free markets rests. The theory of the firm and the theory of agency are based on the 'me first rule'. The theory of agency explains how it is that an agent maximizes the benefit or yield from the holdings of the company owners (shareholders). Maximizing shareholder yield vis-à-vis the cost of guaranteeing that the manager will behave/act in the best interest of the stockholders is one of the key problems in contemporary market structures. Because of the requirement to maximize yield for stockholders, company managers are constantly exposed to pressure to make decisions in the short term that will increase that stockholder yield. Such pressure on managers leads directly to short-termism in running a business, undermining commitment to the bases of sustainable long-term growth and technological advancement that respects ecological standards.

George Soros has well presented the problem of how to shape market expectations and the ambiguous position of actors in the economic system. In his view, the economic sciences are facing major problems because of the constant desire to present the economic system on the basis of equilibrium, which does not exist in reality. What is presented as deviation from equilibrium is not deviation in real life, but the rule. This rule is a consequence of the phenomenon of reflexivity, by which Soros means situations in which market actors find themselves in a double position: on the one hand, they are trying to understand what is actually happening, and so to create an image which corresponds to reality. Soros refers to this function as cognitive. On the other hand, market actors are attempting to influence the real train of events and bend reality to their wishes. Soros calls this function participatory. When both functions are at work and united in the same person (or group of persons), there is a reflexive situation.[8]

Soros' explanation is a fairly representative illustration of the problem of the intellectual validity of rational expectations theory. Contemporary financial theory is based on rational expectations: given that the most important actors in global economic currents, in principle, do very often find themselves in reflexive situations in existing market structures and would find themselves in such situations even more frequently if there were no (public) regulatory institutions responsible for the management of the business cycle, as the rational expectations of school advocates, the logical result would be to increase the weighting applied in forming rational expectations to the subjective expectations of the most important actors on world markets, so that rational expectations would, to a highly significant degree, be a reflection of the reflexive situations in which those actors find themselves. The conclusion which follows from the principles of market economics and modern financial theories based on the 'me first rule' is that rational expectations are a reflection of the desire of the most important actors, in both the markets for commodities and financial markets, to mould the rules of the game around them to their own ends.

Following the definition of the Great Transformation and the Longview project,[9] market fundamentalism denotes the quasi-religious belief that the unregulated market will always somehow produce the best possible results for society. On the other hand, the purpose of this project is to train people to analyse the economy not as an impersonal mechanism which gives effective results, but as a network of institutions which can be shaped to serve the needs of society, and so of people.

In his books *Globalisation and Its Discontents* and *Making Globalisation Work*, one of the best-known contemporary economists, Joseph Stiglitz, presented a number of problems arising from the liberalization of economic activity without a concomitant creation of institutions of global management. Stiglitz stresses that economic globalization has outpaced political globalization and that this represents a major problem for the coordination and management of a world in which we live:

We have a chaotic, uncoordinated system of global governance without global government, an array of institutions and agreements dealing with a series of problems, from global warming to international trade and capital flows. Finance ministers discuss global finance matters at the IMF, paying little heed to how their decisions affect the environment or global health. Environment ministers may call for something to be done about global warming, but they lack the resources to back up those calls.[10]

In *The Crisis of Global Capitalism*, George Soros claims that the global capitalist system is a deformation of the Open Society. In his view, the excesses of global capitalism could be corrected for or avoided more successfully if the principles of the Open Society were better understood.[11]

> Capitalism, with its exclusive reliance on market forces, poses a different kind of danger to open society. The central contention of this book is that market fundamentalism is today a greater threat to open society than any totalitarian ideology. This statement is rather shocking. A market economy is an integral part of an open society. Friedrich Hayek, the greatest twentieth-century ideologist of laissez faire economics, was a firm believer in the concept of an open society. How can market fundamentalism threaten open society? Let me make myself clear.... The concepts of open society and market economy are closely linked and market fundamentalism can be regarded as merely a distortion of the idea of the open society.... Market fundamentalism endangers the open society inadvertently by misinterpreting how markets work and giving them an unduly large role to play.

Soros sees the transfer of market logic based on profit maximization to domains of social activity where it does not properly belong as one of the main drawbacks of the global capitalist system.[12] According to Soros, profit maximization and basing decision-making on the 'first me rule' in politics, as a form of group decision-making, in contrast to the market where individual decision-making is the norm, are causing major damage to market economies and bringing into question the global sustainability of capitalism, while seriously hampering the realization of the idea of the Open Society as outlined by Karl Popper in 1944. Market fundamentalism is, in Soros' opinion, no less dangerous than the totalitarian ideologies which were dominant at the time when Karl Popper was writing his book – that is fascism and the Soviet system.

George Soros' analysis of the dangers of the global capitalist system in this book published not quite ten years ago is newly relevant for two reasons: Soros has published a new book in which he reaffirms the threat the market fundamentalist logic represents for global integration at a time when a new financial crisis generated in the United States of America is spreading to the leading European and Asian economies. The other reason is that Soros himself is one of the leading players on financial markets, so that his views regarding the dangers facing the global system must be accorded due attention.

Economic growth and political democracy

Investigating the correlation between economic growth and political democracy, Robert Barro found no necessary conditionality between economic growth and being a political democracy. What is more, political autocracy has enabled some developing countries, and even some of the members of the OECD, to achieve high rates of economic growth.

> The connection between political and economic freedom is more controversial, as stressed in the theoretical parts of the recent surveys by Sirowy and Inkeles (1990) and Przeworski and Limongi (1993). Some observers, such as Friedman (1962), believe that the two freedoms are mutually reinforcing. In this view, an expansion of political rights – more 'democracy' – fosters economic rights and tends thereby to stimulate growth. But the growth-retarding aspects of democracy have also been stressed.... Authoritarian regimes may partially avoid these drawbacks of democracy. Moreover, nothing in principle prevents nondemocratic governments from maintaining economic freedoms and private property. A dictator does not have to engage in central planning. Examples of autocracies that have expanded economic freedoms include the Pinochet government in Chile, the Fujimori administration in Peru, the Shah's regime in Iran, and several previous and current governments in East Asia. Furthermore, as Schwarz (1992) observes, most OECD countries began their modern economic development in systems with limited political rights and became full-fledged representative democracies only much later.[13]

The result of Robert Barro's empirical analysis of the links between political democracy and economic growth have essentially confirmed Lipset's[14] thesis that political democracies can develop in countries and environments that have already experienced high levels of economic growth, which is to say that economic prosperity is the precondition to the development of political democracy on sustainable and stable bases:

> Despite the lack of a compelling underlying theory, the cross-country evidence examined in this study confirms that the Lipset hypothesis is a strong empirical regularity. In particular, increases in various measures of the standard of living tend to generate a gradual rise in democracy. In contrast, democracies that arise without prior economic development – sometimes because they are imposed by former colonial powers or international organizations – tend not to last.[15]

Religious fundamentalism

The term fundamentalism was originally linked to Protestant culture. The term was officially introduced on the occasion of the Niagara Falls Bible Conference in 1910, which was followed by the publication of a collection of 12 books under the title of 'The Fundamentals'. The mission of the fundamentalist movement in Protestant culture was to protect the fundamental ideas of Christianity, which in the view of the movement had been lost as part of a historical process of the transformation of the Christian teaching after the appearance of Protestantism. The concept of fundamentalism came about as a result of this attempt to define the fundamental principles of Christianity, i.e. the fundamentals, deviation from which was unacceptable in the view of this Protestant movement. As it was related to religion or religious values, the term was later expanded to religious fundamentalism and has, over the past three decades, been used to describe the religious worldview based on the belief that society should be organized solely and exclusively on the basis of strongly codified religious norms of behaviour.

Today, religious fundamentalism has developed amongst the members of certain communities in all the significant world religions: starting from Christianity, through Islam and Judaism to Hinduism. Common to this worldview is the claim by the religious fundamentalists that only their worldview is correct, in other words a claim to absolute and exclusive truth. In essence, religious fundamentalism is a totalitarian ideology, like the totalitarian ideologies and movements based on atheism. In the former socialist countries, which is to say the countries in transition, there is an evident crisis of identity which has resulted in a 'conversion' from atheist totalitarianism to religious totalitarianism or fundamentalism.

In *The Future of Capitalism*, Lester Thurow analysed the impact of social volcanoes on the future economic development of the world. The two most important social volcanoes, with negative consequences for the integration of the world and its organization on sustainable bases, are religious fundamentalism and ethnic separatism.[16] Thurow stresses that the religious fundamentalists are at heart social dictators. They are trying to force others to follow their path. As this author puts it, one of the most interesting consequences has been the political opinions of libertarians and the religious fundamentalists in the United States. They not uncommonly vote for the same party:

> Three out of four Christian fundamentalists voted in 1994 for the Republicans, contributing a total of 29% of the vote. No one doubts the Christian fundamentalists will control the selection of the next Republican candidate for president.... In America, the political expression of these fundamental tensions may best be seen in the Republican party, which is supported by both a majority of the libertarians and a majority of the fundamentalists. They are allies in their antipathy towards the Democrats, but when the regulation of social behaviour is on the agenda, then no two groups are so far from each other.[17]

Religious fundamentalism blossoms during periods of economic instability. Major economic crises provide very fertile social ground, creating major differences in the distribution of national income at the national level as well as in national participation in the creation of world wealth. The particularly unbalanced distribution of world wealth over the past three decades has resulted in a reincarnation of religious fundamentalism in the countries of Asia and Africa, particularly of Islamic fundamentalism. The inability of the international political institutions to solve the problem of Palestine and Israel has increased tensions in the region and strengthened the political position of the Jewish fundamentalists. The terrorist attacks on the United States and the destruction of the World Trade Center in New York on 11 September 2001, carried out by Islamic fundamentalists, produced a radicalization of American politics and immoderate statements and actions on the part of the George Bush administration.

This US president's statements that he would prosecute a crusade (made just before the invasion of Iraq) were hardly words calculated to encourage the process of global integration on a stable basis or the prosecution of an effective struggle against all the terrorists in the world. Such intemperate statements are always counter-productive in the world of international relations and politics. Their 'specific gravity' lay in the fact that they were uttered by the president of the greatest world power. George W. Bush's explicit message was that radicalism would be answered with radicalism. The attack on Iraq, it was thought, was a textbook example of the demonstration of power, but was not fundamentally oriented towards the democratization of Iraq or the true struggle against terrorism, but the battle for oil. Confirmation of the thesis that the Bush administration attacked Iraq because of oil was presented to the world by the former chairman of the Federal Reserve, Alan Greenspan. In the last paragraph of a chapter on the long-term energy squeeze in his book *The Age of Turbulence*,[18] Greenspan stated with regret that the war in Iraq had been about oil.

The political-cultural approach to market economics against the ideology of market fundamentalism

The political-cultural approach to the analysis of market structures has been developed into a consistent sociological model to the operation of contemporary market economies by Neil Fligstein in his book *The Architecture of Markets*.[19] This approach to the analysis of social structures depends on a particular interpretation of the importance of institutions in modern societies. All social action takes place within defined boundaries, which may be termed fields, domains, sectors, or organized social spaces.

> Fields contain collective actors who try to produce a system of domination in that space. To do so requires the production of a local culture that defines local social relations between actors. These local cultures contain cognitive elements ... define social relationships, and help people interpret their own position in a set of social relationships.... Collective actors who benefit the most from current arrangements can be called incumbents and those who benefit less, challengers. Once in place, the interactions in fields become

'games' where groups in the field who have more power use the acceptable cultural rules to reproduce their power. This process makes action in fields continuously conflictual and inherently political.[20]

Fligstein sees states and markets as forms of social order comprised of fields for action:

> States and markets are types of social orders that contain fields.... The social order of the state is a set of fields or policy domains where actors claim the power to make and enforce rules for all of the other actors in society.[21]

Analysing the market structure of the most important world economy in the last two decades of the previous century, drawing on analyses of the real importance of the governments, companies, unions, legal systems, and cultural traditions in the world's most important economies, the author has concluded that both the neoliberal and the neo-Marxist ways of looking at globalization are mistaken and do not correspond to reality. Fligstein's conclusion is that governments in all the major world economies have played and continue to play a very significant role in the creation of conditions for companies in their respective parts of the world to increase their exports and their share in world trade. Moreover, the author concludes that the world is not as globalized as is often presented.

Assuming that this author's conclusions with regard to the most developed world economies are correct (the role of the governments of these economies in creating a better environment and that rules of the game facilitate business expansion), this does not mean the same conclusions regarding the strengthening of the role and the importance of government necessarily hold true for countries in transition and most developing countries (not including the countries of the Far East and Southeast Asia); they cannot be taken as the rule. On the other hand, this does not mean that Fligstein's conclusions on the structure of market economies should not be applied to developing countries, including the countries in transition.

Notes

1 This text was presented at the International Conference on Unity and Plurality organized by International Forum Bosnia in Mostar in August 2008 and subsequently published in *Forum Bosnae 46/2008* on pages 75–88. It is reprinted here with the kind permission of the original publisher. Translated by Desmond Maurer, M.Sc.
2 For more detailed data and analysis on inequalities in the global distribution of GDP between 1980 and 2005 and its relationship to the accelerated process of financial liberalization and globalization, see Fikret Čaušević, *Economic Sovereignty and Global Capital Flows*, International Forum Bosnia, Sarajevo, 2006.
3 For more details, see Jeffrey Sachs, *The End of Poverty – How to Make it Happen in our Lifetimes*, Penguin, London, 2005.
4 Lester C. Thurow, *Budućnost kapitalizma*, MATE, Zagreb, 1997, Chapter 12.
5 Reuven Brenner, *The Force of Finance – Triumph of the Capital Markets*, Texere, New York; London, 2002; see Chapter 9: 'A Financial Twenty-first Century'.

6 George Soros, *The Crisis of Global Capitalism – Open Society Endangered*, Public Affairs, New York, 1999.
7 Robert B. Ekelund Jr. and Robert F. Hebert, *Povijest ekonomske teorije i metode (A History of Economic Theory and Method)*, MATE, Zagreb, 1997, pp. 102–103.
8 George Soros, op. cit. page 7.
9 See: www.greattransformations.org/what-is-market-fundamentalism, accessed 2 August 2008.
10 Joseph Stiglitz, *Making Globalization Work*, W.W. Norton & Company, New York, 2006, p. 21.
11 George Soros, op. cit., Introduction – p. xxii.
12 'One of the great defects of the global capitalist system is that has allowed the market mechanism and the profit motive to penetrate into fields of activity where they do not properly belong', Ibid., p. xxiii.
13 Robert J. Barro, *Determinants of Economic Growth – A Cross-Country Empirical Study*, The MIT Press, Cambridge, MA, 1999, pp. 49–50.
14 Robert J. Barro: 'A common view since Lipset's (1959) research is that prosperity stimulates democracy, an idea often described as the Lipset hypothesis', op. cit., p. 51.
15 Robert J. Barro, op. cit., p. 52.
16 Lester Thurow, op. cit., Chapter 12.
17 Lester Thurow, op. cit., p. 237.
18 Alan Greenspan, *The Age of Turbulence*, Penguin, London, 2007.
19 Neil Fligstein, *The Architecture of Markets – An Economic Sociology of Twenty-First-Century Capitalist Societies*, Princeton University Press, Princeton, NJ, 2002.
20 Neil Fligstein, op. cit., p. 15.
21 Neil Fligstein, op. cit., p. 16.

References

The data for this paper were drawn from the various institutional webpages cited in the endnotes.

Barro, Robert J., *Determinants of Economic Growth – A Cross-Country Empirical Study*, The MIT Press, Cambridge, MA, 1999.

Brenner, Reuven, *The Force of Finance – Triumph of the Capital Markets*, Texere, New York; London, 2002.

Čaušević, Fikret, *Economic Sovereignty and Global Capital Flows*, International Forum Bosnia, 37/06, Sarajevo, 2006.

Ekelund Jr., Robert B. and Robert F. Hebert, *Povijest ekonomske teorije i metode*, MATE, Zagreb, 1997.

Fligstein, Neil, *The Architecture of Markets – An Economic Sociology of Twenty-First-Century Capitalist Societies*, Princeton University Press, Princeton, NJ, 2002.

Greenspan, Alan, *The Age of Turbulence*, Penguin, London, 2007.

Sachs, Jeffrey, *The End of Poverty – How to Make it Happen in our Lifetimes*, Penguin, London, 2005.

Soros, George, *The Crisis of Global Capitalism – Open Society Endangered*, PublicAffairs, New York, 1999.

Stiglitz, Joseph, *Making Globalization Work*, W.W. Norton & Company, New York, 2006.

Thurow, Lester C., *Budućnost kapitalizma*, MATE, Zagreb, 1997.

Part II
Economic challenges in Southeastern Europe and the Western Balkans

Lessons learned in the first decade of the twenty-first century

Part II

5 What type of fiscal policy is needed to foster the economic development of the Western Balkans?[1]

Introduction

The starting point for this short analysis of fiscal policies in the Western Balkans is based on the main propositions of the Mundell–Fleming model, on the one hand, and the recommendations for economic policy-makers presented in 2009 by Mr Dominique Strauss-Khan, on the other.

The Mundell–Fleming model comprises three main points:

- In a small open economy with full financial and trade liberalization, fiscal policy is practically the only active segment of economic policy.
- A small open economy with a fixed exchange rate can increase its national income (and GDP) by expansionary fiscal policy.
- A side effect of expansionary fiscal policy in a small open economy is to increase the trade and current account deficits, as well as foreign debt.

In a speech at the Banco de España on 15 December 2008, Mr Strauss-Kahn advocated demand management through expansionary fiscal policy in the following words:

> Another priority is to support aggregate demand, in the face of what now looks to be a dramatic fall in consumer demand. As often for the Fund, the solution to global economic problems is mostly fiscal but with a twist – it is fiscal expansion, not fiscal contraction that we need. And this has been advocated by the Fund as soon as last January in Davos.[2]

He also made clear his thoughts on how best to support aggregate demand:

> On how fiscal stimulus should be done, a key criterion is to maximize the multiplier effect of different fiscal measures. Transfers to low-income households are important because they are most likely to face credit constraints and – relatedly – because they would be most likely to rise their spending. Some good examples would be greater provision of unemployment benefits, increased tax benefits for low-wage earners, and expansion of

in-kind benefits covering basic needs such as food.... Since the slowdown is expected to be long lasting, investment spending, which typically has a longer gestation period than many other measures, becomes a more appropriate policy tool in the current circumstances.[3]

It remains for us to consider whether the recommended fiscal policy measures can be implemented in the Western Balkans. The following questions are particularly relevant:

- Does the region need a fiscal stimulus?
- If it does, what type of fiscal stimulus does it need?
- How might such a fiscal stimulus be implemented?
- How should an effective fiscal policy be carried out and what might serve as the basis for a sustainable fiscal policy in the region?

Compatibility of fiscal policies in the Western Balkans with EU conditions

Taking as our benchmark the Maastricht Treaty and the fiscal criteria it established (budget deficit of a maximum of 3 per cent of GDP; public debt not exceeding 60 per cent of GDP), the Western Balkan countries (the WBC) have performed relatively well over the last seven years:

- Almost all of the WBC, except Albania, have run budget deficits below the 3 per cent threshold.
- More precisely, their deficits were between 0.3 per cent and 1.8 per cent in 2003, 2004, and 2008. During the period of 2005–2007 the countries of the region had a budget surplus of 0.4 per cent.
- In 2009, the budget deficit averaged 4.1 per cent, less than the average for Central Europe and the Baltic countries (5.4 per cent).
- The public debt of the countries has ranged from 24 per cent in Macedonia, 37 per cent in Serbia, 38 per cent in Montenegro, 43 per cent in Bosnia and Herzegovina, 48 per cent in Croatia, and 55 per cent in Albania.[4]

Comparing the WBC data with that for the EU and Euro-zone countries, we may conclude that fiscal discipline during the period of 2003–2009 was generally fairly good in the Western Balkan region. Rising budget deficits and public debts, in combination with the credit crunch and relatively large current account deficits, are, however, an important factor in making decisions on further steps.

Social and wage needs and fiscal policies

The structure of fiscal expenditures in the region continues to be informed by the circumstance that almost all the countries of the region (except Albania) were directly or indirectly involved in the wars in the former Yugoslavia: from 1991 to 1995 in Croatia and Bosnia and Herzegovina and later in Serbia, Kosovo, and Macedonia (1999–2001). The country in the region most affected by war was, however, Bosnia and Herzegovina.

- The structure of their budgets shows how much of general government spending goes to social security (ranging from 33 per cent in Croatia and 42 per cent in Serbia to 55 per cent in Bosnia and Herzegovina).
- Public administration accounts for another large slice of public spending, ranging from 15 per cent to 22 per cent. It is certainly too high in some countries and could be significantly reduced (especially in Bosnia, but in Serbia as well).[5]

The need for coordination of fiscal and monetary policies

The monetary regimes in the region differ significantly: Albania has a floating regime, while Croatia and Serbia have managed floats; Bosnia and Herzegovina has adopted a currency board arrangement pegged to the euro; Macedonia has a de facto peg to the euro; and Montenegro and Kosovo have unilateral euroization.

There are also different levels of exposure by the national currencies to external shocks. With a view to preparing for EU membership, it might be useful to coordinate exchange rate regimes in line with improving fiscal discipline, while also spurring growth through expansionary fiscal policy based on joint infrastructural projects supported by EU financial resources.

The role of the euro in the region

All the countries in the region have close links with Euro-zone and other EU countries, both in trade and regarding other balance of payments transactions.

- Trade with the EU accounts for 83 per cent of Albania's exports of goods and services and 60 per cent of imports;
- Bosnia and Herzegovina conducts some 60 per cent of its trade with the EU, compared to 31 per cent with neighbouring countries (Croatia 18 per cent and Serbia 13 per cent);
- Trade with the EU accounts for 60 per cent of Croatia's exports and 65 per cent of the country's imports;
- For Macedonia, 65 per cent of export trade and 50 per cent of import trade is with the EU;
- 72 per cent of Serbia's trade is with the EU.[6]

Thus, the euro plays an extremely important role in the economies of the region. External shocks to the region caused by the euro's decline against the US dollar are a consequence of the structure of foreign trade. All the countries are directly or indirectly linked to the Euro-zone in their exports and imports. This means that they cannot take the opportunity to increase exports based on price competitiveness due to their national currencies' falling exchange rates with the US dollar.

Foreign debt, GDP, and exports

The Western Balkan countries succeeded in significantly decreasing their external debt/exports of goods and services ratio (from 174 per cent to 126 per cent) between 2003 and 2008, which compares well to both the Central European and the Baltic countries.[7]

There are, however, significant differences in the Western Balkan region between the different countries' levels of foreign debts and their export performance compared to their external debt. At the end of 2008, Croatia had relatively the largest foreign debt (82 per cent of GDP), but it was Montenegro whose external debt was growing fastest, up 17.9 per cent of GDP in just two years (2006–2008). Of all the countries of the Western Balkans, it is Bosnia and Herzegovina that has made the greatest progress in reducing the ratio of its external debt to export capability, down from 183 per cent to just 61 per cent, which is twice as good as the regional average. It is worth noting that Slovenia's external debt significantly worsened compared to its export capability after it joined the EU and the Euro-zone (the debt to exports ratio rose from 95 per cent to 156 per cent between 2003 and 2008).[8]

Recommendations for the region

The data presented above show the results of fiscal policy management in the countries of the Western Balkans with regard to public and external debt. Due to the spill-over effects of the global financial and economic crisis (global recession), all the countries of the region saw their GDP decrease in 2009 except Albania. Average GDP per capita in the countries of the region reaches some 33 per cent of the average EU GDP per capita. These data clearly show that fiscal expansion based on an increase in investment in capital projects is a key factor capable of a countercyclical effect on the region's economies.

Fiscal expansion based on the issuance of government bonds is one instrument for getting out of recession. Given the declining household consumption caused by the credit crunch in almost all the countries of the region and the decline in business investment (including foreign investment), an active fiscal policy has an important role to play in changing expectations and any anti-recessionary course of action.

Any government bonds issued by Western Balkan countries to finance infrastructural projects would likely require high interest rates. Given that high interest rates on government bonds, when fiscal revenues from tax collection are down, increase the risks of fiscal non-sustainability, the ratings of these bonds would have to be increased. This would depress the required return rate. My proposal, therefore, includes the following:

Introducing Euro-Balkan bonds

These new financial products for the Western Balkans would be issued by the governments (ministries of finance) of the region's countries. They would be used primarily to finance infrastructural projects (e.g. energy and road infrastructure).

These Euro-Balkan bonds would be covered by the guarantees of an EU Guarantee Fund for the Western Balkans. The amount of funds to be approved by the EU would depend on available resources. However, a total value of €15–20 billion for the Fund over the following 7–10 years would provide an explicit basis for the primary goal of this Fund: a meaningful increase in the security level of investment in Euro-Balkan bonds and, consequently, a reduction of the required interest rate.

Such Euro-Balkan bonds would be issued by countries with common (cross-border) projects for the construction of energy facilities and road or railway infrastructure. Countries with such common projects would issue bonds denominated in their respective national currencies in quantities reflecting the extent of their participation in financing the common projects. Issuing such bonds and realizing such projects would help economically connect the region, gradually increase employment, broaden fiscal capacity, and decrease the relative cost of financing. It would also significantly enhance the supply of sounder financial instruments on the financial markets of the Western Balkans. This would allow institutional and other investors in this part of Europe to manage and structure their portfolios more efficiently.

One argument against this recommendation is political in nature, namely the unwillingness of EU countries to support such a project or approve the funds which would be the basis for forming the EU Guarantee Fund for the Western Balkans. There might be opposition due to current problems following on from the spread of the Greek crisis to the countries of the southern Euro-zone and the increase in funds needed to support the value of the euro. Rejecting it could lead to political and economic losses that are much higher than the actual funds needed to allow such a fund to begin operations, however. It is in the common interest of both the EU and the Western Balkans to increase economic cooperation and for the EU to pursue decisions that show that the Western Balkan countries are not 'forgotten' – left alone to deal with the problems of recession.

Establishing a Western Balkan Stock Exchange

The formation of a Western Balkans Stock Exchange is my second recommendation. National capital markets in the Western Balkan area are insufficiently developed and in some cases additionally divided by administrative barriers (Bosnia and Herzegovina). It is necessary to increase the range of financial properties in order to attract investment in the region's stock exchanges.

Electronic connection of the Western Balkan stock exchanges and the dismantling of administrative barriers to cross transactions between Zagreb, Belgrade,

Sarajevo, Podgorica, Pristina, Skopje, and Tirana would increase the prospects for cooperation within the region and the interest for joint projects. No spectacular results would be achieved in the short-term just by forming a joint financial market, but it would provide the basis for conducting transactions with lower costs and a significant increase in interest in investment in financial properties denominated in national currencies or euro-emissions.

The formation of a Western Balkans Stock Exchange (WBSE) is directly connected to the first recommendation – introducing Euro-Balkan bonds. Issuing and trading in these bonds on a single stock exchange would promote realization of the initial goal, or my first recommendation. The reduced transaction costs and lower interest rates on such bonds would increase their price and liquidity, increasing the feasibility of the above-mentioned goal – fiscal expansion with relatively low financial costs.

Notes

1 This text was first presented at a workshop in Dijon on the 10–11 May 2010. The workshop was organized by the NGO Bourgogne Balkans Express and Science Po University of Paris, in cooperation with the European Commission.
2 Dominique Strauss-Kahn, 'The IMF and Its Future', 15 December 2008, The Banco de España (www.imf.org/external/np/speeches/2008/121508.htm).
3 Dominique Strauss-Kahn, op. cit.
4 Sources: CIA – The World Factbook (www.cia.gov/library/publications/the-world-factbook/rankorder/2186rank.html); European Bank for Reconstruction and Development, *Transition Report 2009 – Transition in Crisis?*, London, 2009.
5 Sources: Budgets of the countries posted on the websites of the ministries of finance of the Western Balkan countries.
6 Sources: The World Economic Forum, *The Global Enabling Trade Report 2010*, (www.weforum.org/reports/global-enabling-trade-report-2010); national statistical offices of FYR of Macedonia and Serbia.
7 Source: EBRD, *Transition Report 2009 – Transition in Crisis?*, London, 2009.
8 Source: EBRD, *Transition Report 2009 – Transition in Crisis?*, London, 2009, pp. 135, 151, 159, 167, 219, and 227.

References

The data for this paper were drawn from the various institutional webpages cited in the endnotes.

European Bank for Reconstruction and Development, *Transition Report 2009 – Transition in Crisis?*, London, 2009.

Strauss-Kahn, Dominique, 'The IMF and Its Future', 15 December 2008, Banco de España.

The World Economic Forum, *The Global Enabling Trade Report 2010*, Geneva, Switzerland, 2010.

6 Fiscal policies in the European Union, the United States, and the Western Balkans in the age of global crisis
Controlled fiscal expansion for a New Deal for the Western Balkans[1]

'Fiscal discipline' in the European Union and the United States

The European Central Bank (the ECB), the youngest of the world's leading central banks, was established in June 1998. The European Monetary Institute, which inherited the role of the European Monetary Cooperation Fund, was the predecessor of the European Central Bank. Six months after the ECB was established, the single European currency or the euro was introduced as the first single currency in one of the most developed group of countries in the world. The introduction of the single currency was one of the main objectives of European integration, initiated by the establishment of the Community for Coal and Steel, from which the European Economic Community and the European Community had been developed, as predecessors of the European Union.

In order to stabilize public finances and achieve fiscal discipline in the European Community with the aim of introducing a single currency, rules on monetary and fiscal discipline were introduced by the Maastricht Treaty (February 1992). The Treaty entered into force on 1 December 1993. The two fiscal criteria that should be met, and were determined by the Maastricht Treaty, referred to the allowed budgetary deficit of 3 per cent of GDP (as a maximum level), while the alternative fiscal criterion related to the total public debt. The total public debt was allowed at the level of 60 per cent of GDP.[2]

When the ECB was established, and a single European currency was introduced (January 1999), more than half of the then member states of the Euro-zone had a total debt much higher than the 'allowed' 60 per cent of GDP. The two countries with the highest level of public debt in 1998/1999 were Belgium (124 per cent of GDP) and Italy (122 per cent of GDP). Greece was admitted to the Euro-zone in 2001, having met one of the two fiscal criteria. Specifically, Greece had cut the budget deficit to below 3 per cent of GDP, while its public debt at that time was at a level comparable to those of Italy and Belgium (about 120 per cent of GDP).

Joining the Euro-zone was strictly conditioned by the first criterion – reducing the budget deficit to below 3 per cent of GDP, while countries with substantially higher public debt than the established criteria (60 per cent of GDP) were obliged to reduce that debt gradually to an acceptable and sustainable level. Italy and Belgium were told to reduce their public debt to 90 per cent of GDP by 2005. By the end of that year Belgium had reduced its public debt to below 100 per cent of GDP, while Italy's stood at 104 per cent of GDP.

In October 2002, the then European Commission president, Romano Prodi, gave his famous interview to *Le Monde* in which he emphasized that the fiscal criteria set out in the Maactricht Treaty and the Stability Pact had been too rigid. The rules, confirmed by the European Stability Pact, he called 'these stupid rules'.[3] At the time (the last quarter of 2002), the three most developed countries of the European Union who were Euro-zone member states (Germany, France, and Italy) had all violated the fiscal criterion related to the budget deficit. These countries had their excuses for budget deficits and claimed there was no danger in their violating the fiscal criteria related to the budget deficit. Specifically, their argument was that entering recession would do much greater damage than having budget deficits at the level of 4 per cent of GDP.[4]

The first decade of the twenty-first century in the global economy began with problems in US financial markets with the burst of the dotcom bubble and the terrorist attacks on 9/11. In the last quarter of 2001 and through 2002, the Bush administration basically implemented the recommendations of John Maynard Keynes. Specifically, at the beginning of his first term, George W. Bush and his administration drafted a fiscal programme to reduce the total US public debt to zero by 2010. When Bush took office, the total public debt of the United States amounted to nearly $4.5 trillion. Thanks to highly favourable trends on US financial markets, President Clinton had succeeded for the first time in 30 years in eliminating the budget deficit in 1998. The US was fiscally one of the most successful countries in the world in three consecutive years (1998–2001). Drawing an effective linear projection from the then present to the then future, the Bush administration was planning to eliminate the total public debt by 2010. Instead, they ended up almost $10.6 trillion in public debt by the end of his second term (twice as much in absolute terms as inherited).[5]

Despite Bush's free-market rhetoric, what the Bush administration did in the first two years after the terrorist attacks (2002–2003), as well as in its last two years in office (2007–2008), was to take essentially classical measures of state intervention in the tradition of Keynes – that is, preventing a crash in the business cycle (in the period after the terrorist attacks) and preventing the recession turning into a depression (in the last two years in office) based on rapid growth of public debt. Extremely expansionary fiscal policy was supported by an expansionary monetary policy during both the Greenspan and the Bernanke eras.

The economic strength of the Western Balkans and the relevance of the theory of small open economies for the region

The area of the Western Balkans is approximately 248,000 square kilometres, which is equivalent to 95 per cent of the United Kingdom. The total population of the Western Balkans is 23 million – which is approximately 35 per cent of the population of the UK. The region's GDP in 2010 accounted for 0.25 per cent of world GDP, while its share in world population was 0.32 per cent.

The Western Balkan countries had implemented the main elements of financial and trade liberalization by the end of 2006. Since financial liberalization had been carried out quickly and allowed for the free entry of foreign banks into the banking systems of Western Balkan countries, the banking sector of the Western Balkan countries was in majority ownership of banks from Austria, Italy, France, Slovenia, and Greece.

The monetary and foreign exchange regimes of the Western Balkan countries differ:

- Albania has adopted a free floating exchange rate regime;
- Croatia and Serbia have adopted a managed float regime;
- Bosnia and Herzegovina has operated under a currency board regime with a fixed peg of the national currency to the euro;
- FYR Macedonia has implemented a de facto pegged regime; and
- Montenegro and Kosovo have unilateral euroization.

The ability of the central banks in the region (Albania, Croatia, Serbia, FYR Macedonia) to conduct a discretionary monetary policy is very limited, and in Bosnia and Herzegovina it has been eliminated by the Law on the Central Bank, with the exception of the required reserves policy (the least efficient monetary policy instrument in practice). Since Montenegro and Kosovo have adopted the euro as means of payment, required reserves are also the only monetary policy instrument effectively available to their central banks.

The financial systems of countries in the region are predominantly reliant on financing through commercial banks, although insurance companies, leasing companies, and investment companies are an integral part of the financial system. The supply of additional liquidity to the real sector is almost entirely dependent on the lending activity of commercial banks. Since the banks in the region are majority-owned by banks from the EU, financial cycles in the banking sector of Western Europe have a direct impact on the credit activity of the banks in the region.

Relevance of the Mundell–Fleming model[6]

The theoretical basis for considering the room for active implementation of economic policy instruments in the small open economies in the Western Balkans is the Mundell–Fleming model.[7] According to the model, there is no room in a small open economy that has consistently adopted all the measures of financial and trade liberalization for an active monetary policy. The money supply is completely (or almost completely) endogenous, meaning that the central bank has no scope for influencing the money supply process or the interest rate. The interest rate is determined on the international money market.

Under conditions of perfect capital mobility and openness of markets in goods, money, and bonds, a small economy can increase public expenditures in two ways:

- by issuing public debt (government bonds); and
- by raising tax rates.

The quantity of money is determined endogenously as a result of rapid substitutions between different types of financial assets, at a globally determined interest rate.

Analysis of the effects of public consumption in the theoretical model of perfect capital mobility depends on the exchange rate regime: i.e. fixed or flexible exchange rate policy. Focusing on the pure impact of fiscal policy, in this context, would mean the absence of active monetary policy, as, to the extent that a country follows an expansionary fiscal policy by issuing public debt, the central bank cannot act as a buyer of bonds. Analysis of fiscal policy impact in the context of perfect capital mobility assumes a distinction between short-term and long-term impact under two models:

- the model of fiscal policy based on tax increases (balanced fiscal policy); and
- the model of expansionary fiscal policy based on higher public debt, i.e. on bond issue with a passive central bank (a central bank prevented from buying government bonds).[8]

In the first context, analysis of the impact of fiscal policy relates primarily to the influence of increased government spending based on higher taxes on the levels of production, debt, and interest rates under the two exchange rate regimes. Under a fixed exchange rate regime, expansionary fiscal policy induces changes in the money supply, while under a flexible exchange rate regime, changes are induced in the exchange rate.

The short-term and long-term effects of the unit growth of public consumption in a small economy are financed in one model by debt issuance (bonds), in the other by rising taxes. The interest rate is determined exogenously due to the assumption of unlimited freedom of international capital flows. The production multiplier under a fixed exchange rate regime is typically the simple foreign trade multiplier. This result is logical, as the interest rate is exogenously determined in a small country. The fixity of the interest rate presupposes that the typical crowding-out effect, induced by changes in the interest rate, does not operate in this case.

Under flexible exchange rate conditions, the short-term production multiplier, as a consequence of expansionary fiscal policy, depends for the most part on the effect of debt revaluation induced by changes in the exchange rate. In the absence of such an effect (for example, when the starting debt position is zero), fiscal policy loses the ability to influence disposable income. In line with this, where rising national consumption is financed by bond issues, the production multiplier equals zero, but when financed by higher taxes, it equals one. Generally, the sign and the quantity of the short-term production multiplier depends on the size of already existing debt. In contrast, these quantities do not affect the quantity of the long-term production multiplier. In a world of perfect capital mobility and flexible exchange rates, the long-term value of disposable income would not be affected by fiscal policy.

A very important characteristic of the interaction between fiscal and exchange rate policy in an open economy is the fundamental dependence of the directions of change of basic variables on the resources of fiscal policy, particularly as the shifting away from public consumption based on public debt issue towards higher public consumption financed out of tax changes the signs of the private debt multiplier (βf), total cash holdings (M), and the exchange rate. Higher government spending financed out of higher taxes under a fixed exchange rate induces a balance of payment deficit, reducing both short- and long-term cash holdings (the amount of money as property in the hands of private transactors).[9] On the other hand, a similar rise in government spending financed by public debt issue (bonds) induces a positive balance of payments and increases cash holdings, over both the short and the long term.

Under a flexible exchange rate, higher public spending financed out of taxes causes depreciation over the long term of the local currency, while higher debt-financed spending causes the currency to appreciate over the long term.[10] Similar shifts in the direction of change of the exchange rate also have short-term effects, but whether the currency appreciates or depreciates depends on the size of the debt, which in turn determines the impact of debt-revaluation.

Fiscal policy in Western Balkan countries

According to the average size of public debt, Western Balkan countries are not in the category of countries with a high level of public debt. Still, public debt figures need to be analysed also in the context of total external debt, whose level is very high in some countries of the region (for instance, in Croatia). According to IMF figures, the public debt of all the countries in the region increased in the 2008–2011 period. Albania's public debt was the highest in the region, having increased from 55.1 per cent (in 2008) to 59.4 per cent of GDP (in 2011). In the same period, the public debt of Bosnia and Herzegovina increased from 30.8 per cent to 43 per cent of GDP, that of Croatia from 29 per cent to 47.4 per cent of GDP, that of Montenegro from 31.9 per cent to 44 per cent of GDP, that of Macedonia from 20.6 per cent to 27.4 per cent of GDP, and that of Serbia from 34.2 per cent to 44.1 per cent of GDP.[11]

It is indicative to compare changes in credit activity and fiscal discipline in the countries of the region because of the fact that, according to figures of the European Bank for Reconstruction and Development, International Monetary Fund, and World Bank, Albania appeared to be the only country in the region whose real GDP did not fall. In other words, Albania was the only country in the region and, together with Poland, the only country in Central and Southeastern Europe to have achieved real GDP growth in 2009. To recapitulate, in 2009 Albania had a record high budget deficit in the region. Moreover, its public debt in 2009 was 72 per cent greater than the average in the other five countries of the region (59.8 per cent of GDP, compared to an average of 34.7 per cent of GDP).

The most important institutions in the national financial systems in the region are the commercial banks, whose share in total financial sector assets ranges between 75 per cent and 90 per cent. Commercial banks in Western Balkan countries are predominantly owned by Austrian, Italian, Slovenian, Greek, and French banks (although there are no Greek banks in Bosnia and Herzegovina or Croatia, and no Slovenian banks in Albania, where the second largest bank is Turkish). Lending by commercial banks in the Western Balkans is, therefore, directly influenced by movements in Western European financial markets. Each financial shock that hits Western Europe soon spills over into the region. Foreign trade with Western Europe accounts for approximately three-fifths of the Western Balkan trade. All major banks operating in the Western Balkans hold significant surplus liquidity reserves, as a 'shield' against possible shocks.

Parent banks in Western Europe will have to raise the bank capital to weighted assets ratio from 6 per cent to 9 per cent by the end of June this year (2012). These measures will cause a lower inflow of funds into the region because new credit lines will be reduced significantly (or suspended completely). Banks in Western Balkan countries are facing increasing levels of non-performing loans in the overall loan structure. Between 2009 and the end of 2011, non-performing loans in the total loan portfolio soared from 3 per cent to as high as 15 per cent. Under such circumstances, it is not realistic to expect significant credit expansion in the near future. Stagnation of lending activities, as mentioned earlier, directly affects the fiscal revenues of Western Balkan countries, due to declining or stagnating personal spending and plummeting business investment, coupled with a growing illiquidity of the real sector.

Fiscal discipline, based on cutting expenditures for non-productive purposes, especially administrative expenditures and outlays for a sometimes unreasonable increase in social payments, is very useful and will become necessary. Almost no country in Europe, however, either in its recent or more distant history, has managed to bail out of recession or to prevent recession from growing into depression by means of sharply cutting public spending, particularly expenditures aimed at creating new jobs or economically connecting the region. Of course, I am referring to capital expenditures which are essential for boosting the quality of the business environment and connecting the countries of the region, which, in turn, would pave the way for the implementation of joint business venture projects and the development of cross-border clusters.

Some countries of the region, like Bosnia and Herzegovina and Serbia, and to some degree Croatia, still own dominant or significant shares in large and profitable companies. This ownership may be used as a guarantee for issuing government securities, whose sole purpose would be to finance development projects. I shall conclude my paper on fiscal policy in the Western Balkan countries with a section on my proposal for a possible way out of the 'vicious circle' we have found ourselves in, though I have no illusions with regard to its weaknesses and welcome criticism. In the modern financial market structure that the Western Balkan market is also part of (although regrettably still disunited), the banks and other financial institutions (investment funds and insurance companies) in the region need more secure financial instruments to allow more successful portfolio management and pro-development utilization of idle available potential.

Euro-Balkan bonds and the New Deal for the Western Balkans

My proposal of a possible way out of the 'race to the bottom' at the time of crisis is based on the issue of new types of financial instruments, which can influence simultaneous achievement of the following goals:

- higher profitability of commercial banks;
- more successful bank portfolio management;
- economic development based on financing of cross-border projects; and
- reduced systemic risk.

At first glance, achievement of the above goals may be seen contradictory or, at least, hardly feasible in the short or medium term. On the other hand, my proposal may contribute to achieving them in cooperation with Western European countries. If we take the example of Bosnia and Herzegovina, we can identify one of the main systemic problems. From 2000 to date, commercial banks in Bosnia and Herzegovina have retained excess mandatory reserves in their accounts. These excess reserves have grown over time, to reach between 90 per cent and 110 per cent additional to the mandatory reserve amounts in the last two years. Lately, the Central Bank of Bosnia and Herzegovina has been paying interest to commercial banks on the excess reserves at a money market euro deposit rate payable up to one month (and, in some periods, at an interest rate equal to the overnight rate for interbank lending in the Eurozone).

In other words, commercial banks incur significant opportunity costs in keeping excess reserves on account with the Central Bank, as a 'sacrifice' for avoiding liquidity risk. In this context, Bosnia and Herzegovina is faced with the problem of hyper-liquid banks, on the one hand, and real sector illiquidity, on the other. The government does not issue securities to finance development projects. According to the law, the Central Bank of Bosnia and Herzegovina is not allowed to issue securities. Hence, there is no risk-free reference rate in Bosnia and Herzegovina to serve as a basis for bank portfolio structuring/restructuring. Governments of other Western Balkan countries issue securities denominated in national currencies, but due to a proportionately high level of political and institutional risk, the cost of financing public debt is above average for countries whose national currencies are formally or informally pegged to the euro.

There is great development potential available in the Western Balkan region in terms of road, railway, and energy infrastructure at cross-border level. Unfortunately, this potential is idle. Regional infrastructural development projects could help significantly reduce differences in economic development between the Western Balkans and European Union. Financing such projects through government bond issues denominated in national currencies and with a maturity period of 10–15 years could help upgrade regional economic cooperation and shrink the gap in economic development. In order to reduce the cost of financing capital investment by issuing government bonds to finance cross-border projects, one would have to increase the level of trust of financial investors in such assets and to reduce the required return.

New financial instruments that are of better quality, risk-free (or least risky), capable of boosting the profitability of commercial banks (reducing the need for keeping significant excess reserves) and of prompting faster economic growth and development of the Western Balkans would have to be of such a kind as to ensure a lower level of systemic risk.[12] In other words, issuing Western Balkan government bonds would have to be supported or insured. Who could influence a reduction of the required rate of return on such bonds, while making these financial instruments more attractive?

My proposal relates to issuing Euro-Balkan bonds,[13] so-called because they would be covered by the guarantees of a new fund – an EU Guarantee Fund for the Western Balkans. The new fund would be established by the European Union or Commission. Its main goal would be to offer guarantees for the issue of government bonds by Western Balkan countries with a view to financing or co-financing infrastructural development projects. Priority would be awarded to cross-border infrastructural development projects on a PPP basis (public–private partnership projects).

Issuing such bonds and their purchase by the commercial banks that dominate the Western Balkans would enable more successful portfolio management. The interest rate would be tied to average interest rates on government bonds with the same maturity as in the Euro-zone, augmented by a risk premium for the region. However, the risk premium would be lower than the current one, which is included in the price of government securities issued by Western Balkan countries, because their issue would be covered by the guarantees of an EU Guarantee Fund for the Western Balkans. The Guarantee Fund would have a debt–equity swap option for state-owned infrastructure companies, whose equity would be pledged as collateral.

This proposal will certainly face a series of opposing arguments, partly because of the existing problems in the Euro-zone and intensive discussions on how to bail out unruly Euro-zone members. Nevertheless, these problems must be dealt with simultaneously in Western Europe and in the Western Balkans. The sooner we deal with them, the better. A belated reaction may be too late. The main weaknesses of my proposal include the following:

- the current political situation in the region is unfavourable;
- the current political situation in European Union member states may result in their unwillingness to support such a proposal or similar proposals;

- the ethnically based way of thinking about economic reforms in the region;
- the current capital market in the region is uncoordinated and fragmented;
- spill-over effects of the financial and economic crisis and lower projections of economic growth in the countries of the region for the current year and next year; and
- the existing administrative barriers to doing business in the region.

On the other hand, advantages and opportunities arising from my proposal include the following:

- a funding source based on such instruments is more reliable thanks to its guarantee schemes;
- interest rates on these new bonds would be lower thanks to EU guarantees, as compared to 'classical' local bonds;
- implementation of cross-border infrastructural projects funded with these instruments would enable achievement of higher economic growth rates and provide faster regional connection of companies;
- fiscal sustainability would be a result of new jobs created through these projects and a result of regional connection of companies;
- the quality of financial instruments traded at regional stock exchanges would be upgraded, which would, in turn, improve portfolio management of financial institutions and help keep some part of the current money outflows to Western European countries within the region;
- foreign financial investors would also be more motivated to invest in the region;
- transaction costs would be lower, provided that stock exchanges in the region are connected to a single Western Balkan electronic stock exchange;
- all of this would result in an increase in market capitalization at the stock exchanges in the region, including an increase of funding sources.

The advantages of this proposal exceed its weaknesses. The current political and economic situation is very difficult and dangerous – not only in the Western Balkans. The funds needed for the Guarantee Fund for the Western Balkans would not exceed 5 to 7 per cent of the existing guarantee schemes in the Eurozone. Keeping labour from the Western Balkans in their own countries of residence, as new jobs would be created through the implementation of cross-border projects funded by bonds covered by guarantees of the Western Balkan Fund, would be a much better choice (both in economic and in political terms) for both sides – the European Union and Western Balkans – than just leaving the Western Balkans to deal with the crisis on their own. The feeling of having been abandoned and left 'to one's own devices' may have far-reaching negative consequences for all of us. The Western Balkan region has plenty of natural resources and boasts a rather high level of human capital (all countries in the region have been ranked by UNDP in the group of countries with a high level of human capital). Western Europe, on the other hand, is overpopulated and its resources are depleting. The size of the Western Balkans approximately matches that of Great Britain, but its population is only 35 per cent of Great Britain's. A comparison with the Netherlands is probably even more illustrative. The future of sustainable economic development largely depends on cost-effective spatial management, sources of good quality drinking water, and biodiversity. Short distances in the Western Balkans, as opposed to long distances in Western Europe, make this part of Europe very close and highly promising. The cost of a missed opportunity might be very high for both parts of Europe.

Notes

1 This paper is an extended version of a text published as an Opinion Piece on the webpage of South East European Studies at Oxford (SEESOX), St Antony's College, University of Oxford, in March 2012, when I was 2011/2012 Alpha Bank Visiting Fellow at the SEESOX Centre. The text appears in this collection with the kind permission of SEESOX, St Antony's College, University of Oxford.
2 The Maastricht Treaty – Provisions amending the Treaty establishing the European Economic Community with a view to establishing the European Community, Maastricht, 7 February 1992 (http://europa.eu/legislation_summaries/institutional_affairs/treaties/treaties_maastricht_en.htm).
3 *Le Monde*, Interview with Romano Prodi: 'I know very well that the Stability Pact is stupid because all the decisions made under it are so rigid', 24 October 2002, as reported in the *Daily Telegraph* (www.telegraph.co.uk/finance/2830598/Euro-Stability-Pact-is-stupid-says-Prodi.html).
4 *Guardian*, 'What Is the Stability and Growth Pact?', 27 November 2003 (www.guardian.co.uk/world/2003/nov/27/qanda.business).
5 On the day of Obama's inauguration as US president, total public debt was $10.62 trillion (http://nationaldebtbusters.blogspot.co.uk/).
6 Robert Mundell and Marcus Fleming developed a model of an open economy based on the IS-LM model. The IS-LM model was presented at the Conference of Econometric Society held in Oxford in September 1936 as a model of a closed economy, based on Keynes' *General Theory of Interest, Employment and Money*. The model was developed by John Hicks based on Roy Harrod's paper. The Mundell–Fleming model is also called the IS-LM-BP model and it describes an open economy whereas the IS-LM model deals with a closed economy. The seminal papers for the development of IS-LM-BP model were: Robert A. Mundell, 'Capital Mobility and Stabilization Policy under Fixed and Flexible Exchange Rates', *Canadian Journal of Economic and Political Science* 29 (4): 475–485, 1963; and J. Marcus Fleming, 'Domestic Financial Policies under Fixed and Floating Exchange Rates', *IMF Staff Papers* 9: 369–379, 1962.
7 Presentation of the Mundell–Fleming model for a small open economy can be found at: http://isites.harvard.edu/fs/docs/icb.topic647573.files/1010b_12_mundellfleming.pdf.
8 One of the best books written about the impact of fiscal policies on economic policies in small open and big open economies, to my knowledge, is Jacob Frenkel, Assaf Razin, *Fiscal Policies and the World Economy*, MIT Press, Cambridge, MA, 1987.
9 This theoretical proposition is very important for economic policy-making in developing countries and countries in transition.
10 This theoretical proposition is relevant for the economic policy-making in countries of the centre.
11 Data on the public debts of Western Balkan countries are from the International Monetary Fund 'Country Info' webpage (www.imf.org – 'Country Info').

12 The theoretical basis for the introduction of risk-free or less risky financial assets is Harry Markowitz's portfolio theory. Markowitz's seminal paper was written under the title 'Portfolio Selection' and it was published in March 1952 in *The Journal of Finance* 7 (1): 77–91. Markowitz's book *Portfolio Selection: Efficient Diversification of Investments* was first published in 1959 by John Wiley & Sons.

13 I first presented the idea of Euro-Balkan bonds at a workshop held in Dijon, France, on 10 May 2010, which was organized by the Association Bourgogne Balkan Express. The workshop materials were published in: 'Accession of the Western Balkans to the EU: Evaluating a Process', Sciences Po Paris, Paris, June 2010. The document is available at: http://ec.europa.eu/enlargement/pdf/publication/20100609_att4639135.pdf.

References

The data for this paper were drawn from the various institutional webpages cited in the endnotes.

Čaušević, F., *Capital Market and Portfolio Theory*, The Faculty of Economics, University of Sarajevo, 1991.

Fleming, J. Marcus, 'Domestic Financial Policies under Fixed and Floating Exchange Rates', *IMF Staff Papers* 9: 369–379, 1962.

Frenkel, Jacob and Assaf Razin, *Fiscal Policies and the World Economy*, MIT Press, Cambridge, MA, 1987.

Markowitz, Harry, 'Portfolio Selection', *The Journal of Finance* 7 (1): 77–91, 1952.

Markowitz, Harry, *Portfolio Selection: Efficient Diversification of Investments*, John Wiley & Sons, New York, 1959.

Mundell, Robert A., 'Capital Mobility and Stabilization Policy under Fixed and Flexible Exchange Rates', *Canadian Journal of Economic and Political Science* 29 (4): 475–485, 1963.

The Maastricht Treaty – Provisions amending the Treaty establishing the European Economic Community with a view to establishing the European Community, Maastricht, 7 February 1992.

7 Financial constraints on economic growth in Southeastern Europe[1]

Overview of the business environment in Southeastern Europe

According to the *Doing Business* report,[2] the most successful country in Southeastern Europe (SEE) at reforming its legal and regulatory framework for doing business is the Former Yugoslav Republic of Macedonia (FYR Macedonia). Reforms to simplify procedures for doing business between 2007 and 2011 helped move the country from seventy-fifth to twenty-second place in the rankings, making it the third most successful country in the world in this regard over the last four years. Montenegro was the second most successful reformer in SEE over this period – its ranking improved from eighty-first to fifty-sixth place (see Table 7.1).

FYR Macedonia's progress was greatest with regard to 'procedures for starting a business' and 'protecting investors', taking sixth and seventeenth place

Table 7.1 Ease of doing business and gross national income per capita

Country	Ease of doing business 2008	Ease of doing business 2012	Gross national income per capita 2008 (in US$)	Gross national income per capita 2012 (in US$)
Albania		82	2,960	4,000
Bosnia and Herzegovina	105	125	2,980	4,790
Bulgaria	46	59	3,990	6,240
Croatia	93	67	9,330	13,760
Kosovo	113*	117	1,800*	3,300
Montenegro	81	56	3,860	6,690
Macedonia, FYR	75	22	3,060	4,520
Romania	48	72	4,850	7,840
Serbia	86	92	3,910	5,820

Source: The WB, *Doing Business 2008*; *Doing Business 2012*.

Note
* Data for 2010.

Table 7.2 Doing business in FYR Macedonia

	2008	2009	2010	2011	2012
Starting a business	21	12	6	5	6
Dealing with construction permits	76	152	137	136	61
Registering property	91	88	63	69	49
Getting credit	48	43	43	46	24
Protecting investors	83	88	20	20	17
Paying taxes	99	27	26	33	26
Trading across borders	72	64	62	66	67
Enforcing contracts	84	70	64	65	60

Sources: The IBRD/WB, *Doing Business 2008; 2009; 2010; 2011; 2012.*

respectively for these two criteria (see Table 7.2). The country cut the number of procedures for starting a business from nine to three and the number of days needed from fifteen to three. The cost of business registration reduced from 6.6 per cent to 2.4 per cent of per capita income. The business environment also greatly improved, thanks to 'tax reforms', with lower rates and simpler payment procedures producing a jump of 73 places in the ranking for this criterion. The number of tax payments in a business year was reduced from 52 to 26, while the tax burden was cut from 49.8 per cent to 9.7 per cent of total profits.

It is noteworthy that Montenegro ranked only 108 for 'property registration' in *Doing Business*, even though the country has famously based its economic growth over the last six years primarily on tourism and high capital income through investment into real-estate (primarily from Russian investors). Montenegro's progress in improving the business environment was greatest in 'starting a business' and 'cross-border trade' (see Table 7.3). The number of procedures for starting a business fell from 15 to six, while the number of days needed fell from 24 to ten. The cost of starting a business was reduced from 6.2 per cent to 1.8 per cent of per capita income. In cross-border trade, export expenses per container were reduced from $1,580 to $805, and import expenses from $1,780 to $915.

Table 7.3 Doing business in Montenegro

	2008	2009	2010	2011	2012
Starting a business	98	105	85	51	47
Dealing with construction permits	113	167	160	161	173
Registering property	103	123	131	116	108
Getting credit	84	43	43	32	8
Protecting investors	19	24	27	28	29
Paying taxes	129	139	145	139	108
Trading across borders	113	125	47	34	34
Enforcing contracts	131	130	133	135	133

Sources: The IBRD/WB, *Doing Business 2008; 2009; 2010; 2011; 2012.*

Table 7.4 Doing business in Croatia

	2008	2009	2010	2011	2012
Starting a business	93	117	101	56	67
Dealing with construction permits	162	163	144	132	143
Registering property	99	109	109	110	102
Getting credit	48	68	61	65	48
Protecting investors	122	126	132	132	133
Paying taxes	43	33	39	42	32
Trading across borders	96	97	96	98	100
Enforcing contracts	45	44	45	47	48

Sources: The IBRD/WB, *Doing Business 2008; 2009; 2010; 2011; 2012.*

Between 2007 and 2011, Croatia improved its ranking 27 places overall, simplifying procedures, reducing the costs of starting a business, and improving constructions permit procedures and tax payment systems (see Table 7.4). The number of procedures for starting a business was reduced from eight to six and the number of days from 40 to seven. The cost of starting a business was reduced from 11.7 per cent to 8.6 per cent of per capita income. The number of tax payments per year was reduced from 28 to 17, while tax payments went almost unchanged – the tax burden declined from 32.5 per cent to 32.3 per cent of total profit.

It was Albania, however, whose ranking improved most over the last four years – 54 places (though its overall ranking was higher in 2011 than in 2012). Progress was greatest regarding procedures for starting a business and protecting investors (see Table 7.5). The number of procedures was cut from ten to five, while the number of days needed fell from thirty-six to five. These changes in starting a business improved Albania's ranking on this criterion by 61 places, even though the cost of starting a business actually increased from 20.9 per cent to 25.8 per cent of per capita income. Albania is the highest ranked country in SEE for investor protection. The investor protection index improved from 2.7 to

Table 7.5 Doing business in Albania

	2008	2009	2010	2011	2012
Starting a business	123	67	46	45	61
Dealing with construction permits	168	170	173	170	183
Registering property	82	62	70	72	118
Getting credit	48	12	15	15	24
Protecting investors	165	14	15	15	16
Paying taxes	118	143	138	149	152
Trading across borders	70	77	66	75	76
Enforcing contracts	74	89	91	89	85

Sources: The IBRD/WB, *Doing Business 2008; 2009; 2010; 2011; 2012.*

Table 7.6 Doing business in Serbia

	2008	2009	2010	2011	2012
Starting a business	90	106	73	83	92
Dealing with construction permits	149	171	174	176	175
Registering property	115	97	105	100	39
Getting credit	13	28	4	15	24
Protecting investors	64	70	73	74	79
Paying taxes	121	126	137	138	143
Trading across borders	58	62	69	74	79
Enforcing contracts	101	96	97	94	104

Sources: The IBRD/WB, *Doing Business 2008; 2009; 2010; 2011; 2012.*

7.3 on a scale from 0 (the worst) to 10 (the best). Albania did worst in property registration. Over the last four years, the cost of registering property has increased from 3.5 per cent to 11.9 per cent of the property's value.

Over the last four years, Serbia's overall ranking in *Doing Business* fell six places, with the biggest decline in dealing with construction permits, paying taxes, and trading across borders, and the biggest improvement in registering property (see Table 7.6). The number of days needed to register property fell from 111 to 11 days and the cost was cut from 5.4 per cent to 2.8 per cent of the property's value. It is worth noting that, while the total tax rate, expressed as a percentage of profit, fell from 35.8 per cent to 34 per cent, Serbia's ranking deteriorated 21 places. This may be because of the number of payments per year, which in Serbia is the highest in the region – companies have to pay taxes 66 times per year and spend 279 hours per year paying them.

Bosnia and Herzegovina has had one of the lowest rankings in the region over the last four years. In 2007–2011, its ranking fell 20 places. Although it was one of the most open economies in the region in the last decade (according to the *volume of trade to GDP* ratio, which averaged 95 per cent), Bosnia and Herzegovina's ranking fell 55 places on the trading across borders criterion (see Table 7.7).

Table 7.7 Doing business in Bosnia and Herzegovina

	2008	2009	2010	2011	2012
Starting a business	150	161	160	160	162
Dealing with construction permits	150	137	136	139	163
Registering property	144	144	139	103	100
Getting credit	13	59	61	65	67
Protecting investors	83	88	93	93	97
Paying taxes	142	154	128	127	110
Trading across borders	53	55	63	71	108
Enforcing contracts	126	123	124	124	125

Sources: The IBRD/WB, *Doing Business 2008; 2009; 2010; 2011; 2012.*

Table 7.8 Doing business in Bulgaria

	2008	2009	2010	2011	2012
Starting a business	100	81	50	43	49
Dealing with construction permits	103	117	119	119	128
Registering property	62	59	56	62	66
Getting credit	13	5	4	6	8
Protecting investors	33	38	41	44	46
Paying taxes	88	94	95	85	69
Trading across borders	89	102	106	108	91
Enforcing contracts	90	86	87	87	87

Sources: The IBRD/WB, *Doing Business 2008; 2009; 2010; 2011; 2012.*

Moreover, despite significant cuts in the cost of starting a business, from 30.1 per cent to 17 per cent of income per capita, Bosnia and Herzegovina's ranking on this criterion also fell 12 places. The business environment in the country improved most with regard to paying taxes. The total tax rate as a percentage of profit was cut from 44.1 per cent to 25 per cent.

Bulgaria's overall ranking in the *Doing Business* report deteriorated from forty-sixth to fifty-ninth over the past four years. The country did best in improving conditions for starting a business (see Table 7.8). The number of procedures was cut from nine to four, the number of days from 32 to 18, and the cost from 8.4 per cent to 1.5 per cent of income per capita. In registering property, dealing with construction permits, and protecting investors, Bulgaria's position was worse in 2012 than in 2008.

Romania also fell 14 places in the overall *Doing Business* ranking over the last four years. Unlike Bulgaria, Romania's ranking for starting a business worsened, from 26 to 63 (see Table 7.9). Romania was also downgraded over dealing with construction permits, paying taxes, and trading across borders. Business people in Romania have to pay taxes 113 times per year and have to spend 220 working hours doing so. The country successfully improved its procedures for registering property – rising 53 places in the relevant ranking.

Table 7.9 Doing business in Romania

	2008	2009	2010	2011	2012
Starting a business	26	26	42	44	63
Dealing with construction permits	90	88	91	84	123
Registering property	123	114	92	92	70
Getting credit	13	12	15	15	8
Protecting investors	33	38	41	44	46
Paying taxes	134	146	149	151	154
Trading across borders	38	40	46	47	72
Enforcing contracts	37	31	55	54	56

Sources: The IBRD/WB, *Doing Business 2008; 2009; 2010; 2011; 2012.*

It is worth comparing the rankings for Bulgaria and Romania with regard to the effects and acceleration of institutional reforms for doing business, as these are the only EU members among the SEE countries (since 1 January 2007). From the data presented above, it can be seen that the quality of the business environment in Bulgaria and Romania has worsened since joining the EU, while access to credit in both became significantly easier (in the reports for 2008 and 2012, both countries were equally ranked for access to credit, while moving up from thirteenth to eighth).

On the other hand, over the past four years, Croatia, a country that has met all the criteria for joining the EU and will join in 2013, improved its rank by 26 places. It has already been pointed out that FYR Macedonia was the most successful reformer in the period, while Montenegro and Albania also made very significant progress in their business environment. A special type of paradox, evident from the above presentation of the rankings for the SEE countries, is that those that have already joined the EU have seen their business environment worsen, rather than improve, while those in the process of meeting EU membership requirements have put a lot of effort into attracting investors through rapid changes to their regulatory frameworks.

Even though Greece and Turkey do not formally belong to the region, it is useful to consider their positions in their *Doing Business* reports, since they both have significant geographical and economical influence on how business is done in other countries of the region. Greece's ranking was downgraded from 100 to 109 during 2007–2010, but restored to 100 in 2011 (see Table 7.10). Greece has improved its ranking in relation to procedures for starting a business, investor protection, access to credit, and tax payment. The biggest improvement was in the procedures for starting a business, while the main decline was in real-estate registration and cross-border trade.

Turkey was downgraded from 57 to 71 over the last four years (see Table 7.11), which is comparable to Bulgaria and Romania. In the latest report, Turkey was ranked just below Romania and 29 places above Greece. In contrast to the

Table 7.10 Doing business in Greece

	2008	2009	2010	2011	2012
Starting a business	152	133	140	149	135
Dealing with construction permits	42	45	50	51	41
Registering property	93	101	107	153	150
Getting credit	84	109	87	89	78
Protecting investors	158	150	154	154	155
Paying taxes	86	62	76	74	83
Trading across borders	65	70	80	84	84
Enforcing contracts	87	85	89	88	90
OVERALL RANK	100	96	109	109	100

Sources: The IBRD/WB, *Doing Business 2008; 2009; 2010; 2011; 2012.*

Table 7.11 Doing business in Turkey

	2008	2009	2010	2011	2012
Starting a business	43	43	56	63	61
Dealing with construction permits	128	131	133	137	155
Registering property	31	34	36	38	44
Getting credit	68	68	71	72	78
Protecting investors	64	53	57	59	65
Paying taxes	54	68	75	75	79
Trading across borders	56	59	67	76	80
Enforcing contracts	34	27	27	26	51
OVERALL RANK	57	59	73	65	71

Sources: The IBRD/WB, *Doing Business 2008; 2009; 2010; 2011; 2012*.

countries discussed above, Turkey's position did not improve in any ranking criterion. Nonetheless, between 2007 and 2010 Turkey's nominal GDP per capita improved some 9.2 per cent and Bulgaria's 15 per cent, while Greece and Romania's fell 2.4 per cent and 4 per cent, respectively.[3]

Comparing economic growth rates and changes in the rankings for Western Balkan countries, we reach an at-first-glance paradoxical conclusion about the impact of change in business environment quality on economic growth. We have already mentioned that Albania's ranking improved 54 places, FYR Macedonia's 53, Croatia's 26, and Montenegro's 25. By contrast, the two countries downgraded were Serbia (down six places) and Bosnia and Herzegovina (down 20 places) (see Figure 7.1).

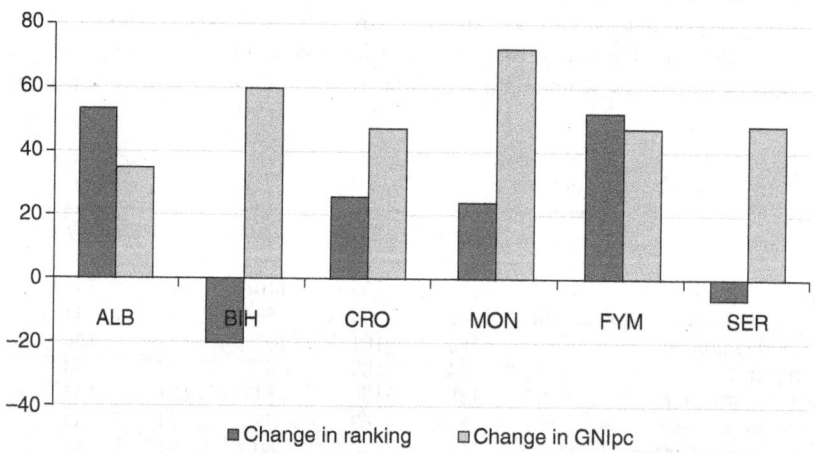

Figure 7.1 Change in ranking and GNI per capita of the Western Balkan countries, 2008–2012 (change in ranking = number of ranks; change in GNIpc in %) (sources: the IBRD/WB, *Doing Business 2008; Doing Business 2012*, Washington).

Compare changes in GNI per capita, however, and one might rather conclude that the most successful countries during the period were Montenegro and Bosnia and Herzegovina. From 2007 to 2011, GNI per capita increased by 73.3 per cent in Montenegro and by 60.8 per cent in Bosnia and Herzegovina. Serbia saw GNI per capita increase by 48.8 per cent, as well, which is better than the most successful reformer in the region – FYR Macedonia. During this period, FYR Macedonia's GNI per capita increased by 47.7 per cent. From this data, one might conclude that the speed at which reforms are implemented in the medium run is not a direct condition of economic growth and that ranking countries by the criteria used above fails to cover all the factors that significantly influence economic growth rates. These data do not, for example, include criteria on the quality of the available workforce, labour costs, productivity, or the cost of money capital (interest rates). Actual GNI per capita growth rates in Western Balkan countries resulted from the very different rates of external debt growth, based on the import of capital, as a result of rapidly widening current account deficits. Economic growth in SEE countries was fastest during the 2004–2008 period.

The fastest growing economy in the Western Balkans was Montenegro, with GDP per capita up nearly 2.5 times in 2004–2008 (see Figure 7.2). This rapid economic growth was, however, financed by high capital inflows, as reflected in an enormous increase in the current account deficit – from 8 per cent to 51 per cent of GDP (see Figure 7.3). While it had been cut to 25 per cent of GDP by 2010, high money borrowing in 2006 and 2007 caused non-performing loans to

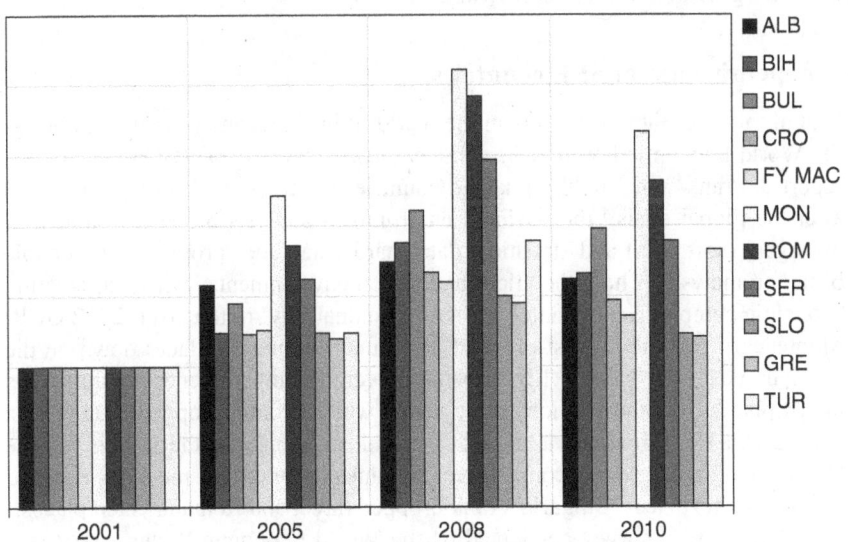

Figure 7.2 Change in GDP per capita in SEE countries, 2001–2010 (2001 = 100) (source: the author's calculations based on the World Bank data, http://data.worldbank.org/indicator/NY.GDP.PCAP.CD).

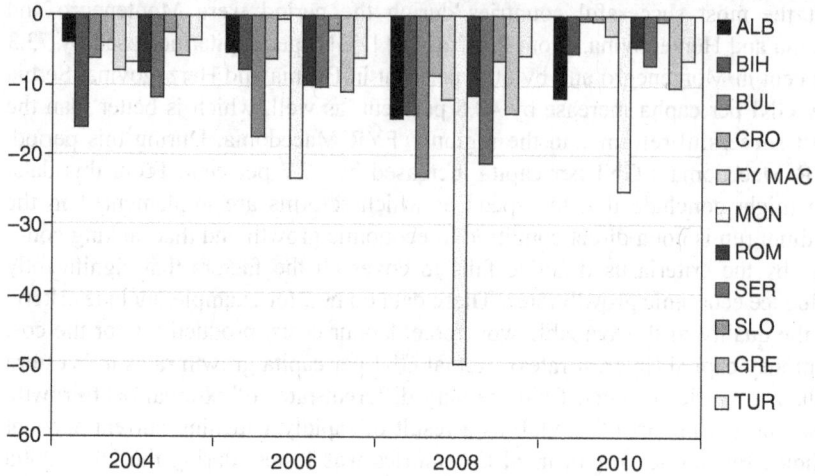

Figure 7.3 Current account balances of SEE countries, 2004–2010 (per cent of GDP) (source: IMF, *World Economic Outlook: Slowing Growth, Rising Risks*, Washington, September 2011, pp. 197–198).

grow fast and lending to drop in 2008–2010. This credit crunch continued into 2011. The basic model for economic growth in all the SEE countries has been characterized by domestic demand-driven economic growth based primarily on intensive growth in foreign borrowing.

Competitiveness of SEE countries

One of the most famous reports in the world of business and economic policy is the World Economic Forum's *Global Competitiveness Report* (GCR). While the report did rank some highly indebted countries relatively high just prior to and after the global crisis,[4] the business environment analysis based on surveys of managers (soft data) and statistical data (hard data) does provide a reasonable basis for analysis of how the micro and macro environments interact in creating economic competitiveness and long-term sustainability. In the 2011–2012 GCR, Montenegro was the highest-ranked SEE country, albeit 11 places down on the previous year (see Table 7.12). Albania's overall competitiveness ranking was up 18 places over the previous three years, while Croatia dropped four places. Bosnia and Herzegovina was the lowest ranked country in the region. Unlike Croatia and Serbia, whose competitiveness ranks dropped, Bosnia's position had improved nine places. Bulgaria's rank dropped three, and Romania's ten places.

The managers' survey conducted by the World Economic Forum every year in the countries in the report provides insight into managers' opinions on barriers to business. Comparing the five factors ranked highest over the past three years, we see how their opinions have changed. In Albania, Bosnia and Herzegovina,

Table 7.12 Competitiveness of SEE countries: ranking of Southeastern European countries in the *Global Competitiveness Report*

Country	2011–2012 (out of 142)	2010–2011 (out of 139)	2009–2010 (out of 133)
Albania	78	88	96
Bosnia and Herzegovina	100	102	109
Croatia	76	77	72
Macedonia FYR	79	79	84
Montenegro	60	49	62
Serbia	95	96	93
Bulgaria	74	71	76
Romania	77	67	64
Greece	90	83	71
Turkey	59	61	61

Source: World Economic Forum, *The Global Competitiveness Report 2011–2012*, Geneva, 2011.

FYR Macedonia, and Montenegro, access to financing is now considered the main obstacle to doing business, while three years ago it was not a significant barrier in any of them (see Tables 7.13 and 7.14). It is the third most problematic factor in Serbia. Croatia is the only Western Balkan country in which it was not considered a major barrier last year.

The other factors most frequently cited as major barriers to business are the tax rates, tax system, inefficient government bureaucracy, and corruption. Regarding the global financial cycle's influence on economic growth rates and managers' attitudes as to which 'economic' and 'non-economic' factors represent the most significant barriers, the data in the tables below suggest that access to financing was not considered a problem in 2008, while factors like the quality of institutions and of governance were, so long as there was high loan activity by internationally active banks, the most significant of which for the Western Balkans were from Austria, Italy, France, Slovenia, and Greece.

In Bulgaria and Romania, access to financing also emerged as one of the top five barriers to doing business (fourth largest) in the GCR 2011–2012 (see Table 7.15). Three years ago, it was not on the list. In both these countries, however, political factors such as corruption and inefficient government bureaucracy are amongst the top five, which is somewhat surprising given that they are both EU members.

Along with spill-over of the global financial crisis from Western Europe, access to financing is now the second largest barrier to business in Greece, even if three years ago managers there did not place it in the top five. Managers in Turkey, however, singled out tax rates and the tax system (see Table 7.16).

This analysis of what managers consider the most problematic factors for doing business and investment activity in SEE, based on the GCR 2011–2012 survey, shows that access to financing is now the greatest barrier to doing business in four of the ten countries (Albania, Bosnia and Herzegovina, FYR Macedonia, and Montenegro), the second largest in one (Greece), third largest in one

Table 7.13 The most problematic factors for doing business in Albania, Bosnia and Herzegovina, and Croatia

	1	2	3	4	5
Albania 2011	Access to financing	Tax rates	Corruption	Tax regulations	Ineff. gov. bureaucracy
Albania 2008	Corruption	Inad. supply of infrastr.	Ineff. gov. bureaucracy	Tax regulations	Tax rates
Bosnia and Herzegovina 2011	Access to financing	Tax rates	Ineff. gov. bureaucracy	Corruption	Tax regulations
Bosnia and Herzegovina 2008	Government instability	Policy instability	Ineff. gov. bureaucracy	Inadequate supp. of infrastruct.	Corruption
Croatia 2011	Ineff. gov. bureaucracy	Corruption	Policy instability	Tax rates	Corruption
Croatia 2008	Ineff. gov. bureaucracy	Corruption	Tax regulations	Inadeq. edu. workforce	Access to financing

Sources: The World Economic Forum, *The Global Competitiveness Report 2011–2012*, and *The Global Competitiveness Report 2008–2009*.

Table 7.14 The most problematic factors for doing business in Macedonia FYR, Montenegro, and Serbia

	1	2	3	4	5
Macedonia FYR 2011	Access to financing	Ineff. gov. bureaucracy	Inadeq. edu. workforce	Poor work ethic	Corruption
Macedonia FYR 2008	Policy instability	Ineff. gov. bureaucracy	Access to financing	Poor work ethic	Corruption
Montenegro 2011	Access to financing	Tax rates	Restrictive labour regul.	Inadeq. supp. of infrastr.	Ineffic. gov. bureaucracy
Montenegro 2008	Ineff. gov. bureaucracy	Inadeq. supp of infrastr.	Inad. educat. workforce	Restrictive labour regul.	Poor work ethic
Serbia 2011	Ineff. gov. bureaucracy	Corruption	Access to financing	Inflation	Governm. instability
Serbia 2008	Policy instability	Corruption	Ineff. gov. bureaucracy	Inadeq. supp of infrastr.	Crime and theft

Sources: The World Economic Forum, *The Global Competitiveness Report 2011–2012*, and *The Global Competitiveness Report 2008–2009*.

Table 7.15 The most problematic factors for doing business in Bulgaria and Romania

	1	2	3	4	5
Bulgaria 2011	Corruption	Inefficient gov. bureau.	Inflation	Access to financing	Inadeq. supp of infrastr.
Bulgaria 2008	*Corruption*	*Inefficient gov. bureau.*	*Inadequate educat. work*	*Inadeq. supp of infrastr.*	*Inflation*
Romania 2011	Tax rates	Inefficient gov. bureau.	Policy instability	Access to financing	Corruption
Romania 2008	*Policy instability*	*Tax rates*	*Tax regulations*	*Inefficient gov. bureau.*	*Inadequate supp. of infrastruct*

Sources: The World Economic Forum, *The Global Competitiveness Report 2011–2012*, and *The Global Competitiveness Report 2008–2009*.

Table 7.16 The most problematic factors for doing business in Greece and Turkey

	1	2	3	4	5
Greece 2011	Inefficient gov. bureaucracy	Access to financing	Corruption	Tax regulations	Policy instability
Greece 2008	*Inefficient gov. bureaucracy*	*Tax regulations*	*Restricted labour regul.*	*Corruption*	*Tax rates*
Turkey 2011	Tax rates	Inefficient gov. bureaucracy	Tax regulations	Inadeq. educat. work	Foreign currency regulations
Turkey 2008	*Inefficient gov. bureaucracy*	*Tax regulations*	*Policy instability*	*Access to financing*	*Tax rates*

Sources: The World Economic Forum, *The Global Competitiveness Report 2011–2012*, and *The Global Competitiveness Report 2008–2009*.

(Serbia), and fourth largest in two (in Bulgaria and Romania). Their view is confirmed by analysis of changes in lending between 2004 and 2010. In the four SEE countries whose managers ranked financing as the main problem in the last survey, we find a decline in lending, along with associated problems.

Figure 7.4 shows the changes in credit activity, in total assets, and nominal GDP growth rates in Albania and FYR Macedonia for 2005–2010. Lending in Albania was most intense in 2005, when loans to business rose 72 per cent and loans to households were up nearly 80 per cent over the previous year. Credit expansion continued in 2006–2007. A sharp decline in growth was recorded in 2009–2010, with a concomitant increase in the share of NPLs (non-performing loans) in total assets. Lending activity in FYR Macedonia grew fastest in 2005–2007. In 2009 and 2010, credit activity reduced sharply, contributing to the 2009 recession there. During 2011, credit activity in both countries was very moderate.

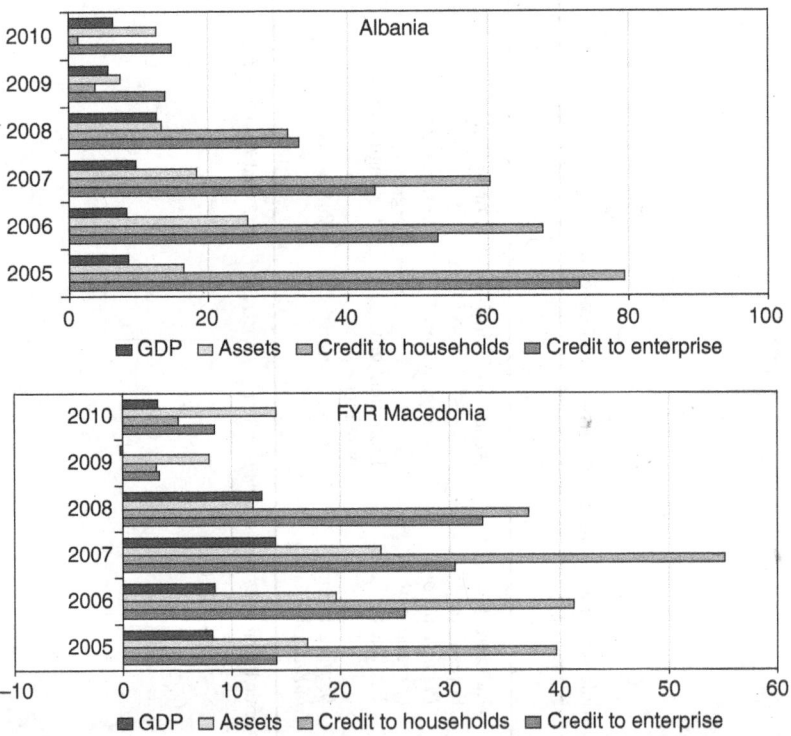

Figure 7.4 Credit activity in Albania and FYR Macedonia, 2005–2010 (percentage change year-on-year).

Note
The author's calculations and figures are based on Bank of Albania data (www.bankofalbania.org/web/Time_series_22_2.php?evn=agregate_parent_sel&evb=agregate&Cgroups=36&periudha_id=5) and National Bank of FYR Macedonia data (www.nbrm.mk/?ItemID=A55FFC32FC478E4A89444507A6C02C45).

Loans grew significantly less, on average, in Bosnia and Herzegovina than in Albania or FYR Macedonia and less again than in Montenegro in 2006–2008 (see Figure 7.5). One reason for this moderate (but still high) increase was the intensity of lending activity in 2002–2005. The loan to GDP ratio in Bosnia and Herzegovina was, at that point, well above those in Albania, FYR Macedonia and Montenegro. Thus, in 2005 the business loans to GDP ratio had been 23.1 per cent in Bosnia and Herzegovina, 15.9 per cent in FYR Macedonia, 13.2 per cent in Montenegro, and 10.2 per cent in Albania. The household loans to GDP ratio was 20.7 per cent in Bosnia and Herzegovina, 7.9 per cent in FYR Macedonia, 5.7 per cent in Montenegro, and 4.7 per cent in Albania.

In 2006 and 2007, however, Montenegro became the absolute record holder in lending in SEE and the world, with an average percentage increase in loans to both enterprises and households of 175 per cent (each year). There was a sharp drop in lending in Montenegro in 2008 (a sharp decline in the growth rate), with

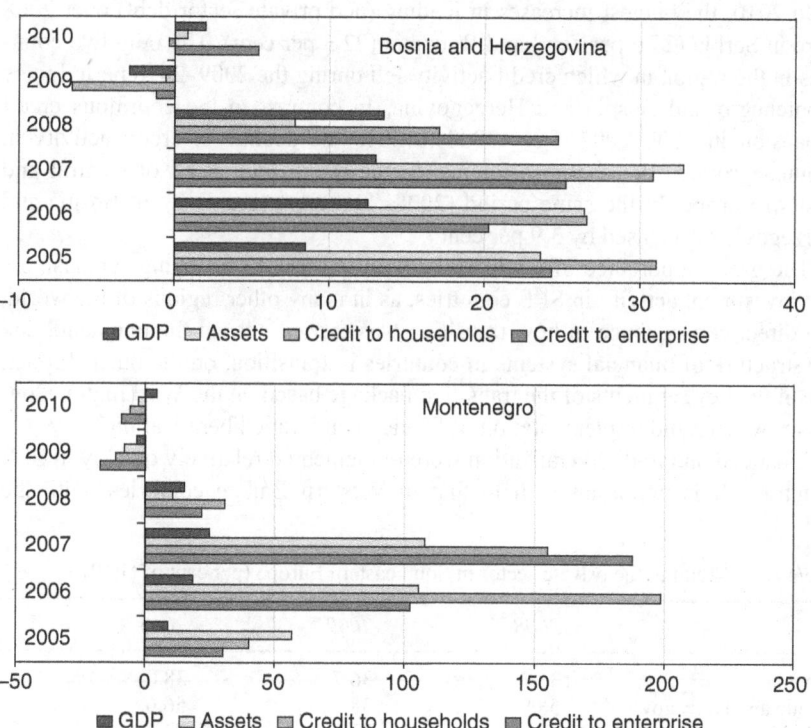

Figure 7.5 Credit activity in Bosnia and Herzegovina, and Montenegro, 2005–2010 (percentage change year-on-year).

Note
The author's calculations and figures are based on data published by the Central Bank of Bosnia and Herzegovina (www.cbbh.ba/index.php?id=33&lang=en&sub=mon&table=konsolidovani_bilans_komercijalnih_banaka_bihh) and the Central Bank of Montenegro (www.cb-mn.org/eng/index.php?mn1=statistics&mn2=monetary_statistics).

absolute decline following in 2009 and 2010 and continuing into 2011. An enormous credit expansion in 2006–2007 caused high rates of economic growth, but was also associated with an enormous increase in the current account deficit (from 10 per cent in 2005 to 51 per cent of GDP in 2008). The result was a rapid increase in external indebtedness.

Credit activity measured by the loan to GDP ratio (loans to the private sector) reveals a significant difference in private sector indebtedness and in changes in indebtedness between SEE countries in 2008–2010. During that period, the average loan to GDP ratio in the region increased from 54.7 per cent to 56.3 per cent (see Table 7.17). At the end of 2008, four SEE countries had higher than average private sector debt for the region. Private sector indebtedness in Montenegro was 61.8 per cent above the average, compared to 27.6 per cent in Bulgaria, 17.7 per cent in Croatia, and 7.8 per cent in Bosnia and Herzegovina. Two years later (in 2010), it was highest in Bulgaria and Croatia, at 32.5 per cent and 24.5 per cent above the SEE average, respectively.[5]

In 2010, the biggest increases in lending (and private sector debt) over 2008 were in Serbia (25.6 per cent) and Romania (22.3 per cent). The only two countries in the region in which credit activity fell during the 2009–2010 period were Montenegro and Bosnia and Herzegovina. In contrast to the enormous credit expansion in 2006–2007, from 2008 to 2010 the decline in credit activity in Montenegro was the sharpest not just in the region but in all of Central and Eastern Europe. In the same period (2008–2010), credit activity in Bosnia and Herzegovina decreased by 3.9 per cent.

The great importance of credit activity and access to financing for business and investment activity in SEE countries, as in many other regions of the world, is a direct consequence of how transition was carried out, on the one hand, and the structure of financial systems in countries in transition, on the other. In fact, one of the key segments of the transition package based on the Washington Consensus was a rapid implementation of financial and trade liberalization.[6]

Financial and trade liberalization were implemented relatively quickly in SEE countries. It is important to note that in Western Balkan countries, with the

Table 7.17 Credit to the private sector in Southeastern Europe (per cent of GDP)

	2008	2009	2010
Albania	35.2	36.7	38.0
Bosnia and Herzegovina	58.9	58.7	56.6
Bulgaria	69.8	73.3	74.6
Croatia	64.4	65.9	70.1
Macedonia, FYR	42.4	43.9	45.6
Montenegro	88.5	77.7	68.8
Romania	37.7	39.5	46.1
Serbia	40.3	45.2	50.6

Source: EBRD, *Transition Report 2011 – Crisis and Transition: The People's Perspective*, London, 2011.

exception of Albania, economic reforms were not possible in 1991–1995 (Croatia, Bosnia and Herzegovina, Serbia, Montenegro) or 1999–2000 (Serbia, Kosovo, FYR Macedonia) because of war. Measures of financial and trade liberalization were, however, implemented in a relatively short period of time after the end of these wars. Financial liberalization in the region, including full freedom of access by foreign banks to the countries' financial sectors, was conducted over an average of three years, while trade liberalization was implemented in 2000–2006.[7] The structure of the financial systems in the region was based on the dominant role of commercial banks in financing companies and households. Private sector loans were, in the first decade of this century, by far the most important source of financing for working capital needs and, in part, for the purchase of fixed assets, as well as the dominant source of growth in household purchasing power.

Comparing the data on changes in credit activity and private sector indebtedness between 2010 and 2009 (the year of recession) reveals various factors that influenced the recession. Although Romania saw credit growth of 16.7 per cent over the previous year, it was unable to avoid recession. Romania reduced its current account deficit from 11.6 per cent to 4.3 per cent of GDP between 2008 and 2010. Romania and Croatia were, however, the only countries in the region with a decline in real GDP from 2009 to 2010 (see Table 7.18). The Serbian economic recovery in 2010 was partly supported by a growth in private sector loans of 11.9 per cent against a year earlier, and it was followed by a sharp reduction in the current account deficit, from 20.9 per cent to 7.2 per cent of GDP.

The growth of credit activity in Bulgaria in 2010, against the previous year, was very modest (1.8 per cent). The country did succeed in almost eliminating its current account deficit, however. The deficit was reduced from 22.9 per cent to only 1 per cent of GDP (2008–2010). During 2009–2010, the growth of credit activity in Croatia of 8.9 per cent was associated with significant reduction in the current account deficit (from 8.6 per cent to 1.1 per cent of GDP). Croatia, however, faced a decline of GDP in both years. The 7.8 per cent increase in credit activity in Albania in 2009–2010 was followed by a reduction in the current account deficit, but not to an extent comparable with other countries in the region. At the same time, Albania was the only country in the region not facing recession in 2009.

Bosnia and Herzegovina and Montenegro were the only two SEE countries to see a decrease in credit activity in 2009–2010. This was associated with a slight increase in real GDP in 2010 (year-on-year) and a sharp decline in the current account deficit in both countries. Bosnia and Herzegovina's current account deficit fell from 14.2 per cent in 2008 to 5.6 per cent of GDP in 2010. In the same period, Montenegro succeeded in cutting its current account deficit nearly in half – from an enormous 51.3 per cent (2008) to 25.6 per cent of GDP (2010).

The importance of credit activity for economic growth and investment in most developing and developed countries without arm's-length financial systems has been confirmed by recently published studies. In a recent study by Kalemli-Ozcan, Kamil, and Sanchez-Villegas about the factors influencing the fall in

Table 7.18 Current account balance, real GDP growth, and credit growth in SEE countries

Country	Current acc. balance as % of GDP			Real GDP growth			Credit growth (in %)		
	2008	2009	2010	2008	2009	2010	2008	2009	2010
Albania	−15.6	−15.2	−11.8	7.5	3.6	3.8	17.3	4.3	3.5
Bosnia and Herzegovina	−14.2	−6.3	−5.6	5.7	−2.8	0.7	7.0	−0.3	−3.6
Bulgaria	−22.9	−8.8	−1.0	6.2	−5.5	0.2	15.2	5.0	1.8
Croatia	−8.6	−5.0	−1.1	2.2	−6.0	−1.2	3.0	2.3	6.6
Macedonia, FYR	−12.6	−6.4	−2.8	5.0	−1.0	1.8	19.4	3.5	3.9
Montenegro	−51.3	−30.1	−25.6	6.9	−5.7	2.5	13.8	−12.2	−11.5
Romania	−11.6	−4.3	−4.3	7.4	−7.1	−1.3	8.4	4.8	16.7
Serbia	−20.9	−6.9	−7.2	3.8	−3.5	1.0	16.9	12.2	11.9
Average	−19.7	−10.4	−7.4	5.6	−3.5	0.9	12.6	2.5	3.7

Sources: EBRD, *Transition Report 2011*; EBRD, *Transition Report 2010*; the author's calculations.

Note
Credit growth in per cent is derived from the level of indebtedness based on data for the loan to GDP ratio for respective countries.

investment in Latin America, the authors conclude that in a period of twin-crisis domestic exporters could not finance their businesses due to a lack of access to financing, causing a sharp decline in both exports and economic activity. In their conclusion, they point out:

> Our main result is that foreign-owned exporters with dollar debt perform better than domestic exporters with dollar debt only during twin crises, where domestic firms' access to finance is limited given the troubled banking sector.... During twin crises, however, domestic exporters suffer from the problem of illiquidity and hence contract investment and production, as opposed to foreign-owned exporters. Our results have important policy implications. First, to the best of our knowledge, this paper is first in quantifying the significant real effects of shocks to the banking sector using firm-level investment data. Second, short-term foreign currency borrowing may not be detrimental to firms' balance sheets as long as their access to finance is not limited during periods of instability. Hence it is important to provide liquidity to the banking sector during financial crises, especially if the domestic banking sector is the main source of financing for the firms.[8]

Although this research was done on a sample of companies in Latin America, lack of financial resources due to a fall in lending especially for export-oriented domestic enterprises has had a similar direct impact on declining investment activity, the fall or very slow growth of real GDP, and the decline of fiscal capacity in Eastern European countries. The fall in fiscal capacity due to lower business investment and the consequent decline of wages, salaries, and employment, has caused an increase in foreign public debt in the countries hit by the crisis. This chain of events has also been confirmed in SEE countries and in most of the other countries in transition as well. A recent study of the impact of credit activity on investments and economic growth, published by the ECB, demonstrates the key role of banking and credit activity in the business cycle in Eastern European countries (including SEE countries). In a study based on a representative sample of enterprises in the countries in transition, the authors found:

> Indeed, according to the Institute of International Finance (IIF), Emerging Europe is the region most directly affected by the declining international capital flows. According to the BIS definition, Emerging Europe consists of the Eastern European countries in our sample, minus Slovenia, plus Belarus, Moldova, Montenegro, Turkey, and Ukraine. This severe contraction in refinancing of the region's banking sector immediately raises the question of which firms in Eastern Europe will most likely face tighter credit constraints and what the credit contraction implies for the economic performance of the entire region. Our results suggest that especially export-orientated firms, which have the highest credit demand, may be hit hardest by a potential credit crunch, while smaller firms, with their lower demand for bank credit, may be less affected.[9]

Brown, Ongena, Popov and Yesin also emphasized that there were highly significant differences in the degree of indebtedness and access to loans in Eastern European countries:

> Despite the substantial resources invested in improving credit availability in Eastern Europe, less than half of the firms in the region actually have bank credit.... The use of bank credit does however vary strongly across the region. The share of firms with a bank loan varies from 29 percent in Macedonia to more than 66 percent in Croatia. While the use of bank credit seems to be low in Eastern Europe, it is only slightly below that of selected Western European countries. Indeed, four countries in Eastern Europe (Croatia, Slovenia, Bosnia, and Hungary) have loan incidences which exceed the average for the sample of Western European firms.[10]

In a working paper published in December 2010, Christian Friedrich, Isabel Schnabel, and Jeromin Zettelmeyer examined the impact of financial integration on Emerging Europe's economic growth.[11] They found that the impact of financial integration was highest in the countries politically most integrated with the EU. They also found that the financial integration of Emerging Europe was different from other developing regions. The effects of the financial integration of the region on economic growth were above the average in other regions, and, although the growth was associated with a rapid increase in current account deficits, it was not due to falling savings but to investments rising faster than average. In their paper, the authors point to the importance of financial integration despite the negative effects of the global crisis:

> Our results have important policy implications. They suggest that the negative side effects of financial integration that became evident in the current crisis, such as credit booms, overindebtedness of firms and households, and especially a high exposure to foreign currency debt, must be weighed carefully against clear evidence that financial integration has had significant growth effects in the transition region. This does not imply that the risks associated with financial integration do not need to be taken seriously, but it does suggest that policy should seek various ways to better manage those risks, rather than push back against financial integration per se (see also European Bank for Reconstruction and Development, 2009, 2010).[12]

The main feature of credit activity in SEE for 2004–2008 (the period of fastest growth in credit activity) was that household loans grew faster than corporate ones. The average growth rates for loans to households and loans to companies in Western Balkan countries during this period were: in Albania, 59.7 per cent and 50.7 per cent, respectively; in Bosnia and Herzegovina, 26.4 per cent and 23.6 per cent; in Croatia, 18 per cent and 15.2 per cent; in FYR Macedonia, 45.8 per cent and 25.8 per cent; in Montenegro, 106.2 per cent and 85.3 per cent; and in Serbia, 60.8 per cent and 27.5 per cent. On average, therefore, in all the

Western Balkan countries, loans to households grew more than business loans, in percentage terms. This percentage change is derived from the amounts of loans approved rather than the change in the level of credit activity shown in Tables 7.17 and 7.18, which is expressed as the loan to GDP ratio.

This credit expansion, based on faster growth of loans to households than of loans to companies and the breakdown of loans to companies by sector, which was initially dominated by the service sector (trade, real estate, and construction), combined to produce a sharp increase in the marginal propensity to import, so that loans approved to households and the service sector contributed to higher trade and current account deficits. Export-oriented companies and projects were not priorities. From 2004 to 2008, almost all the countries in the region doubled their trade and current account deficits.

Since the most important export markets for SEE exporters were Western European (on average about 60 per cent of all SEE exports),[13] the 2009 recession in Western Europe directly caused a sharp decline in trade volume and the incomes of SEE exporters. Decreasing export revenues due to falling demand for SEE goods on Western European markets influenced a decline in domestic demand during 2009, causing wages and employment in export-oriented enterprises to fall.

The chain reaction of tax revenues falling as a result of failing aggregate demand in SEE countries forced Bosnia and Herzegovina, FYR Macedonia, Romania, and Serbia to conclude financial arrangements with the IMF. These arrangements contributed to a significant increase in the external public debt of these countries (see Table 7.19). Unlike these countries, the largest increase in Bulgaria's external debt was a consequence of economic expansion in 2004–2008 and was primarily due to private debt. In 2008–2010, Bulgaria did not conclude an arrangement with the IMF, as the country was able to reduce imports sharply, increase exports, and almost eliminate the current account deficit. This resulted in a slight reduction of total external debt. During the crisis,

Table 7.19 The external debt to GDP ratio of Southeastern European Countries (per cent of GDP)

	2000	2004	2008	2010
Albania	31.8	20.8	20.4	36.6
Bosnia and Herzegovina	59.2	51.3	42.5	56.9
Bulgaria	88.6	70.1	103.5	101.6
Croatia	60.6	70.0	82.4	102.1
Macedonia, FYR	41.5	52.4	49.1	59.0
Montenegro	–	23.6	52.7	100.2
Romania	27.7	39.3	42.2	76.4
Serbia	105.0	59.8	60.4	83.1

Source: EBRD, *Transition Report 2005 – Business in Transition*, London, 2005, pp. 97, 113, 117, 121, 133, 169, 177; EBRD, *Transition Report 2009 – Transition in Crisis?*, London, 2009, pp. 132–226: EBRD, *Transition Report 2011 – Crisis in Transition: The People's Perspective*, London, 2011.

Table 7.20 Percentage change in the level of indebtedness of SEE countries

	2008/2004	2010/2008	2010/2004
Albania	−1.9	+79.4	+76.0
Bosnia and Herzegovina	−17.2	+33.9	+10.9
Bulgaria	+47.6	−1.8	+44.9
Croatia	+17.7	+23.9	+45.9
Macedonia, FYR	−6.3	+20.2	+12.6
Montenegro	+123.3	+90.1	+324.6
Romania	+7.4	+81.0	+94.4
Serbia	+1.0	+37.6	+39.0

Source: EBRD, *Transition Report 2011 – Crisis and Transition: The People's Perspective*, London, 2011.

Croatia, like Bulgaria, also avoided an agreement with the IMF, but was not successful in coping with declining GDP. Croatia's external debt increased sharply in 2008–2010.

The data in Table 7.20 show very different rates of change in the external indebtedness of SEE countries. Montenegro's external indebtedness has sharply increased. Extremely high rates of credit growth during 2006 and 2007 were directly related to the growth of external debt based on credit lines from abroad, which were the primary source of funding for economic growth. Due to the very small number of export-oriented companies in Montenegro, the country was unable to increase exports.

Romania and Serbia have emerged as the countries with the highest burden of debt to the IMF in the region (see Table 7.21). In March 2009, Romania signed a Stand-by Arrangement (SBA) with the IMF.[14] The total amount approved was SDR11.44 billion, of which Romania has drawn SDR10.57 billion (1,026 per cent of its quota with the IMF). In January 2009, Serbia also signed a SBA with the IMF. The total amount approved was SDR2.62 billion (292 per cent of the country's quota with the IMF) of which Serbia has drawn SDR1.37 billion.[15] The highest burden of debt repayment comes due in 2013 and 2014. Bosnia and Herzegovina is the third largest debtor in the SEE to the IMF. The country signed a SBA with the IMF in July 2009.[16] The total amount approved was SDR1.02 billion, of which the country has drawn SDR338 million.

Table 7.21 Projected payments to the IMF based on existing use of resources and present holdings of SDRs (millions of SDR)

	2012	2013	2014	2015
Romania	1,592	4,295	3,950	1,242
Serbia	191	580	502	117
Bosnia and Herzegovina	27	140	248	33

Source: See endnotes 16, 17, and 18.

Kosovo is the youngest member of the IMF from the region (it became a member in June 2009). In July 2010, Kosovo signed a SBA with the IMF. The total amount approved was SDR92.7 million and the amount drawn by the end of 2011 was SDR18.8 million.[17] FYR Macedonia signed a PLL (Precautionary and Liquidity Line) with the IMF in January 2011. The total amount approved was SDR413.4 million and the amount drawn by the end of 2011 was SDR197 million.[18] Rapid expansion of international banking activity and growth of international capital flows from 2000 to 2008 had a direct impact on the credit activity of banks in SEE countries.[19] Relatively high growth in FDI in the region was a direct consequence of the rapid increase in international capital flows during the same period (see Table 7.22). In the first decade of this century, the largest FDI per capita in SEE was in Bulgaria and Croatia ($5,960 and $5,000, respectively).[20] The third largest recipient was Romania. The highest inflow of FDI was realized in 2004–2008, corresponding to the high rates of economic growth associated with rapidly growing external debt. This was especially true of Bulgaria, which in 2004–2008 increased its level of external indebtedness by 47.6 per cent.

In both Bulgaria and Croatia, there was a strong correlation of rapid growth in FDI with growth in the external debt (as a result of the growth in private external debt) in 2004–2008. Such trends can be explained by the structure of FDI. In both countries, the overall structure of FDI was dominated by investments in finance, real estate and trade. Out of the total FDI in Bulgaria, the largest share went to real estate (21.7 per cent) and finance (19.1 per cent). The combined share of FDI represented by real estate, finance, and trade in Bulgaria was 57.5 per cent, whereas manufacturing represented only 18.3 per cent.[21] The structure of FDI in Croatia was similar. Most FDI went to finance (34.2 per cent). The combined share of finance, trade, telecommunications, and real estate was 57.5 per cent.[22]

Portfolio and capital market theory and possibilities for the development of capital markets in Southeastern Europe

Representatives of the SEE countries met at the Regional Cooperation Council in Sarajevo and signed a Memorandum of Understanding on 27 March 2012. The aim of signing this document was the formation of a single electronic platform for the development of capital markets in SEE countries. The capital markets of Southeastern Europe, especially the Western Balkan countries, are too atomized. The administrative barriers hindering economies of scale in financial markets are the most serious obstacles to lowering transaction costs and the successful structuring of portfolios.

Starting from the fundamentals of portfolio as founded by Harry Markowitz and of capital market theory as developed by Sharpe, Lintner, and Treynor, the structuring of a successful financial portfolio is based on the dispersion of risk, for which the existence of risk-free or at least less risky securities is a precondition.[23] The possibility of structuring a portfolio of financial institutions and

Table 7.22 Foreign direct investment in SEE (US$ millions)

Year	Albania	Bosnia and Herzegovina	Bulgaria	Croatia	FYR Macedonia	Romania	Serbia
2000	143	150	998	1,085	176	1,051	25
2001	204	130	803	1,407	439	1,154	165
2002	135	266	876	591	77	1,080	475
2003	178	382	2,070	1,927	118	2,156	1,365
2004	324	708	2,879	732	322	6,368	966
2005	258	608	4,005	1,551	95	6,587	1,550
2006	315	718	7,583	3,194	424	10,957	4,264
2007	647	2,087	11,433	4,736	700	9,629	2,523
2008	874	908	9,187	4,706	601	13,606	2,714
2009	924	245	3,525	1,617	186	4,934	1,881
2010	1,098	199	1,936	452	292	3,583	1,141
Total	5,100	6,401	45,295	21,998	3,430	61,105	17,069
US$ per capita	1,594	1,684	5,960	5,000	1,715	2,740	2,276

Source: EBRD, *Transition Report 2005 – Business in Transition*, London, 2005; EBRD, *Transition Report 2009 – Transition in Crisis?*, London 2009.; EBRD, *Transition Report 2011*, London, 2011.

investors in capital markets that are atomized and where no risk-free (or very low risk) securities exist is very limited. In other words, capital markets characterized by the predominance of risky financial securities mean financial investors cannot structure their portfolios successfully. Such financial markets operate on a sub-optimal level, in comparison with financial markets based on a sufficient range of financial assets – from risk-free to risky financial assets. To put it another way – in such circumstances, financial investors cannot achieve the target level of return with a minimum of risk, compared to financial markets where financial assets are on offer over a wide range, starting from risk-free securities (bonds of countries with high ratings, the bonds of international institutions and financial agencies) and ending with high-risk securities (shares of companies with highly uncertain profit potential).

The EBRD's 2010 Transition Report's third chapter emphasized the need to develop a financial market based on financial assets denominated in domestic currencies in the countries of Southeastern Europe (and other countries in transition) as an important element in reducing the tendency of banks to borrow in foreign currencies.[24] The report also particularly emphasized the very important role of institutional investors in the development of capital markets in domestic currencies. Returning again to the basis of the theory of capital markets and to the valuation of financial assets, where the risk-free rate is one of the fundamental elements in financial assets pricing, the main question that arises is how to enable the development of domestic capital markets in SEE countries without risk-free financial instruments. In fact, government bonds in all the SEE countries (with the exception of Bosnia and Herzegovina, where there are none on the domestic capital market) are basically risky financial assets, as the countries' ratings are low or relatively low. The fact that assets denominated in local currencies in SEE tend to be high risk has meant that institutional investors reduce their portfolio risk by holding a significant proportion of their assets in foreign securities (Western European countries' bonds), with a consequent outflow of financial capital.

I have previously presented one possibility that could possibly contribute to successful structuring of institutional investors' portfolios in SEE capital markets in a text on small open economies in the Western Balkans.[25] The basic idea is based on issuing government bonds of the Western Balkans (SEE countries) denominated in domestic currencies, but guaranteed by an EU Guarantee Fund for the Western Balkans. I call them Euro-Balkan bonds. Revenues from the sale of these financial assets, with maturities of 10–15 years, would be used exclusively for funding the development of cross-border projects. The EU Guarantee Fund would have the right to review public finances every six months in SEE countries issuing such bonds, with a guarantee-to-equity option (as compensation for bearing the guarantee risk). In other words, the Fund would be given the right to convert the guarantee into common stocks of the public utilities controlled by the governments in the region.

Issuing such bonds on the domestic capital markets of SEE would broaden and deepen the regional financial markets, based on the emergence of risk-free financial instruments with low interest rates. These financial instruments denominated in the national currencies of the Western Balkan and other SEE countries would provide the basis for much more successful structuring of institutional investors' portfolios in SEE domestic capital markets, while linking the economies of the region and supporting economic growth on a more sustainable basis.

Concluding remarks

Analysis of the main factors affecting investment and sustainable economic growth negatively suggests that institutional weaknesses like inefficient government bureaucracy and unstable and corrupt institutions were the predominant barriers in the pre-crisis period. Nonetheless, all the SEE countries did achieve relatively high rates of economic growth at that time. These growth rates were based on the large credit expansion generated by the presence of banks from the EU which improved the technology of financial operations and contributed to easier access to financing from Western Europe.

Since the crisis, access to financing, tax rates, and tax systems have emerged as major obstacles. A sharp decline in credit activity in the region has directly affected household consumption and business investment. In the business sector, export-oriented companies were among the most affected. Economic growth throughout the region has been based on domestic demand-led growth. There is a lack of clearly defined strategies to attract export-oriented FDI. There is also a lack of well-established and sufficiently capitalized financial institutions responsible for financing export-oriented companies and projects. Such institutions could be crucial for a shift from domestic demand-led to export-led growth in SEE countries.

In this sense, SEE countries should redefine their strategies to attract foreign direct investors and provide significant tax relief for investors with a long-term export-orientation and that can integrate local businesses with international production chains. Another important conclusion from this paper is that SEE countries should establish stronger financial institutions to finance export-oriented projects. These two measures, combined with tax incentives for domestic investors with export potential, can contribute to a change in the dominant development model practised in SEE countries for the past two decades.

The development of domestic capital markets in SEE countries and especially the Western Balkans is critically dependent on a supply of new and less risky financial instruments to be used to finance economic growth based on capital projects. For the SEE countries to offer the new types of risk-free or minimum risk financial instruments needed to restructure domestic financial institutions' portfolios, they must have the support of the EU guarantee schemes. In that sense, the idea is to issue new types of government bonds backed by EU guarantee schemes that would allow better and more efficient portfolio management of domestic financial institutions, while supporting economic growth and linking economies in Southeastern Europe.

Notes

1 This is an extended version of a text written while on the Alpha Bank Visiting Fellowship programme in 2011/2012. The text was presented in April 2012 in this broader version. A shortened version was published by SEESOX, St Antony's College, University of Oxford in March 2013 in the book *Defining a New Reform Agenda – Paths to Sustainable Convergence in South East Europe*, edited by Othon Anastasakis, Peter Sanfey, and Max Watson. The text appeared as Chapter 4: 'Financial Constraints on Economic Growth in South East Europe' (pp. 69–86). I am grateful to the SEESOX Centre and St Antony's College for their kind permission to publish this text in this collection.
2 The International Bank for Reconstruction and Development/The World Bank, *Doing Business 2012 – Doing Business in a More Transparent World*, Washington, 2012.
3 The World Bank: http://data.worldbank.org/indicator/NY.GDP.PCAP.CD.
4 For example, in the *2011–2012 Global Competitiveness Report*, Hungary and Latvia are ranked forty-sixth and sixty-fourth, even though their foreign debt was 143 per cent and 145 per cent of GDP, respectively, according to IMF data. The data on foreign indebtedness and SBA for Hungary are available at: www.imf.org/external/np/fin/tad/exfin2.aspx?memberKey1=415&date1key=2012-02-23; www.imf.org/external/np/sec/pn/2012/pn1204.htm; and for Latvia at: www.imf.org/external/np/fin/tad/exfin2.aspx?memberKey1=575&date1key=2012-02-23; www.imf.org/external/pubs/ft/scr/2012/cr1231.pdf.
5 The analysis of changes in credit activity is based on data published in European Bank for Reconstruction and Development, *Transition Report 2011 – Crisis and Transition: The People's Perspective*, London.
6 John Williamson, 'A Short History of the Washington Consensus', a paper commissioned by Fundación CIDOB for a conference 'From the Washington Consensus towards a new Global Governance', Barcelona, 24–25 September 2004, published on the webpage: www.iie.com/publications/papers/williamson0904-2.pdf.
7 All SEE countries signed bilateral free trade agreements from December 2000 to October 2003. These bilateral free trade agreements were replaced by a regional free trade agreement signed in December 2006 – the CEFTA (available at: http://rtais.wto.org/UI/PublicShowMemberRTAIDCard.aspx?rtaid=4).
8 Sebnem Kalemli-Ozcan, Herman Kamil, and Carolina Villegas-Sanchez, 'What Hinders Investment in the Aftermath of Financial Crisis: Insolvent Firms or Illiquid Banks?', NBER Working Paper 16528, 2010, (www.nber.org/papers/w16528).
9 Martin Brown, Steven Ongena, Alexander Popov, and Pinar Yesin, 'Who Needs Credit and Who Gets Credit in Eastern Europe', *European Central Bank, Working Paper Series, No 1421*, 2011, pp. 7–8.
10 Martin Brown, Steven Ongena, Alexander Popov, and Pinar Yesin, op. cit., p. 4.
11 Christian Friedrich, Isabel Schnabel, Jeromin Zettelmeyer, 'Financial Integration and Growth – Is Emerging Europe Different?', *EBRD, Working Paper No. 123*, 2010.
12 Christian Friedrich, Isabel Schnabel, Jeromin Zettelmeyer, op. cit., p. 29.
13 Data on the geographical distribution of trade can be found at the WTO website: http://rtais.wto.org/UI/PublicSearchByMemberResult.aspx?MemberCode=070&lang=1&redirect=1.
14 www.imf.org/external/np/fin/tad/exfin2.aspx?memberKey1=818&date1key=2012-02-21.
15 www.imf.org/external/np/fin/tad/exfin2.aspx?memberKey1=1072&date1key=2012-02-21.
16 www.imf.org/external/np/fin/tad/exfin2.aspx?memberKey1=75&date1key=2012-02-21.
17 www.imf.org/external/np/fin/tad/exfin2.aspx?memberKey1=555&date1key=2012-02-21.
18 www.imf.org/external/np/fin/tad/exfin2.aspx?memberKey1=618&date1key=2012-02-21.
19 See the Bank for International Settlements statistics on international banking at www.bis.org/statistics/consstats.htm.
20 Based on data published in the EBRD Transition Reports for 2005, 2009, and 2011.

21 InvestBulgaria Agency – http://bulgarico.com/wp-content/uploads/2011/02/Bulgaria-The-Right-EU-Location.pdf.
22 Croatian National Bank: www.hnb.hr/statistika/hstatistika.htm.
23 The theoretical basis for the introduction of risk-free or less risky financial assets is Harry Markowitz's portfolio theory. Markowitz's seminal paper was written under the title 'Portfolio Selection' and it was published in March 1952 in *The Journal of Finance* 7 (1): 77–91. Markowitz's book *Portfolio Selection: Efficient Diversification of Investments* was first published in 1959 by John Wiley & Sons and was reprinted by Basil Blackwell in 1991. For the Sharpe model of capital asset pricing and the index model of portfolio selection, see William F. Sharpe, 'Capital Asset Prices – A Theory of Market Equilibrium Under Conditions of Risk', *Journal of Finance* XIX (3): 425–442, 1964, and idem, *Portfolio Theory and Capital Markets*, McGraw-Hill, New York, 1970.
24 European Bank for Reconstruction and Development, *Transition Report 2010 – Recovery and Reform*, London, Chapter 3, pp. 56–58.
25 Fikret Čaušević, 'Small Open Economies in the Western Balkans: Controlled Fiscal Expansion for a New Deal for the Western Balkans', Opinion Piece, SEESOX, St Antony's College, University of Oxford, March 2012. This text forms the basis of the essay printed in this volume as 'Fiscal policies in the European Union, the United States, and the Western Balkans in the age of global crisis: controlled fiscal expansion for a New Deal for the Western Balkans'.

References

The data for this paper were drawn from the various institutional webpages cited in the endnotes.

Brown, Martin, Steven Ongena, Alexander Popov, and Pinar Yesin, 'Who Needs Credit and Who Gets Credit in Eastern Europe', *European Central Bank, Working Paper Series, No. 1421*, February 2012.

Čaušević, Fikret 'Small Open Economies in the Western Balkans: Controlled Fiscal Expansion for a New Deal for the Western Balkans', Opinion Piece, SEESOX, St Antony's College, Oxford, March 2012.

Christian, Friedrich, Isabel Schnabel, and Jeromin Zettelmeyer, 'Financial Integration and Growth – Is Emerging Europe Different?', *EBRD, Working Paper No. 123*, December 2010.

European Bank for Reconstruction and Development, *Transition Report 2005 – Business in Transition*, London, 2005.

European Bank for Reconstruction and Development, *Transition Report 2009 – Transition in Crisis*, London, 2009.

European Bank for Reconstruction and Development, *Transition Report 2010 – Recovery and Reform*, London, 2010.

European Bank for Reconstruction and Development, *Transition Report 2011 – Crisis and Transition: The People's Perspective*, London, 2011.

Kalemli-Ozcan, Sebnem, Herman Kamil, and Carolina Villegas-Sanchez, 'What Hinders Investment in the Aftermath of Financial Crisis: Insolvent Firms or Illiquid Banks?', *NBER Working Paper 16528*, November 2010.

Markowitz, Harry, 'Portfolio Selection', *The Journal of Finance* 7 (1): 77–91, 1952.

Markowitz, Harry, *Portfolio Selection: Efficient Diversification of Investments*, John Wiley & Sons, New York, 1959.

Sharpe, William F., 'Capital Asset Prices – A Theory of Market Equilibrium under Conditions of Risk', *Journal of Finance* XIX (3): 425–442, 1964.

Sharpe, William F., *Portfolio Theory and Capital Markets*, McGraw-Hill, New York, 1970.
The International Bank for Reconstruction and Development/The World Bank, *Doing Business 2008*, Washington, 2008.
The International Bank for Reconstruction and Development/The World Bank, *Doing Business 2009*, Washington, 2009.
The International Bank for Reconstruction and Development/The World Bank, *Doing Business 2010 – Reforming Through Difficult Times*, Washington, 2010.
The International Bank for Reconstruction and Development/The World Bank, *Doing Business 2011 – Making a Difference for Entrepreneurs*, Washington, 2011.
The International Bank for Reconstruction and Development/The World Bank, *Doing Business 2012 – Doing Business in a More Transparent World*, Washington, 2012.
The International Monetary Fund, *World Economic Outlook: Slowing Growth, Rising Risks*, Washington, 2011.
The International Monetary Fund, *2011–12 Global Competitiveness Report*, Washington, 2012.
The World Economic Forum, *The Global Competitiveness Report 2009–10*, Geneva, Switzerland, 2010.
The World Economic Forum, *The Global Competitiveness Report 2010–11*, Geneva, Switzerland, 2011.
The World Economic Forum, *The Global Competitiveness Report 2011–12*, Geneva, Switzerland, 2012.
Williamson, John, 'A Short History of the Washington Consensus', Fundación CIDOB, Barcelona, 2004.

Part III
Economic challenges in post-Dayton Bosnia and Herzegovina

Part III

8 Macroeconomic management in Bosnia and Herzegovina on the road to EU accession
1996–2006[1]

Macroeconomic trends and the structure of the Bosnian business sector

Major characteristics of the post-conflict economic situation in Bosnia and Herzegovina

The economic conditions in Bosnia and Herzegovina after the war have been marked by many mutually conflicting goals, most of which should have been attained relatively quickly after the end of what was, after all, the most important war-related disaster on the soil of Europe since World War II. This fact has severely affected the dynamic of economic and employment growth and the labour market equilibrium. The extent of devastation during the war (1992–1995) particularly affected the quantity and quality of human capital, as well as infrastructure and industrial/commercial property, and meant that economic recovery was entirely dependent on resources authorized by the international community (donor conferences). The degree of wartime devastation may be illustrated by the following indicators:

- The total number of recorded deaths from 1992 to 1995 was estimated between 102,600 (the lowest estimation) and 200,000.[2]
- The number of missing persons still being sought is around 40,000.
- The number of persons who fled abroad because of the war and have not returned is around 450,000.
- The Foreign Trade Chamber of Bosnia and Herzegovina estimates the extent of wartime damage to personal and commercial/industrial property to be in the range of US$30 to 50 billion.[3]
- The total gross domestic product (GDP) losses over the four-year period amounted to about US$30.4 billion (the pre-war GDP of BiH was approximately US$10.3 billion in 1991 US$ terms and average GDP during the war was estimated at US$1.2 billion).[4]

Between 1996 and 2000, financial resources were largely channelled into the reconstruction of housing, infrastructure, and public services. Resources available for business sector development were much more modest and limited in scope. Employment growth between 1996 and 1999 was therefore largely due to large-scale reconstruction projects in the aforementioned sectors and their closure in turn brought about a reduction in demand for that type of job on the labour market. Leaving public services to one side, employment had been concentrated in industry, so that problems privatizing state companies, modest market share, and low levels of exports all contributed to a declining capacity to maintain employment.

Production and output

Only three pre-war Yugoslav republics had positive individual balances of foreign trade between 1985 and 1991 and one of them was Bosnia and Herzegovina. In fact, three of the five largest exporters in the former Yugoslavia were from Bosnia and Herzegovina, two of them taking turns at the top of the list during the final ten years of that ex-country's existence: Energoinvest Sarajevo (production of electrical equipment, engineering, oil refining, and the production of petroleum derivatives, metallurgy, clay, and aluminium) and Unis Sarajevo (the auto-industry, metallurgy, and military industries). During the 1980s, the largest car factory in the Balkans was located in Sarajevo (in 1990, annual production was 32,000 Golf cars) thanks to a joint investment by Volkswagen and Unis (TAS – Tvornica Automobila Sarajevo/The Sarajevo Car Factory). The company with most employees in the former Yugoslavia was also from Bosnia and Herzegovina – Šipad of Sarajevo, which was really a wood processing and manufacturing cluster with some 80,000 employees.

Between 1970 and 1991, the contribution to Bosnia and Herzegovina's gross domestic product of manufacturing, particularly metal working, the car industry, electricity, wood processing, and chemicals, increased markedly. The military industry was a significant source of pre-war income, but did not appear in the official statistics of the former Yugoslavia. The increasing importance of middle and higher value-added products in GDP led to significant economic progress and an increased standard of living in Bosnia and Herzegovina between 1970 and 1991. It was also very important for the Republic's pre-war economic development that Sarajevo hosted the XIVth Winter Olympic Games in 1984 and that between 1978 and 1984 around US$1 billion was invested in the development of winter and rural tourism, while the city infrastructure was fully overhauled. Agriculture and the food industry also saw significant progress and pre-war Bosnia and Herzegovina was home to a number of very significant food and drinks producers (UPI Sarajevo, Bosanka Doboj, Vitaminka Banja Luka). The Sarajevo Tobacco Company produced one of the best cigarettes in Europe, in cooperation with American Marlboro (the well-known 'Sarajevo Marlboro').

Bosnia and Herzegovina's GDP was greatly reduced by extensive war-related destruction. At the end of the war in 1995, the IMF and the World Bank estimated Bosnia and Herzegovina's GDP at around US$1.2 billion at current prices. Particularly important for analysis of the economic impact of the war was the drop in population from 4.37 million, according to the 1991 census,[5] to 3.35 million in

Table 8.1 Gross domestic product – Bosnia and Herzegovina, 1991–2006

Year	GDP in millions of KM (local currency)	GDP in millions of US$ (current prices)	GDP per capita in US$ (current prices)
1991	17,750	10,250	2,305
1996	3,150	2,150	595
1998	7,650	4,343	1,189
2000	10,713	5,056	1,337
2001	11,599	5,307	1,397
2002	12,829	6,177	1,614
2003	13,443	7,755	2,024
2004	14,678	9,316	2,424
2005	17,218	10,947	2,849
2006	19,333	12,398	3,226

Sources: Statistics Agency of Bosnia and Herzegovina. Data for 1991 are from the Statistical Bulletin of Bosnia and Herzegovina 1992, Institute for Statistics of Bosnia and Herzegovina, Sarajevo, May 1992.

1995, according to the estimates of demographic experts.[6] Between 1996 and 2006, the population was estimated as having risen to 3.83 million. Table 8.1 shows GDP rising from US$2.15 to 5.05 billion between 1996 and 2000 in current prices at an average annual US dollar rate for the relevant years. That GDP grew by a factor of 2.3 over this period was largely due to the World Bank-coordinated and implemented priority renewal and reconstruction programme. During the period in question, according to the World Bank mission to Bosnia and Herzegovina, some US$5.3 billion was spent on the reconstruction of basic infrastructure, educational, and healthcare institutions/facilities, and repair and reconstruction of housing.

In the following period, from 2001 to 2006, economic growth was predominantly based on enabling greater capacity exploitation in business and industry, privatization, restructuring, strengthening the financial sector, and attracting foreign direct investment. During this period, GDP rose from US$5.3 to 11.3 billion, or from KM 11.6 to 17.3 billion. Given that the domestic currency was pegged to the euro throughout (€1 = 1.956 KM), one gets a better idea of GDP growth in Bosnia and Herzegovina from the local currency figure than the figure in US dollars. The fall of the US dollar against the euro by more than 52 per cent between 2001 and 2006 means that GDP data in dollars do not express real GDP growth. Taking an average rate of inflation of 3.5 per cent in the US as a rough guide for comparing the value of the US dollar in 2006 to its value in 1991, however, suggests that Bosnia and Herzegovina's GDP in 2006 (US$11.27 billion at current prices) was equivalent to US$6.73 billion in 1991 terms, or to 65.6 per cent of the country's GDP in 1991. As this GDP was produced by 14 per cent fewer people, per capita GDP in Bosnia and Herzegovina in 2006 works out at US$1,770 (1991 value), or 76.8 per cent of per capita GDP for 1991, which was US$2,305. This rough measure of GDP per capita calculated in 1991 US dollars does not take into account the performance of other countries in the

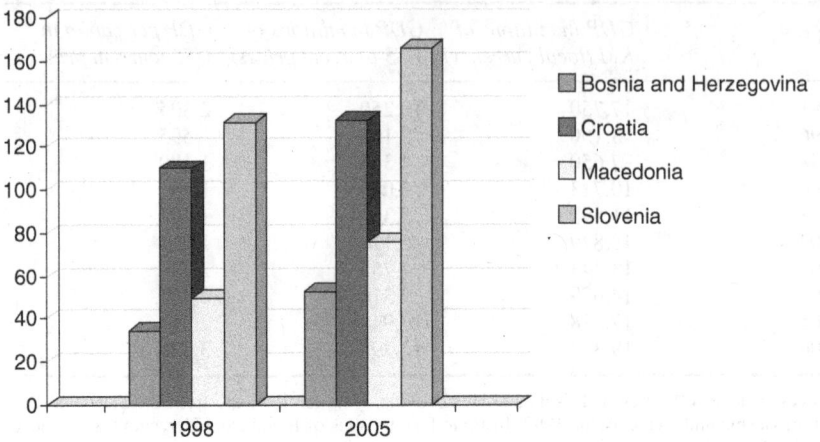

Figure 8.1 Change in the level of relative economic positions of the Former Yugoslav republics in relation to their economic position in 1991 (1991=100).

Note
The relative economic positions of the countries of the Former Yugoslavia are calculated on the basis of their wealth coefficients for the relevant years (1991, 1998, and 2005). The wealth coefficient is the ratio of a country's share in world GDP to its share in world population.

world. A more precise measure of the relative economic position of a country is the wealth coefficient (see Figure 8.1 and associated note). According to this measure, Bosnia and Herzegovina's economic position in 2005 was only 52.5 per cent of what it had been in 1991.

Major trends in the structure of the Bosnian economy

A distinguishing feature of Bosnia's gross domestic product (GDP) over the 2000–2006 period has been comparative growth in the role of service industries within the business sector (trade, transport and communications, business services, financial mediation, tourism and catering). The significance of manufacturing and mining has been reduced relative to before the war (1990–1991), but manufacturing retains a key role in the development of Bosnia's competitive capabilities for entering regional integration processes of trade, cluster development, and establishing the single Bosnian economic space.

In 1999–2001, the business sector's share in GDP decreased from 61.7 per cent to 58.8 per cent (see Table 8.2).[7] The major fall, from 61.7 per cent to 57.4 per cent, occurred between 1999 and 2000, and was primarily due to agricultural and forestry production falling by almost KM 100 million, while salaries grew faster for public employees (including healthcare and education) than in the business sector. During this three-year period (1999–2001), growth of added-value was greatest in transport and the communications (33.4 per cent), trade (31.8 per cent), and financial services and intermediation

Table 8.2 Sectoral distribution of GDP in Bosnia and Herzegovina, 1999–2001

	1999		2000		2001	
	'000 KM	– in %	'000 KM	– in %	'000 KM	– in %
Agriculture, forestry, and hunting	1,138,611	13.25	1,038,134	10.71	1,112,585	10.62
Fishery	2,405	0.03	2,609	0.03	1,636	0.02
Mining	148,630	1.73	182,202	1.88	172,696	1.65
Manufacturing	920,528	10.70	993,384	10.25	1,073,504	10.24
Electricity generation and distribution, gas and water	574,000	6.67	628,971	6.49	691,678	6.60
Construction	452,263	5.26	459,574	4.74	439,286	4.19
Wholesale and retail trade	755,880	8.79	759,697	7.84	995,708	9.50
Tourism and catering	171,046	1.99	183,295	1.89	202,941	1.94
Transport, communication, and warehousing	710,563	8.26	798,519	8.24	947,658	9.04
Financial services	258,875	3.01	322,943	3.33	329,570	3.14
Real estate, renting, and business services	172,556	2.00	195,028	2.01	199,915	1.90
Total business sector	**5,305,357**	**61.67**	**5,564,356**	**57.41**	**6,617,177**	**58.84**
Gross domestic product	**8,603,006**	**100.00**	**9,692,332**	**100.00**	**10,479,957**	**100.00**

Source: BiH Statistics Agency, Nacionalni računi – National Accounts, Tematski bilten – Thematic Bulletin – TB 01, December 2005.

(26 per cent). The leading factor in this high added-value growth rate in transport and communications was telecommunications, which saw the highest investment rates in the post-war period. Total investment in this sector in 1996 to 2000 amounted to KM 700 million, largely financed by reinvestment of profits. This resulted in a sudden increase in subscribers to both fixed and, more particularly, mobile telephony and so high growth in income and added value.[8]

As regards trade, foreign direct investors from France, Slovenia, and Austria, availed of incentives under the Law on Foreign Direct Investment Policy in Bosnia and Herzegovina, opened large retail centres in major cities (Sarajevo, Banja Luka, Mostar, Tuzla, and Zenica). Domestic companies and individuals also invested in expanding trade facilities, resulting in high income growth. In financial services, the introduction of international banking standards much improved banking control and supervision. The introduction of a single currency, the arrival of foreign investors (the Raiffeisen Bank, the Zagrebačka Banka, and the Hypo-Alpe-Adria Bank), reform of internal payment system, and the conversion of national Euro-zone currencies all contributed to a tripling of foreign currency reserves and a 48.5 per cent increase in the Bosnian banking sector assets. In contrast to the three fastest growing industries, added value fell in agriculture, forestry, and construction between 1999 and 2001.

Over the next three-year period (2002–2004), the fastest added-value growth was achieved in the generation and distribution of electricity (37.3 per cent), real estate and business services (36.9 per cent), and trade (31.3 per cent) (see Table 8.3). High growth rates were also achieved in mining (26.2 per cent), tourism and catering (27.3 per cent), and financial mediation (26 per cent).

The rapid expansion of electricity generation and distribution was due to significantly improved operations in the three public electricity companies: JP Elektroprivreda BiH d.d. Sarajevo, JP Elektroprivreda RS a.d. Trebinje and JP Elektroprivreda HB d.d. Mostar. Loans approved by the World Bank (IBRD) and the European Bank for Reconstruction and Development (EBRD) and the application of business auditing (2001–2002) together resulted in significantly lower losses in electricity transmission, as well as in improved revenue collection. Although the financial results as presented in the profit and loss balances show losses over the last five years, losses have actually been decreasing and none of the three enterprises is facing any problems with cash flows (see Table 8.4). In 2004, for instance, the biggest electricity producer in Bosnia and Herzegovina, JP Elektroprivreda BiH d.d. Sarajevo, showed a KM 55 million loss, but there were positive cash flows of approximately KM 40 million. Production growth in mining is directly related to electricity generation, since around a fifth of Bosnian electricity is produced in thermal plants. JP Elektroprivreda BiH d.d. Sarajevo and JP Elektroprivreda RS a.d. Trebinje have also become very significant exporters.

Production growth in mining was also affected by foreign investments in the Zvornik-based Birač company (alumina production) and Ljubija mines. Birač is owned by Lithuanian partners and is directly related to the exploitation of

Table 8.3 Sectoral distribution of GDP in Bosnia and Herzegovina, 2002–2004

	2002		2003		2004	
	'000 KM	– in %	'000 KM	– in %	'000 KM	– in %
Agriculture, forestry, and hunting	1,141,355	9.80	1,063,196	8.64	1,272,269	9.43
Mining	220,957	1.90	241,829	1.97	278,619	2.06
Manufacturing	1,161,969	9.97	1,260,269	10.24	1,364,461	10.11
Electricity production and distribution, gas and water	592,292	5.08	715,657	5.82	813,040	6.02
Construction	482,291	4.14	561,416	4.56	522,656	3.87
Wholesale and retail	1,224,352	10.50	1,327,452	10.79	1,607,473	11.91
Tourism and catering	238,967	2.05	265,953	2.16	303,427	2.25
Transport, communications, and warehousing	1,045,010	8.97	1,145,750	9.31	1,211,725	8.98
Financial services	389,855	3.35	445,977	3.62	490,245	3.63
Real estate, renting, and business services	221,994	1.90	264,921	2.15	304,543	2.26
Total business sector	**6,721,277**	**57.68**	**7,294,083**	**59.27**	**8,170,945**	**60.54**
Gross domestic product	**11,651,119**	**100.00**	**12,303,008**	**100.00**	**13,497,134**	**100.00**

Source: BiH Statistics Agency, Nacionalni računi – National Accounts, Tematski bilten, TB 01, December 2005.

Table 8.4 Biggest exporters in Bosnia and Herzegovina, 1999–2004 (in thousands of KM)

Company name	1999	2000	2001	2002	2003	2004
1 «ALUMINIJ» d.d. Mostar	174,666	305,611	302,939	276,638	259,605	327,210
2 «ELEKTROPRIVREDA BiH» d.d. Sarajevo	33,997	64,322	84,377	102,270	81,099	131,002
3 «ELEKTROPRIVREDA» RS Trebinje	80,804	55,936	77,051	54,546	79,261	96,127
4 FABRIKA GLINICE «BIRAČ» AD Zvornik	11,683	103,337	25,587	718	19,398	80,405

Source: Companies' Departments of Finance and Accounting; quoted from Čaušević, F., *Impact of Foreign Trade Policy on the Current Account and Competitiveness of Bosnia and Herzegovina*, Economics Institute Sarajevo, Sarajevo, July 2005.

bauxite ore (the Milići bauxite mine near Vlasenica), while the Mittal Company bought the iron ore mines in Ljubija and is using them for their own transnational production system.

The average (annual) added-value growth rates of the Bosnian and Herzegovinian economy in 1999 to 2004 show that the fastest-growing industries included trade, financial mediation, and mining (see Table 8.5). The average growth rate in trade in these five years amounted to 16.8 per cent, while in financial mediation it was 13.9 per cent. The growth rates in these two industries are directly positively correlated. The accelerated expansion of the financial sector in 2000 to 2004, particularly following the arrival of foreign banks (the Raiffeisen Bank, the Hypo-Alpe-Adria Bank, the Hypo Vereisbank-Bank Austria, and the UniCredit-Zagrebačka banka), and the increased security this provided the banking sector, resulted in an increase in personal savings from a mere KM 250 million in 1999 to KM 2.9 billion in 2004. The major expansion in residential lending stimulated demand for final (consumer) commodities, generating an expansion of consumption-oriented imports and, consequently, growth in the trade deficit.

The following economic trends were characteristic of 1999–2004:

1 In *agricultural production*, cyclic variability due to weather and labour fluctuation and the financial resources available to the sector led to a decrease in production in 2000 and 2003 compared to 1999 and 2002, respectively. Investment in the food and drink industries and better organized purchasing of primary agricultural produce resulted, however, in increased agricultural production in 2004 compared to all previous years.
2 In *mining and excavation*, increased demand for electric power, on both domestic and foreign markets, resulted in increased production, primarily in the coal mines whose output provides the essential raw material for generation at the Tuzla, Kakanj, Ugljevik, and Gacko power plants. The aforementioned foreign direct investment and increased production at Birač directly resulted in high growth rates of bauxite production at the Milići mine near Vlasenica (eastern Bosnia and Herzegovina), while acquisition of the Ljubija mine by the ISPAT company brought about a great increase in production at this mine (iron-ore mines in Western Bosnia and Herzegovina).
3 *Manufacturing* achieved stable growth over the last five years, despite facing major restructuring issues and a major surplus labour burden compared to other industries. Manufacturing accounts for 90 per cent of all exports from the Bosnian economy and is therefore of special significance for competitiveness. A stimulus for industrial development also came from foreign investors, the most significant being in steel. Mittal Steel bought the B-H Steel company in Zenica, while Slovenian CIMOS bought the TMD Ai factory in Gradačac (the automotive industry), the German Schieder Group bought Standard d.d. Sarajevo (furniture), and German Meggle bought the Bihać dairy. The significance of the investment by Meggle is reflected in the impact it had on creating permanent employment for over 4,000 contract

Table 8.5 Growth rates of the business sector in Bosnia and Herzegovina, 1999–2004

Business sector	2000	2001	2002	2003	2004	Average 1999–2004
Agriculture, forestry, and hunting	−8.8	+7.2	+2.6	−6.8	+19.7	+2.8
Mining	+22.1	−4.9	+27.7	+9.5	+15.3	+13.9
Manufacturing	+7.9	+8.1	+8.3	+8.4	+8.3	+8.2
Electricity production and distribution, gas and water	+9.6	+10.0	−14.3	+20.9	+13.5	+7.9
Construction	+1.5	−4.4	+9.8	+16.4	−6.8	+3.3
Wholesale and retail	+0.5	+31.1	+22.9	+8.4	+21.1	+16.8
Tourism and catering	+7.0	+10.9	+17.7	+11.3	+13.9	+12.2
Transport, communication, and warehousing	+12.2	+18.8	+10.2	+9.7	+5.8	+11.3
Financial services	+24.7	+2.2	+18.2	+14.4	+9.9	+13.9
Real estate, renting, and business services	+12.7	+2.6	+11.0	+19.4	+14.7	+12.1

Source: The author's calculations using data from the BiH Statistics Agency.

farmers in the region. Lithuanian investors bought the aluminium factory near Zvornik and the pipe factory at Derventa. The building materials industry saw investment by German and Austrian investors (cement plants at Kakanj and Lukavac), and in 2003 a Croatian investor from Našice bought the Sarajevo-based GP Put (a construction and building materials business), facilitating their application for an EBRD loan to develop a brickworks near Sarajevo. Support to development of the pharmaceutical industry in Bosnia and Herzegovina came from the International Financial Corporation (IFC), a member of the World Bank group, with a loan that was then converted into shareholder equity in the Bosnalijek company in Sarajevo. The company tripled its total income between 1999 and 2004. In addition to Meggle, food industry development was spurred by the establishment of domestic companies in the meat and meat processing industries. The biggest exporters are in metal production, however (Aluminijum d.d. Mostar is the biggest exporter), and the highest export and income growth rates were achieved by companies in metal processing (TMD Ai d.o.o. Gradačac in the automotive industry and Feal d.o.o. Široki Brijeg in the production of aluminium parts and profiles).

4   The *construction industry* fluctuated over the five-year period, reflecting conditions related to the restructuring of infrastructure. During post-war reconstruction (1995–1999), the construction industry saw relatively high growth rates thanks to widespread major infrastructural rebuilding (roads, bridges, schools, hospitals, residential facilities). In the five years that followed, investment in infrastructure was much lower. The declared plan to begin construction of a highway on the Vc corridor through Bosnia and Herzegovina (connecting Central Europe and the Adriatic via central Bosnia) would provide a major stimulus to development. A number of large domestic construction companies exist with experience in major projects in the Middle East and North Africa before the war. Since the war, some of them have managed to revive business contacts and even a presence on international markets (during the war, some companies continued to do business in Uganda, Kenya, Algeria, Libya through subsidiaries). Put d.d. Sarajevo is one such company and is also one of the few construction companies privatized by the tender method, through a strategic partner. Hidrogradnja d.d. Sarajevo was one of the largest civil engineering or construction companies in the former Yugoslavia and managed to overcome post-war problems, particularly those relating to its surplus workforce, but it has not been privatized yet. A large number of small private construction companies have also been established, particularly during the period of renewal and reconstruction (1995–2000). These companies are now very competitive for smaller-scale works like family homes, catering facilities, or hotels.

5   Much advantage has been taken in the *retail and wholesale trades* of the benefits offered by the BiH FDI Policy Law, particularly the exemption from paying profit tax in full, where a foreign entity or individual owns 100 per cent of the equity. As already pointed out, trade development was

greatly stimulated by the entry of foreign investors into banking, producing increased confidence and an expansion of residential lending unprecedented in the previous five decades in the region. This increased purchasing power was exploited by foreign investors in the retail and wholesale trades, who multiplied their income. Added value achieved went up from KM 775 in 1999 to KM 1.6 billion in 2004 (a 113 per cent increase). The most significant foreign investments in this field were: Mercator (Slovenia), Interex (France), Wisa (Austria, in cooperation with a local partner), Velpro (Croatia), and Robot (Croatia, in cooperation with a local partner). Domestic investors also invested intensively (FIS Vitez, Economic Vitez, and MIMS Sarajevo). Foreign direct investments in Bosnia and Herzegovina also led to improvements in the procedures and control of indirect tax collection, as payment and collection systems in large shopping centres are transparent and far easier to control from a financial perspective than a greater number of small stores with uncoordinated purchasing, inventory and sales systems.

6 *Financial mediation* has been the second fastest growing industry in Bosnia and Herzegovina in the post-war period (after trade), as well as the first industry in which foreign direct investors are absolutely dominant as owners of capital. By the end of 1998, as many as 70 banks had registered in the banking sector, but average bank equity was very low (around KM 7 million) and interest rates were the highest in Europe (55 per cent on the annual level). The arrival of foreign banks and increased minimum equity capital requirements, up from KM 5 to 15 million, the establishment of the Central Bank of Bosnia and Herzegovina, and the introduction of a single currency throughout the country made the Bosnian banking sector one of the best in all of Southeastern Europe. In early 2006, 33 commercial banks were doing business in Bosnia and Herzegovina and average interest rates had fallen to 8.7 per cent. From 1998 to 2005, banking sector assets grew from KM 3.7 to 11.9 billion (221 per cent growth). The highest growth rates were achieved in the area of residential loans. Over the past five years, this segment of assets grew by an average 41 per cent rate. Together with service charges for internal payment transactions, interest on residential loans was the most significant source of income for banking. Insofar as the expansion of residential lending stimulated increased demand for imports, the correlation between banking sector growth rates and those of GDP was not at a level that could secure higher economic growth rates accompanied by new employment opportunities (see Table 8.6).

7 *Tourism and catering* and *business services (including real estate)* had approximately equal (annual) growth rates over the five-year period in question (12.2 per cent and 12.1 per cent, respectively). The former industries, tourism and catering, have great development potential for the formation of a cluster that would link primary agricultural production, transport, the food industry, construction, and business services with real estate rentals. In truth, Bosnia and Herzegovina enjoys very favourable geographic conditions for the development of winter tourism. The rich experience inherited from the

Table 8.6 Ratio of the growth of banking sector assets and GDP growth

	2000/1998	2002/2000	2003/2002	2004/2003	2005/2004
Growth of banking sector assets (in %)	14.3	48.8	21.2	22.3	26.4
Growth of GDP (in %)	35.1	15.9	5.6	9.7	6.0
Ratio of banking sector asset growth to GDP growth	2.46	0.33	0.26	0.44	0.23

Source: The author's calculations using data from the BiH Statistics Agency and the Central Bank of Bosnia and Herzegovina.

organization of the XIVth Winter Olympics, combined with the development of spa and cottage tourism and of coastal tourism, constitute objectively good prospects for the accelerated expansion of this industry or cluster. The US Agency for International Development (USAID) has been financing development of the tourism cluster in the country. In the preceding (post-war) period, over KM 150 million was invested in the development of winter and spa tourism. The most significant destinations for winter tourism include the Olympic mountains of Bjelašnica, Igman, and Jahorina near Sarajevo, while the mountain of Vlašić, another Olympic venue, has already become a popular winter-holiday destinations for tourists from neighbouring Croatia. By attracting foreign investors and with suitable promotion in Central and West European countries, the spa and healthcare complexes in Sarajevo (Ilidža), Fojnica, Olovo, Kladanj, and Teslić (all in central Bosnia), and the Guber spa near Srebrenica (northeast Bosnia) offer great development prospects and exceptional opportunities for generating employment and contributing to better-balanced regional development. Besides being familiar with the Olympic mountains, foreign tourists have already learned of the beauties of one of the most gorgeous rivers in Southeastern Europe – the River Una (in Northwest Bosnia). Ambassadors of the US, UK, Germany, Austria, Canada, Malaysia, Turkey, and all the countries of former Yugoslavia have taken part in the Una regatta, a unique summer attraction. The promotion of Bosnian and Herzegovinian attractions, conducted through all the major embassies in the country, represents a good basis for a more active approach by local tourist agencies and foreign investors. Up to now, foreign investors in tourist facilities have come from Austria (the Holiday Inn hotel in Sarajevo), Slovenia (the spa and recreational centre in Ilidža-Sarajevo), Croatia (winter resorts on Vlašić and Kupres), and Serbia and Montenegro (the Jahorina winter resort). Intensive investment by partners from Austria and, to a lesser degree, Germany are in progress on the Olympic mountains of Bjelašnica and Igman.

Labour market trends – employment and unemployment

In 1998–2003, official employment fell by 2.6 per cent. This downward trend in official employment was halted in 2004. On the other hand, the tendency for official unemployment to grow steadily did not stop at any point during the entire period under analysis. Official unemployment grew from 398,000 in 1998 to 508,000 in 2005 (an average annual growth of unemployment of 3.5 per cent) (see Figure 8.2).

The breakdown of employment by branch reveals that manufacturing, mining, and electricity production accounted for 2.1 times the jobs that retail and wholesale do and that the concentration of employees in the formal (officially recorded) labour market in manufacturing alone is greater than in all three fast-growing service industries taken together: trade, financial mediation, and tourism and catering (see Table 8.7). The special significance of manufacturing, mining, and electricity generation for the formal labour markets is reflected in the far larger relative burden of financing social welfare that this sector bears, insofar as the main concentration of informal employment, which plays no role in financing the public sector, is to be found in agriculture, construction, trade, and tourism and catering.

The regional distribution of population, employment (including informal employment), and unemployment provides a good insight into the major regional variations affecting the economic status of the population (see Table 8.8). In the FBiH, Sarajevo, Western Herzegovina, and Herzegovina-Neretva are the best-off cantons. The ratio of formal employment to population is in fact 37 per cent higher in Sarajevo canton than anywhere else in the FBiH. The same canton also accounts for a higher percentage of total unemployment in the FBiH than its

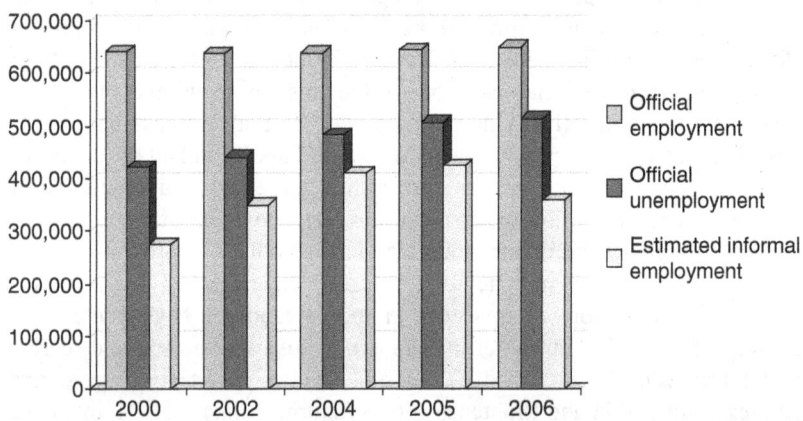

Figure 8.2 Employment and unemployment in Bosnia and Herzegovina, 2000–2006 (sources: BiH Labour and Employment Agency; BiH Statistics Agency; data on informal employment are estimates based on the World Bank Labour Market Surveys in Bosnia and Herzegovina, carried out in 2002 and 2005, and the author's own research in 2003–2006).

Table 8.7 Breakdown of formal employment in Bosnia and Herzegovina

Industry	Sectoral distribution of employment
Agriculture, forestry, and hunting	7.64
Mining	4.18
Manufacturing	19.34
Electricity generation and distribution, gas and water	3.73
Construction	6.19
Wholesale and retail	13.29
Tourism and catering	3.73
Transport, communication, and warehousing	7.03
Financial services	2.36
Real estate, renting, and business services	2.39
Public administration, police, and defence	11.76
Education	8.56
Health and social protection	7.00
Other public and social services	2.79
Total	**100.00**

Source: The author's calculations based on data from the BiH Labour and Employment Bureau, the FBiH Institute for Employment, and the RS Institute for Employment.

population would warrant, however, by some 13.5 per cent, though this greater percentage of unemployed is less important for the population's social status, insofar as the canton has a better developed informal labour market in the service sector, particularly in catering, trade, and construction, than other cantons.

Tuzla, Bosnia-Podrinje, and Una-Sana cantons are the worst off regarding the ratios of population to employment and unemployment. The ratio of employment to population in Una-Sana canton is as much as 35 per cent lower than the average for the FBiH, while the percentage of unemployment is higher. In Tuzla canton, the ratio of employment to population is 14.2 per cent lower and that of unemployment to population is 11.3 per cent higher than the average.

Regional differences in the RS are also very significant and reveal great deviations in the level of economic well-being and capacity for generating new employment. In terms of total trade in goods and services and the capacity to generate new employment through locally initiated projects and loans by microcredit organizations, the western RS, i.e. the Banja Luka and Prijedor regions, are in a far better position than the central (Doboj region) and particularly the eastern parts of the RS, except – to a degree – for the municipalities of Doboj and Trebinje themselves.

Trends in registered employment over the past two years show accelerating growth in official unemployment and the numbers entitled to social welfare, primarily healthcare services. A fairly significant reduction in unemployment in the RS in 2000–2001 was partly due to a new registration process, with the exclusion of Brčko District from the RS unemployment statistics.

Table 8.8 Breakdown of population, employment, and unemployment by canton and region, in accordance with ILO standards (including employment on informal labour markets), June 2005 (in per cent)

Cantons/regions	Population	Employment	Unemployment
Una-Sana canton	8.00	5.23	6.65
Posavina canton	1.14	0.96	1.18
Tuzla canton	13.28	11.43	14.59
Zenica-Doboj canton	10.38	11.24	12.21
Bosnia-Podrinje canton	0.92	0.68	0.91
Middle Bosnian canton	6.27	5.80	7.02
Herzegovina-Neretva canton	5.67	6.30	6.24
Western Herzegovina canton	2.12	2.89	1.45
Sarajevo canton	10.44	14.32	11.12
Livno canton	2.18	1.67	1.52
Banja Luka region	10.97	12.96	10.80
Bijeljina region	8.02	6.90	5.82
Doboj region	6.52	6.02	5.45
Prijedor region	6.44	6.39	5.88
Sarajevo region	3.33	3.05	4.14
Trebinje region	2.42	2.18	3.33
Brčko district	1.90	1.98	1.68
Total Bosnia and Herzegovina	**100.00**	**100.00**	**100.00**

Source: The author's calculations based on data from the BiH Labour and Employment Bureau and the FBiH and RS Institutes for Employment.

Problems of the fiscal structure and its negative consequences on employment

The central problems of the Bosnian fiscal system are the significant differences in tax burden between the FBiH and RS, on the one hand, and the un-harmonized state-level policy regarding direct and indirect taxation, on the other. The RS has enacted and, over the past three years, been implementing a Law on Personal Income Tax and a Law on Corporate Profit. These laws stipulate a 10 per cent rate for both personal income tax (including salary tax) and profit.[9] In the FBiH, the Law on Income Tax is before parliament and has not been enacted yet. The existing Law on Salary Tax and Law on Profit provide for a 5 per cent salary tax (on net salary, after social welfare contributions and levies) and for 30 per cent company profit tax.[10] Foreign investors are exempt from profit tax for five years in the FBiH, i.e. they enjoy favourable tax treatment compared to domestic investors. In the RS, foreign investors have the same rights and obligations as domestic ones in terms of any exemptions from profit tax.

From the employer viewpoint, one of the biggest problems is labour costs, i.e. the fiscal burden on net salaries. The total fiscal burden on salaries is lower in the RS than in the FBiH, the key reason being major disproportions in the rates of social welfare contribution. The aggregate rate of social welfare contributions (pension, healthcare, and employment insurance in the FBiH; the RS also has a children welfare contribution) amounts to 42 per cent of net salary in the RS and 64.4 per cent in the FBiH. The total fiscal burden (contributions plus income tax) is therefore 52 per cent for RS employers and 69.4 per cent for FBiH employers. Labour costs in the formal sector of the FBiH economy are therefore 17.4 per cent higher than in the RS. The significant differences in direct tax levels are further increased by an additional tax levied in the FBiH on total personal income, which is set by the cantonal assemblies and ranges from 10 per cent to 30 per cent depending on the canton.

Bosnia's economic position in Southeastern Europe

Geographically, Bosnia and Herzegovina is centrally placed in the region of the former Yugoslavia and Southeastern Europe. Bosnia and Herzegovina is therefore a spatial link between Central Europe and the Adriatic, a location that affords it a significant position on European corridors – both in the road and railway transportation networks and in future oil and gas transport corridors (pipelines) from the Mediterranean to Central Europe. Southeastern Europe is inhabited by approximately 55 million people and Bosnia and Herzegovina accounts for 6.9 per cent of that population. Post-war renewal and reconstruction of infrastructure and residences, followed by the restructuring of the business sector, resulted in above-average GDP growth rates compared to other Southeastern European countries, but because of the war the base for calculating the growth rate in Bosnia and Herzegovina was far lower than in the other countries of the region (except Albania and Macedonia, to a degree). Consequently, GDP growth has not sufficed to reduce the lag Bosnia and Herzegovina suffers in relation to the more developed countries of the region.

As noted above, Bosnia and Herzegovina's major problems include its trade and current account deficits. This problem takes on added prominence when compared with the condition in other Southeastern European countries. Despite improved coverage of imports by exports over the past four years, Bosnia and Herzegovina's trade balance remains weaker compared to the other countries in the group (see Table 8.9).

In 2004, Bosnia's current account deficit (as a percentage of GDP) was 3.6 times the average of the other Southeastern European countries (24.7 per cent compared to 6.9 per cent). The trade deficit was also far above the average for the other countries of the region (45.6 per cent compared to 17.9 per cent). On the other hand, Bosnia and Herzegovina has a very favourable foreign debt to GDP ratio (see Table 8.10). In 2004, the ten most indebted transition countries (as a percentage of GDP) were: the Kyrghyz Republic (102.9 per cent), Moldova (89.2 per cent), Latvia (82.6 per cent), Croatia (82.1 per cent), Kazakhstan (76.8 per cent), Estonia (70.5 per cent), Bulgaria (69.3 per cent), Tajikistan (64.8 per cent), Serbia and Montenegro (62.4 per cent), and Hungary (62.3 per cent).[11]

Bosnia and Herzegovina's foreign debt to GDP ratio is 36 per cent less than the average of the Southeastern European countries and, in fact, half that of Serbia and Montenegro and 2.3 times less than Croatia's. The impact of foreign

152   *Economic challenges in post-Dayton BiH*

Table 8.9 Current account and trade balances of the SEE countries, 2004 (in US$ millions)

	Current account balance (CAB)	Trade balance (TB)	CAB as % of GDP	TB as % of GDP
Albania	−460	−1,579	−6.1	−20.8
Bosnia and Herzegovina	−2,035	−3,436	−24.7	−45.6
Bulgaria	−1,806	−3,353	−7.5	−13.8
Croatia	−1,641	−8,346	−4.8	−24.6
FYR Macedonia	−415	−1,122	−8.2	−21.7
Romania	−5,468	−6,612	−7.5	−9.0
Serbia and Montenegro	−3,129	−7,434	−13.1	−31.3
Slovenia	−416	−1,258	−1.3	−3.9

Source: EBRD, *Transition Report 2005*, October 2005, pp. 97, 113, 117, 121, 133, 169, and 177.

Table 8.10 Foreign debt of the SEE countries, 2004

Country	Total foreign debt in billions of US$	Foreign debt in % of GDP	GDP per capita US$	GDP per capita US$ PPP
Albania	1.67	22.0	2,372	4,929
Bosnia and Herzegovina	2.57	31.1	2,172	7,168
Bulgaria	16.71	69.3	3,109	8,026
Croatia	30.20	82.1	7,721	12,336
FYR Macedonia	2.03	44.8	2,581	6,767
Romania	22.80	31.2	3,376	8,413
Serbia and Montenegro	14.88	62.4	2,864	–
Total debt and average values (SEE)	90.86	49.0	3,456	7,940
Slovenia	20.95	65.1	16,172	20,853
Total debt and average values	111.81	51.0	5,046	9,784

Source: EBRD, *Transition Report 2005*, October 2005, pp. 97, 113, 117, 121, 133, 169, and 177.

debt on GDP creation varies in different world regions and is not unrelated to a country's ability to use foreign debt to drive export-oriented growth. Indeed, even for countries experiencing problems with rising current account deficits, foreign debt can have a crucial impact on GDP growth, insofar as it allows budget expenditures and domestic production to grow, thanks to an increased capability to import the required components.

Table 8.11 clearly shows that Bosnia and Herzegovina is the only Southeastern European country to achieve considerable GDP growth between 2000 and 2004, while at the same time *reducing* foreign debt, i.e. without incurring additional debts. For every per cent of GDP growth over this period, Bosnia and

Table 8.11 Foreign debt and gross domestic product of the SEE countries, 1999 and 2004

Country	Gross domestic product (US$ billions)		Foreign debt (US$ billions)		Growth of GDP 2004/1999 (in %)	Growth of foreign debt 2004/1999 (in %)
	1999	2004	1999	2004		
Albania	3.43	7.59	1.11	1.67	+121.3	+50.5
Bosnia and Herzegovina	4.68	8.25	3.10	2.57	+76.3	−17.1
Bulgaria	12.97	24.25	10.91	16.71	+87.0	+53.2
Croatia	20.11	33.97	10.14	30.20	+68.9	+197.8
FYR Macedonia	3.67	5.16	1.49	2.03	+40.6	+36.2
Romania	35.66	73.26	9.22	22.80	+105.4	+147.3
Serbia and Montenegro	17.40	23.77	10.74	14.88	+36.6	+38.6
Slovenia	21.45	32.34	8.10	20.95	+50.8	+158.6

Source: EBRD, *Transition Report 2005*, October 2005, pp. 97, 113, 117, 121, 133, 169, and 177.

Herzegovina's foreign debt fell 0.22 per cent. By way of contrast, every per cent of GDP growth was accompanied by a foreign debt increase of 2.9 per cent in Croatia, 3.1 per cent in Slovenia, and 1.4 per cent in Romania. On average, the seven Southeastern European countries, not including Bosnia and Herzegovina, financed each per cent of GDP growth by a 1.48 per cent increase in their foreign debt.

In this context, the approach to Bosnian GDP should be revised, to take into account the country's capability to take on additional foreign debt up to the average level for Southeastern Europe, which would open up room for accelerated economic growth, while the economic results achieved by other countries in the region, particularly those with above average debt (Croatia, Serbia and Montenegro, and Bulgaria) should be viewed in the context of the availability of such resources to finance growth.

Conclusions

Over the past ten years, Bosnia and Herzegovina has undergone three stages of political and economic reform. According to the available data, during the first post-war stage of renewal and reconstruction (1996–1999), some 5.3 billion US dollars were invested in Bosnia and Herzegovina, mainly as donor resources for reconstruction. This period also saw the establishment of the first state-level institutions charged with initial integration of a national economic space (the Central Bank of Bosnia and Herzegovina). Still, almost total economic disintegration was a major characteristic of this period.

The next reform stage (2000–2003) was characterized by further steps in reform, with full support from the international community and the Office of the High Representative for Bosnia and Herzegovina. Increased political stability and more significant steps towards economic integration resulted in greater foreign investor confidence, most prominently in the banking sector. In fact, the banking sector was soon largely in foreign investors' hands (over 80 per cent), increasing the domestic population's confidence in savings and foreign investors' interest in investing in manufacturing. During this period, the privatization of small and medium-sized businesses, as well as of some large companies, was completed. Restructuring could not be carried out quickly, but gradual restructuring in export-oriented companies (metal production and manufacturing, wood products and furniture production) did result in laying the groundwork for faster export growth.

The third reform stage took place between 2003 and early 2006 and was characterized by fiscal reform aimed at introducing a uniform indirect taxation authority, improving customs operations and increasing public revenues. During this period, foreign investors invested in manufacturing, resulting in increased confidence among international financial institutions with regard to approving loans to the business sector. The best examples of positive signs, despite the problems of the high foreign trade deficit and high unemployment, are the loans approved by the European Bank for Reconstruction and Development for the reconstruction of railway infrastructure and to finance production in the metal processing sector and the building materials industry.

Notes

1 This text was presented at a conference on 'Business Education and the Economic Development of Bosnia and Herzegovina', held in June 2006 in Sarajevo and organized by the Faculty of Business Management of the University of Turin, the School of Economics and Business of the University of Sarajevo, and the Faculty of Economics of the University of Seville. The conference was financially supported by the Tempus Joint European Project – Upgrading the University of Sarajevo MBA to international standards.
2 The number of 102,622 killed persons is according to the following source: Ewa Tabeau-J. Bijak, 'War-Related Deaths in the 1992–1995 Armed Conflict in Bosnia and Herzegovina: A Critique of Previous Estimates and Recent Results', *European Journal of Population* 21 (2–3): 187–215, 2005. An estimate of 200,000 killed persons in Bosnia and Herzegovina is according to: Rony Blum, Gregori H. Stanton, Shira Sagi, and Elihu D. Richter, '"Ethnic Cleansing" Bleaches the Atrocities of Genocide', *European Journal of Public Health* 18 (2): 204–209, 2008.
3 Institute for the Research of Crimes Against Humanity and International Law of the University of Sarajevo, *The War Damages in Sarajevo 1992–1995*, Sarajevo. An early post-war internal assessment of war-related damages in Bosnia and Herzegovina according to the Chamber of Commerce of Bosnia and Herzegovina had ranged between US$30 billion and US$50 billion.
4 The European Commission and the World Bank, *Bosnia and Herzegovina – 1996–1998 Lessons and Accomplishments – Review of the Priority Reconstruction Program and Looking Ahead Towards Sustainable Economic Development*, a Report Prepared for the May 1999 Donors Conference, May 1999, p. 47.
5 Yugoslav Federal Institute for Statistics, *Statistical Yearbook 1991*, Belgrade, 1991, p. 441.
6 Population estimates for the 1995–2000 period as published by Dr Ilijas Bošnjević in the *Human Development Report – Bosnia and Herzegovina 2002*, UNDP and the Economics Institute, Sarajevo, 2002 (Annex 2).
7 Since 1999, the Statistics Agency of Bosnia and Herzegovina has published analytical data on GDP.
8 According to *The Global Competitiveness Report 2005* (World Economic Forum), in 2005 Bosnia and Herzegovina ranked number 55 out of the 114 countries included in the report with regard to number of mobile phone subscribers per 100 inhabitants.
9 These laws are available on the RS government website: www.vladars.net, or in the RS Official Gazette for 2001 and 2002.
10 See the FBiH government website: www.fbihvlada.gov.ba, or the FBiH Official Gazette for 2000 and 2001.
11 See the EBRD's *Transition Report 2004*, October 2004 (Part III – Country Assessments).

References

The data for this paper were drawn from the various institutional webpages cited in the endnotes.

Blum Rony, Gregory H. Stanton, Shira Sagi, and Elihu D. Richter, '"Ethnic Cleansing" Bleaches the Atrocities of Genocide', *European Journal of Public Health* 18 (2): 204–209, 2008.

Čaušević, Fikret, *Impact of Foreign Trade Policy on the Current Account and Competitiveness of Bosnia and Herzegovina*, Economics Institute Sarajevo, Sarajevo, July 2005.

European Bank for Reconstruction and Development, *Transition Report 2004 – Infrastructure*, London, 2004.

Tabeau, Ewa and J. Bijak, 'War-Related Deaths in the 1992–1995 Armed Conflict in Bosnia and Herzegovina: A Critique of Previous Estimates and Recent Results', *European Journal of Population* 21 (2–3): 187–215, 2005.

The European Commission and the World Bank, *Bosnia and Herzegovina – 1996–1998 Lessons and Accomplishments – Review of the Priority Reconstruction Program and Looking Ahead Towards Sustainable Economic Development*, a Report Prepared for the May 1999 Donors Conference, May 1999.

United Nations Development Programme, Sarajevo Economics Institute, *Human Development Report – Bosnia and Herzegovina 2002*, Sarajevo, 2002.

World Economic Forum, *The Global Competitiveness Report 2005*, Geneva, Switzerland, 2005.

Yugoslav Federal Institute for Statistics, *Statistical Yearbook 1991*, Belgrade, 1991.

9 Bosnia and Herzegovina's trade policy and competitiveness, 1996–2008

A policy brief[1]

Brief summary

Bosnia and Herzegovina's trade deficit fell from 71 per cent to 38 per cent of GDP and its current account deficit from 30 per cent to 15 per cent of GDP between 1998 and 2008. During the same period, GDP grew 270 per cent. The growth of real GDP per capita between 2000 and 2007 placed Bosnia and Herzegovina in the group of 25 fastest growing economies in the world. Despite relatively favourable results in 2000–2007, over the last three years Bosnia and Herzegovina has lagged behind most other countries in transition. One reason is a significantly lower rate of growth of private external debt than in most of the fastest growing countries in transition and the world. Another more important reason is the decline in competitiveness caused by institutional weaknesses, complicated administrative structures, non-enforcement of reforms, and reducing investment. Transfer of the global economic crisis from Western European markets only enhanced already existing problems. According to the latest *Global Competitiveness Report*, Bosnia and Herzegovina ranked 109 out of 133 countries, while *Doing Business 2010* ranked Bosnia and Herzegovina 116 out of 183 economies.

This policy brief critically assesses some of the major failures of trade and fiscal policy in Bosnia and Herzegovina. The misguided trade and foreign direct investment policies are a major problem for stimulating competitiveness. To improve the country's competitiveness, the laws on foreign direct investment and on corporate income tax in both entities should urgently be changed with a view to stimulating foreign direct investors. A new law on foreign direct investment should differentiate clearly between foreign direct investors who increase export potential and those oriented towards the domestic market. It should provide tax relief to those investors who achieve significant net exports. There should also be urgent measures to improve the business environment, related to reducing the time managers waste making tax payments, reducing the procedures required to start up a new business from 12 to six, and certifying institutions for quality control of imports.

Context and importance of the problem

Between the end of the war (1992–1995) in Bosnia and Herzegovina and the end of the third quarter of 2009, a series of reforms was introduced which enabled relatively fast economic growth, the development of institutional structures common to both entities of Bosnia and Herzegovina (the Federation of Bosnia and Herzegovina – FBiH, and the Republika Srpska – RS), as well as gradual integration of the country into the SEE region. Thanks to the adoption of the Quick Start Package (1997), five extremely important laws for the economic reintegration of Bosnia and Herzegovina were passed, namely: the Law on Foreign Trade Policy, the Law on a Uniform Basis for Customs Policy, the Law on Customs Tariffs, the Law on Foreign Direct Investments, and the Law on the Central Bank of Bosnia and Herzegovina.

In 1998–2004, Bosnia and Herzegovina was the thirteenth fastest growing economy in the world, while in 2000–2007 the country's average growth put it in twenty-third place in the world.[2] However, in 2004–2007, the country's average growth rate was below that of 20 of the 29 countries in transition. Following passage of the Law on Foreign Trade Policy (1998), between December 2000 and October 2003, Bosnia and Herzegovina signed nine bilateral free trade agreements with all the countries of Southeastern Europe, including Turkey. These agreements involved dismantling customs barriers to exports from Bosnia and Herzegovina on most goods, while customs on imports were gradually cut down over a period of three to four years. These bilateral agreements on free trade were replaced by the CEFTA agreement, signed by the Southeastern European countries in December 2006. Bosnia and Herzegovina signed a Stabilization and Association Agreement (SAA) with the EU in June 2008, assuming an obligation to do away with customs on imports of most goods from the EU.

In 2000–2008, the total volume of trade in merchandise increased from €4.52 billion to €11.86 billion (up 162.3 per cent), while the trade deficit grew from €2.21 billion to €4.82 billion (up 118 per cent). Over the past eight years, Bosnia and Herzegovina's GDP increased from €4.9 billion to €12.6 billion (up 157 per cent). Bosnia and Herzegovina's trade in goods expressed as a percentage of GDP increased from 92.1 per cent to 93.4 per cent, while the trade deficit fell from 45 per cent to 38.1 per cent. The current account deficit fell from 26.5 per cent of GDP in 2000 to 10.2 per cent of GDP in 2007. In 2008, however, the current account deficit increased to 15.2 per cent of GDP, largely due to an increase in the trade deficit of €720 million.[3]

Over the past two years, Bosnia and Herzegovina's most important export partners were the EU countries (57.3 per cent), Croatia (18.4 per cent), Serbia (13.7 per cent), and the rest of world (10.6 per cent), while the most important countries of origin of imported goods were again the EU countries (47.9 per cent), Croatia (17.6 per cent), Serbia (10.2 per cent), Turkey (5.8 per cent), China (4.3 per cent), and then the rest of world (10.2 per cent).[4] Over the last five years, the average trade deficits were €623 million with Croatia, €484 million with Germany, and €297 million with Serbia. Over that period, the trade deficit with Croatia increased from €524 million to €829 million (58 per cent), with Serbia it increased from €256 million to €401 million (57 per cent) and with Germany from €426 million to €512 million (20 per cent). The Bosnian exports of goods were up 241 per cent to Germany, 111 per cent to Serbia, and 90 per cent to Croatia, while imports from Croatia were up 70 per cent, from Germany 74 per cent, and from Serbia 82 per cent between 2004 and 2008.[5] In the first three quarters of 2009, the country's trade deficit fell €1 billion (28 per cent), but the driving force behind that decrease was not expanding exports but the impact of the current global economic crisis spilling over onto Bosnia and Herzegovina.

In spite of the fact that over the past eight years Bosnia and Herzegovina has cut its current account and trade deficit to GDP ratios from 45 per cent to 36 per cent and 26 per cent to 15 per cent, respectively, in the latest *Global Competitiveness Report* (the GCR for 2009–2010) Bosnia and Herzegovina ranked 109 out of 133 countries.[6] The other countries of Southeastern Europe ranked as follows: Albania (96), Bulgaria (76), Croatia (71), the former Yugoslav Republic of Macedonia (84), Montenegro (62), Romania (64), and Serbia (93).[7] The major differences in ranking between the countries of the region cannot be explained by any major difference in export capabilities between Bosnia and Herzegovina and other countries of SEE. In 2004 and 2007, the ratio of external debt to exports of goods and services were: Albania (119 per cent; 94 per cent, for 2004 and 2007, respectively), Bosnia and Herzegovina (173 per cent; 117 per cent), Bulgaria (124 per cent; 166 per cent), Croatia (161 per cent; 181 per cent), FYR Macedonia (98 per cent; 70 per cent), Romania (110 per cent; 138 per cent), and Serbia (254 per cent; 222 per cent).[8] Bulgaria and Romania are the most egregious examples. In spite of the clear decline in export capacity (and competitiveness in the original meaning of the word), these two countries achieved better rankings in the GCR, 33 and 45 places above Bosnia and Herzegovina, respectively.

Comparing the competitiveness rankings in the last GCR with the rankings of United Nations member states by the human development index (HDI) suggests an even greater paradox.[9] In the GCR, Namibia ranked 74, Sri Lanka 79, Gambia 81, Guinea 90, Kenya 98, and Nigeria 99. Consequently, these countries are more competitive than Bosnia and Herzegovina. More competitive Namibia, 35 places ahead of Bosnia and Herzegovina, has an average life expectancy of 51.6 years, compared to Bosnia and Herzegovina's 74.5 years. Average life expectancy in Gambia, ranked 28 places ahead of Bosnia and Herzegovina in the GCR, is 58.8 years. One finds a yet starker paradox again, regarding the great competitiveness gap between these two countries found by the GCR, when one looks at the education index (one of the three sub-indices used for calculating the HDI). Gambia's education index is 0.450, compared to 0.874 for Bosnia and Herzegovina – approximately half.

The average human development index value for developing countries in the 2005 HDR was 0.691, and Bosnia and Herzegovina counts as a developed country, that is to say a country with an HDI 16.2 per cent higher than the average for the developing countries. Bosnia and Herzegovina's HDI is also 15 per cent higher than the average for the middle-income countries and on exactly the same level of human development as the average for the Latin American countries. On the other hand, Bosnia and Herzegovina is some 14 per cent behind the average for the OECD countries, which is 0.916. Bosnia and Herzegovina is just 0.6 per cent lower than the average for the countries of Central and Eastern Europe and ranks higher than Albania or the FYR of Macedonia, when it comes to the countries of Southeastern Europe.

It was necessary to review the above data to arrive at a more objective understanding of the potential for economic growth and the actual economic results achieved by Bosnia and Herzegovina in comparison to those countries. Presenting Bosnia and Herzegovina as the most economically backward country in Southeastern Europe, as well as the least competitive economy, is simply not consistent with basic economic indicators, particularly given the scale of the losses the Bosnian economy suffered between 1992 and 1995, both with regard to human capital and in the form of physical capital (plant and infrastructure), and the actual rate of economic growth achieved with a below-average level of foreign debt. Still, and in spite of these results, it must be admitted that the Bosnian economy has not made optimal use of the generous potential for economic growth. The basic question is why has this happened and is it continuing to happen?

The answer to this question, again somewhat paradoxically, is to be found in the GCR and the World Bank's *Doing Business 2010*[10] report. According to the GCR, the main barriers to economic development and competitiveness in Bosnia and Herzegovina are government instability, political instability, the inefficient government bureaucracy, the tax rates, and corruption. According to *Doing Business*, the lowest rankings received by Bosnia and Herzegovina related to: complicated procedures for starting a business, procedures for the issuing of operational licences, inefficient registration of ownership, and procedures for paying taxes. Of these barriers to the development of business and the national economy, only the tax rates represent a classic economic problem or barrier deriving directly from the economic system. The other main barriers are of an institutional and political nature.

While this GCR ranked Bosnia and Herzegovina two places lower than the two previous ones (2007 and 2008), *Doing Business 2010* ranked the country three places higher than in 2009. Most progress was made in the 'Paying taxes' group of criteria, where the country improved its ranking by 27 places. During 2008 and early 2009, two new laws on direct taxation were prepared and passed in the FBiH, one of the two Bosnian entities. They were the Law on Personal Income Tax and the Law on Corporate Income Tax. According to the Law on Corporate Income Tax in the FBiH, the tax rate was cut from 30 per cent to 10 per cent, while a very complicated system of direct taxation at the cantonal level was finally eliminated by the Law on Personal Income Tax. Implementation of these two laws has eliminated a big asymmetry between the entities and balanced tax rates at 10 per cent in both entities. This has significantly enhanced tax harmonization in Bosnia and Herzegovina. Social insurance contributions for health and unemployment were also cut, reducing the labour tax wedge.

According to the data from *Doing Business 2010*, the fiscal burden on labour costs in Bosnia and Herzegovina is 27.6 per cent lower than the average for OECD countries and 23.5 per cent lower than the average for Eastern Europe and Central Asia (EECA). The tax burden of corporate income tax in Bosnia and Herzegovina is also 69.6 per cent lower than in OECD countries and 54.6 per cent lower than the EECA. The total tax burden on entrepreneurs in Bosnia and Herzegovina expressed as a percentage of realized profit is 39.1 per cent lower than in the OECD countries and 37.6 per cent lower than in the EECA. The tax system in Bosnia and Herzegovina does however entail other problems related to the number of payments the average entrepreneur has to make over the year: three times as many as in OECD countries (51 times compared to 12.8 times per year). Consequently, the average entrepreneur in Bosnia and Herzegovina has to spend 117 per cent more working hours annually dealing with tax payments than the OECD average (422 hours in Bosnia and Herzegovina and 194 hours in the OECD).

As regards the registration of ownership, Bosnia and Herzegovina was up ten places in the *Doing Business* rankings. In comparing openness to foreign trade (the 'Trading across borders' criteria), *Doing Business 2010*, like the previous two reports (*Doing Business 2009* and *Doing Business 2008*), put Bosnia and Herzegovina in the top third of countries, at 63, while Albania, Serbia, Turkey, Croatia, and Bulgaria rank less well. In this group of indicators, import cost (per container) was 4.9 per cent lower in Bosnia and Herzegovina than the OECD average and 38.5 per cent than to EECA countries, while export cost (per container) was 3.2 per cent higher than the OECD average, but 28.9 per cent lower than the EECA average. The time required for export and import in Bosnia and Herzegovina is 52.4 per cent longer than in the OECD.

The relatively high ranking of Bosnia and Herzegovina in *Doing Business 2010* in the area of 'Trading across borders' is confirmed by the *Global Enabling Trade Report for 2009*.[11] In this report, with regard to the group of data called 'Efficiency of import–export procedures', five of the seven listed criteria were classified as representing competitive advantage (time for import, documents for import, the import cost, time for export, and documents for export). Bosnia and Herzegovina ranked lowest for the group of criteria relating to institutional arrangements and administrative procedures, performing worst with regard to the eighth pillar – the 'Regulatory environment' (property rights, ethics and corruption, undue influence, government inefficiency, business impact of rules on FDI). Efficiency of customs administration also ranked very poorly. In *Doing Business 2010*, Bosnia and Herzegovina's lowest ranking was for the group of criteria dealing with 'Starting a business', where the country ranked 160 out of 183.

Critique of the current policy approach

Foreign trade in Bosnia and Herzegovina as conducted over the past ten years has been formally based on the Law on Foreign Trade passed in 1998, the provisions of the bilateral free trade agreements in the SEE in 2000–2006, and then the provisions of the CEFTA agreement from 2007 and the rules arising from signing the SAA with the EU (June 2008). Until the signing of the SAA, Bosnia and Herzegovina had most favoured nation status in trade with EU countries. After signing, Bosnia and Herzegovina abolished customs duty on imports of over 1,100 industrial products from the EU.

One of the biggest weaknesses and contradictions in Bosnia and Herzegovina's trade policy lay in the Law on a Uniform Basis for Customs Policy and the Law on Customs Tariffs, especially after signing the bilateral free trade agreements. Most of the inputs used by Bosnian enterprises (especially major exporters) are imported either from the EU or from third countries – i.e. not from SEE. In accordance with the Law on a Uniform Basis for Customs Policy and the Law on Customs Tariffs, until the SAA was signed, Bosnian companies were required to pay high tariffs on imports of equipment and materials which could not be produced in the domestic market and on which any increase in the productivity and competitiveness of Bosnia and Herzegovina exporters largely depends.

On the other hand, with the abolition of duty on final products produced in the SEE region under free trade agreements, effective tariff protection for over half of imports of goods turned into a negative effective tariff protection that disadvantaged most domestic producers. This customs policy problem was partially eliminated by signing the SAA, but illogical application of Article 162 of the Law on Customs Policy, under which producers are obliged to pay duty on imports of equipment and materials from non-EU countries, continues to discourage Bosnian companies from increasing their competitiveness by importing relevant inputs.

The weaknesses of these two laws could have been at least partially reduced by well thought out strategies and policies to attract FDI based on appropriate legislation. The Law on Foreign Direct Investment in Bosnia and Herzegovina was adopted in 1998 and was then a good basis to start attracting FDI. Unfortunately, it was not revised or enhanced and especially not in the segment relating to the Law on Corporate Income Tax (regarding tax exemptions). According to it, foreign direct investors are exempt from tax on profits for a period of five years to the same percentage as their share in the ownership of the Bosnian company, applied equally in all sectors and industries. In other words, the laws on corporate income tax in both entities make no distinction between foreign direct investors as net exporters and foreign direct investors oriented primarily to domestic markets. In that sense, all foreign direct investors have been freed from paying corporate income tax, regardless of whether or not they are net importers or exporters.

A further systemic weakness related to excise policy. After signing first the bilateral free trade agreements and then the CEFTA agreement, the most important regional trade partners compensated for lost fiscal revenues from customs by a new system of higher excises. To illustrate this policy, we may use the status of Drina cigarettes in Croatia: a product of the Sarajevo Tobacco Factory, Drina cigarettes have been classified as belonging to the highest quality group of cigarettes in Croatia. The reason is simple – the highest quality products are taxed at the highest rate of excise. An important obstacle to conducting trade policy at state level in Bosnia and Herzegovina is the lack of key institutions for quality control of imported goods, certification of export products, and simplifying export procedures. This is a direct product of the current institutional structure of Bosnia and Herzegovina, in which the entities attempt to dominate even in areas of economic policy where they have no responsibilities.

Policy recommendations

Over the next ten months, that is until the general elections in October 2010, politicians currently in office in Bosnia and Herzegovina (at state and entity level) should take the following measures to promote competitiveness:

- The most important step towards improved competitiveness and cutting the trade and current account deficits is an initiative to change the Law on Foreign Direct Investment and legislation governing fiscal and trade policy related to its implementation.
- The new version of the Law on Foreign Direct Investment should be based on a clear definition and differentiation of exemption from corporate income tax for manufacturing companies which export at least 20 per cent more than they import. Net exporting Bosnian companies should be exempt from corporate income taxes for five to seven years. Attracting foreign direct investors also entails an immediate cut in the extremely high costs of construction permits, which are ten times higher in Bosnia and Herzegovina than in OECD countries. An immediate target should be cutting these costs to 10 per cent below the EECA average.
- Since the proposed tax exemptions for foreign direct investors could cause a decrease in fiscal revenues, the measure should be followed by introduction of two VAT rates – a low VAT rate of 5 per cent for basic goods and services and a high rate of 20 per cent for all other goods and services.
- The Law on Customs Policy should be changed in the paragraphs related to customs tariffs on imported equipment and machinery and raw materials not produced in Bosnia and Herzegovina. Customs tariffs on imports of equipment and machinery produced in non-EU or non-SEE countries should be abolished.
- There is an urgent need to impose quality control on all imported goods. Due to the lack of domestic certifying institutions responsible for quality control, goods of very low quality are being imported. Introducing quality controls will entail speeding up the procedures for issuing licences to the domestic institutions responsible.

- Customs procedures for export-oriented companies, especially large exporters, must be improved. There is an ongoing process and project to improve customs procedures, financed by the EU. Certification licences should be issued to at least 100 exporters over the next five months.
- The time entrepreneurs spend on dealing with their taxes must also be cut from 422 hours to 336 hours per year, which is the average time for paying taxes in EECA countries.
- The number of procedures involved in starting a new business should be cut from 12 to 6 procedures. Over the past two years, some municipalities in the RS have succeeded in shortening the time required to start new businesses. Good examples from the RS should be followed in other municipalities in Bosnia and Herzegovina.

Notes

1. This policy brief was presented at an international conference held in Tirana on 16–17 November 2009 and organized by the London School of Economics and Political Science and the International Finance Corporation (IFC) of the World Bank Group.
2. The author's calculations based on the World Bank: Data and Publications (http://web.worldbank.org/WBSITE/EXTERNAL/DATASTATISTICS/0,,contentMDK:20535285~menuPK:1192694~pagePK:64133150~piPK:64133175~theSitePK:239419,00.html). See also: Fikret Čaušević, *Economic Sovereignty and Global Capital Flows*, Icfai University Press, Hyderabad, 2008, pp. 176–184.
3. Sources: The author's calculations based on data from the Statistics Agency of Bosnia and Herzegovina (www.bhas.ba) and the Central Bank of Bosnia and Herzegovina (www.cbbh.ba).
4. World Economic Forum, *The Global Enabling Trade Report 2009*, p. 128, (www.weforum.org/pdf/getr09_dev/GETR09_Fullreport.pdf, accessed 8 November 2009).
5. The author's calculations based on Central Bank data (www.cbbh.ba).
6. The World Economic Forum, *Global Competitiveness Report 2009–2010* (www.weforum.org/reports/global-competitiveness-report-2009-2010, accessed 10 October 2014).
7. The World Economic Forum, *Global Competitiveness Report 2009–2010* (www.weforum.org/reports/global-competitiveness-report-2009-2010, accessed 10 October 2014).
8. EBRD, *Transition Report 2008 – Growth in Transition*, London, pp. 95, 99, 103, 107, 111, 115, 119, 123, 127, 131, 135, 139, 143, 147, 151, 155, 159, 163, 167, 171, 175, 179, 183, 187, 191, 195, 199, 203.
9. The data on human development indexes for the countries compared in the text are from the United Nations Development Programme, *Human Development Report 2007/2008 – Fighting Climate Change: Human Solidarity in a Divided World*, New York, pp. 229–232.
10. IBRD/The World Bank, *Doing Business 2010 – Comparing Regulation in 183 Economies* (www.doingbusiness.org/reports/global-reports/doing-business-2010/, accessed 10 October 2014).
11. World Economic Forum, *The Global Enabling Trade Report 2009*, pp. 128, 130 (www.weforum.org/pdf/getr09_dev/GETR09_Fullreport.pdf, accessed 8 November 2009).

References

The data for this paper were drawn from the various institutional webpages cited in the endnotes.

Čaušević, Fikret, *Economic Sovereignty and Global Capital Flows*, Icfai University Press, Hyderabad, 2008.

European Bank for Reconstruction and Development, *Transition Report 2008 – Growth in Transition*, London, 2008.

The World Bank, *Doing Business 2010 – Comparing Regulation in 183 Economies*, Washington, 2010.

The World Economic Forum, *Global Enabling Trade Report 2009*, Geneva, Switzerland, 2009.

The World Economic Forum, *Global Competitiveness Report 2009–2010*, Geneva, Switzerland, 2010.

United Nations Development Programme, *Human Development Report 2007/2008 – Fighting Climate Change: Human Solidarity in a Divided World*, New York, 2008.

10 Economic perspectives on Bosnia and Herzegovina in the period of global crisis[1]

Bosnia and Herzegovina as a small open economy

Bosnia and Herzegovina is a small open economy whose share in world GDP over the past five years has been 0.035 per cent and whose share in world population has been 0.048 per cent.[2] Due to the war in Bosnia (1992–1995), the country's GDP fell from US$10.7 billion (1991) to US$3.2 billion (1996). From 2001 to 2010, the country managed to increase GDP per capita from 25 per cent to 75 per cent of the world average.[3]

The Central Bank of Bosnia and Herzegovina was established in August 1997 and the single currency (the Convertible Mark – KM) was introduced in June 1998. Since its establishment, the Bank has functioned as a currency board. The exchange rate of the KM is fixed (€1 = KM 1.95583). The only monetary policy instrument available to the Bank is the required reserves. In accordance with the Law on the Central Bank of Bosnia and Herzegovina, the Bank is not allowed to exercise a lender of last resort function and is prevented from conducting open market operations. Therefore, the Bank is completely isolated from any possibility of influencing interest rates or the money supply.

Using the Mundell–Fleming IS-LM-BP model,[4] the money supply in Bosnia and Herzegovina is fully endogenous. Monetary policy is therefore a passive segment of economic policy and exchange-rate policy is based on a fixed exchange rate (in other words, it is also a passive segment of economic policy).[5] Since financial liberalization was carried out in 1998–2003, the banking system in Bosnia and Herzegovina has been privatized and is now fully in the hands of foreign banks. Current account convertibility has been fully adopted, while capital account convertibility, with the exception of buying a majority stake in companies in the military industry, games of chance, or the media, has also been conducted.

In other words, Bosnia and Herzegovina is a classic example of a small open economy where the only active segment of macroeconomic policy is fiscal policy. Bosnia and Herzegovina is also an economy to which we can fully apply the Mundell–Fleming impossible trinity of macroeconomic policy.[6] How one approaches fiscal policy, therefore, has a great significance on the direction of the business cycle and the balance of payments equilibrium. In line with the

Mundell–Fleming model, an increase in government spending can be financed in the two following ways: by increasing taxes or by issuing public debt (government bonds). Issuing long-term government bonds to finance infrastructural (capital) projects has not been practised in Bosnia and Herzegovina since the war. The only long-term bonds issued in Bosnia and Herzegovina have been government bonds of the entities (the Federation of Bosnia and Herzegovina, FBiH, and the Republika Srpska, RS). These bonds were issued to compensate for the so-called pre-war frozen foreign currency savings as an internal public debt inherited after the breakup of the former Yugoslavia.

Economic growth and reforms in the 1997–2007 period

According to the Economist, BiH was the seventeenth fastest growing economy in the world in the ten years from 1997 to 2007. The average growth rate for the period was 11.2 per cent in real terms.[7] From 1996 to 2000, the average growth rate was above 25 per cent. This was mainly due to the very low base (in 1991, Bosnian and Herzegovinian GDP was US$10.2 billion, while in 1996 it was only US$3.2 billion). Between 1996 and 2000, financial resources were largely channelled into the reconstruction of housing, infrastructure, and public services. Resources available for business sector development were much more modest and limited in scope. Employment growth between 1996 and 2000 was largely due to the large scale of reconstruction projects in the aforementioned sectors.

In the following period (2001–2008), economic growth was predominantly based on enabling greater capacity exploitation in business and industry, privatization, restructuring, strengthening the financial sector, and attracting foreign direct investment. Tender privatization brought certain major foreign investors to manufacturing in Bosnia and Herzegovina, most prominent among them: Arcelor Mittal Zenica (steel production), Global ISPAT Company (coke production), Heidelberg Cement Gmbh (cement production), Neftegazovaya Innovatsionnaya Korporatsiya OAO (oil refinery), Prevent Group (leather seat covers for cars), the Birač Alumina Factory Zvornik (alumina and zeolit), CIMOS TMD Gradačac (cars), Mann Hummel Tesanj (cars), Alloy Wheels Jajce (cars), Meggle (milk and dairy production), and Hayat-Natron-Kastamone Entegre (paper and pulp production).

After the war, thorough and speedy reforms were carried out in the banking sector. Thanks to a new legislative framework in line with European and international standards, the banking sector in Bosnia and Herzegovina has progressed rapidly. A Law on Foreign Direct Investment (1998) was passed in the meantime, allowing non-residents to buy stakes and shares in domestic private and state-owned banks or to establish new commercial banks. At the end of 2000, the Raiffeisen Bank became the first commercial bank from Western Europe to enter the Bosnian market. The Raiffeisen Bank Sarajevo became a market leader in Bosnia and Herzegovina between 2000 and 2011, with a market share of 17.9 per cent in 2011. The next five biggest banks are: UniCredit Mostar (17.2 per cent), the Hypo-Alpe-Adria Group (Banja Luka and Mostar – 16.9 per cent), the

NLB Group (Tuzla and Banja Luka – 9.9 per cent), Intesa Sanpaolo Sarajevo (6.1 per cent), and Nova Banka Banja Luka (4.2 per cent). In 2011, Austrian banks controlled 42.3 per cent of the market share, Italian banks 23.3 per cent, and Slovenian banks 14.1 per cent.[8]

From 2004 to 2010, total banking sector assets grew 124 per cent, business loans were up 143 per cent, and personal loans up 136 per cent. This represented a growth in total assets from 59.6 per cent to 86.1 per cent of GDP, of business lending from 20.2 per cent to 31.6 per cent of GDP, and of personal lending from 17.1 per cent to 26.1 per cent of GDP. Credit expansion and increasing assets were most remarkable in 2005–2008, when the average annual rate of growth of business lending was 23.6 per cent, while personal lending and total assets grew by 26.4 per cent and 22.7 per cent. respectively.

Economic trends in Bosnia and Herzegovina in the period of crisis: 2008–2011

The global financial and economic crisis spilled over from Western Europe to Bosnia in the last quarter of 2008. The spill-over effects were confirmed by data on falling GDP and lending in the first two quarters of 2009 (see Figure 10.1). In the year of recession, GDP fell 3.1 per cent[9] and personal lending was down 6.6 per cent, while business lending was down 1.2 per cent on the previous year. Total lending to households and enterprises was therefore down 3.9 per cent, in marked contrast to the remarkable growth seen in 2008, when lending to enterprises and

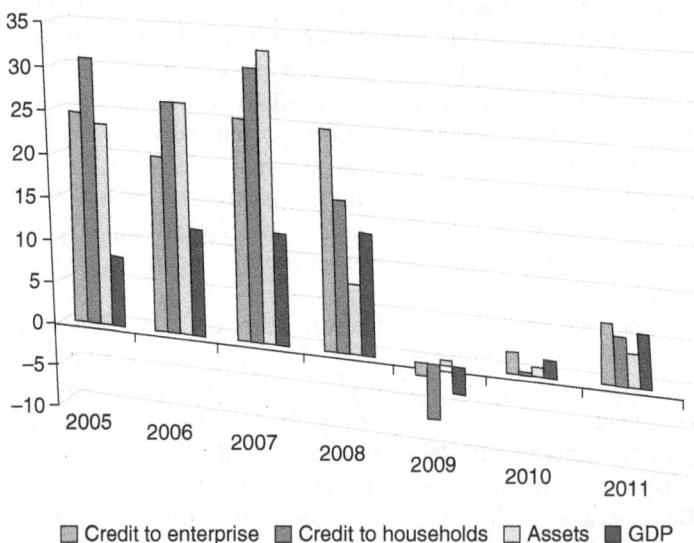

Figure 10.1 Percentage change in credit activity and assets, and nominal GDP growth rates (year-on-year): Bosnia and Herzegovina, 2005–2011 (source: based on Central Bank of Bosnia and Herzegovina data).

households increased by 22.8 per cent.[10] This major difference in lending between 2008 and 2009 caused a sharp decrease in household consumption and business investment.

Due to the tightening of procedures for approving loans and the growth of non-performing loans in the credit portfolio of commercial banks in Bosnia and Herzegovina, lending to enterprises was up only 2.8 per cent in January to May of 2010, against December of 2009. This increase was followed by a reduction in lending between May and September. In December, outstanding loans to enterprises increased compared to the previous three months and was up 5.3 per cent on the previous year. In contrast to this modest growth of lending to enterprises, lending to households reduced. Total loans extended in December 2010 was slightly down (0.4 per cent) on December 2009.

In 2011, credit activity (business and households) grew 5.5 per cent, while household savings grew 6.1 per cent and total deposits were up 5.8 per cent.[11] Access to credit has become more difficult, due to stricter credit approval procedures, caused by the growth of non-performing loans (NPLs). The NPLs to total credit ratio has increased from 5.8 per cent to 11.2 per cent.[12] This modest increase in lending in 2010 and 2011 was not enough to create the increase in household consumption and business investment required to spur economic growth. According to IMF data, real economic growth in Bosnia and Herzegovina was 0.5 per cent in 2010. Comparing this figure with the decline in economic activity in 2009, it is obvious that not enough has been done to bring the economy back on track. According to the IMF staff mission report for 2011, the IMF has cut its growth projection for 2011 from 2.2 per cent to 1.7 per cent.

In 2008–2011, commercial banks' foreign liabilities fell by 33.8 per cent (€1.09 billion) as a result of the impact of the financial crisis on mother-banks in Western Europe. The drop in foreign liabilities was offset by growth in domestic deposits of 18.9 per cent (€993 million) (see Figures 10.2–10.4).

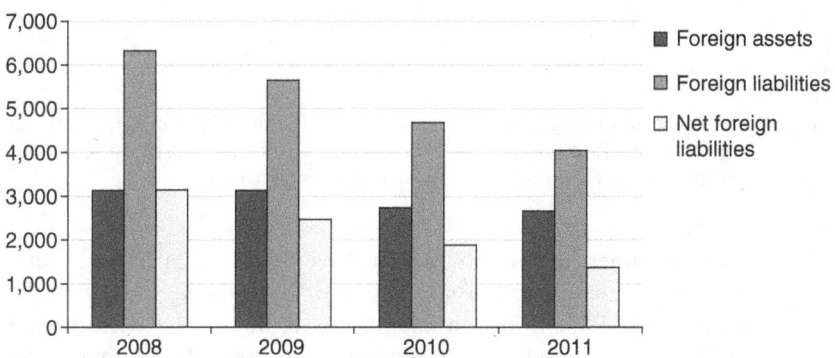

Figure 10.2 Foreign assets, foreign liabilities, and net foreign liabilities (foreign liabilities minus foreign assets) of commercial banks in Bosnia and Herzegovina, 2008–2011 (in millions of KM) (source: based on data published by the Central Bank of Bosnia and Herzegovina).

170 *Economic challenges in post-Dayton BiH*

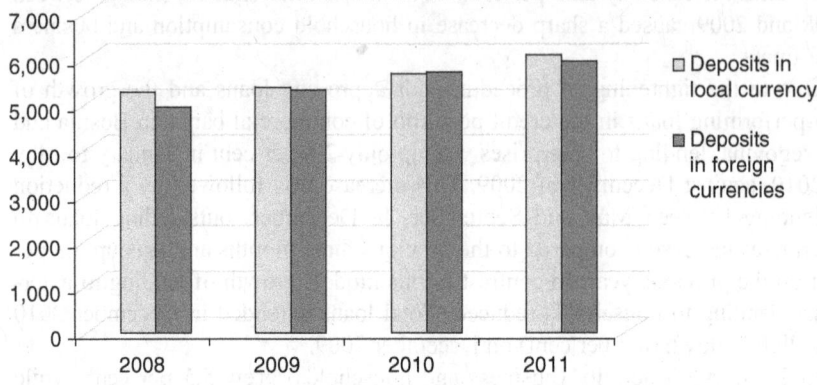

Figure 10.3 Deposits of commercial banks in Bosnia and Herzegovina, 2008–2011 (in millions of KM) (source: based on data published by the Central Bank of Bosnia and Herzegovina).

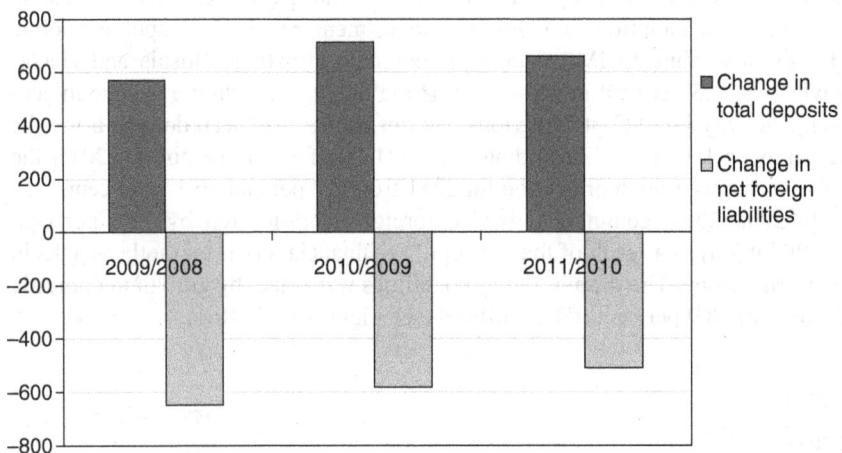

Figure 10.4 Change in total deposits and net foreign liabilities of commercial banks in Bosnia and Herzegovina (in millions of KM) (source: based on data published by the Central Bank of Bosnia and Herzegovina).

Net foreign liabilities, or the difference between the foreign liabilities and foreign assets of commercial banks in Bosnia and Herzegovina, fell during the same period by €1.75 billion: foreign liabilities were down from €3.23 billion (2008) to €2.14 billion (2011), while foreign assets were down from €1.59 billion (2008) to €1.39 billion (2011).

On the other hand, one positive effect of the economic crisis on the Bosnian economy was a significant reduction in the trade and current account deficits in 2009–2010. In 2009, the trade deficit was down 27.7 per cent. This reduction

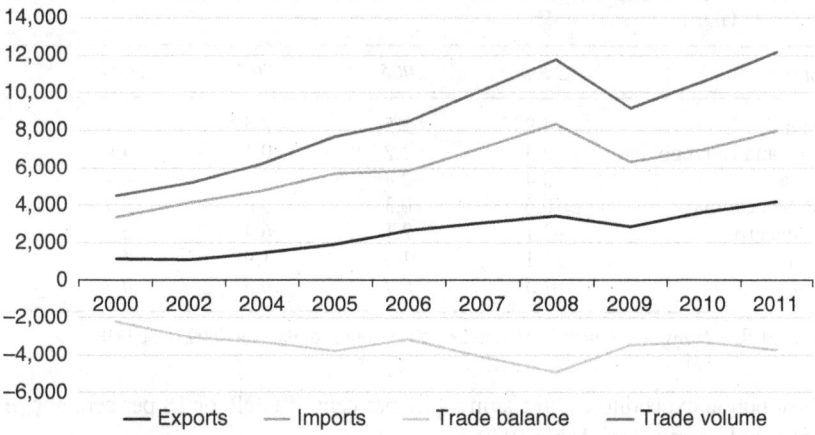

Figure 10.5 Exports, imports and trade balance of Bosnia and Herzegovina (in millions of EUR) (source: Central Bank of Bosnia and Herzegovina).

was not caused by any increase in exports, however, in contrast to trends in 2010, when the Bosnian economy saw its highest ever increase in exports of goods, which were up 15 per cent, reducing the trade deficit by 12 per cent, even though credit activity was very modest. In 2011, despite an increase in exports of 18 per cent, the trade deficit was up on 2010 by around 10 per cent, due to a significant increase in imports during 2011 (see Figure 10.5).[13]

Fiscal discipline and fiscal sustainability

Fiscal discipline in Bosnia and Herzegovina, which was fairly high in 2003–2007, was disrupted by spill-over of the financial and economic crisis and the absence of a cost-effective structure of public spending (given the predominant role played by social security). In the pre-crisis period of 2003–2008, Bosnia and Herzegovina and other Western Balkan countries showed a higher level of fiscal discipline than other regions or countries in transition. While the average budget deficit of transition countries ranged between 2.1 per cent and 0.3 per cent of GDP in 2003 and 2005, respectively, the budget deficit of Western Balkan countries stood at 1.5 per cent in 2003 and their budget surplus was 0.4 per cent in 2005. When the global economic crisis struck in 2008, the average budget deficit of the Western Balkan countries was slightly lower than the average for transition countries.

While the budget deficit of Western Balkan countries averaged 1.2 per cent of GDP, Bosnia and Herzegovina had an average budget surplus of 2.2 per cent of GDP in 2003–2005 (see Table 10.1). On the other hand, when measured in terms of the ratio of total public spending to GDP, average spending in the Western Balkans was 37.3 per cent of GDP in 2003–2008, or 2.7 per cent of GDP higher than the average for transition countries in the same period. Bosnia and Herzegovina had the

Table 10.1 Consolidated budget balances of Western Balkan countries (in per cent of GDP)

Country	2003	2005	2007	2009
Albania	−4.9	−3.5	−3.5	−7.4
Bosnia and Herzegovina	2.3	2.2	−0.1	−4.0
Croatia	−3.4	−2.8	−2.3	−4.1
FYR Macedonia	−0.6	0.3	0.6	−2.7
Montenegro	−3.1	2.1	6.4	−5.3
Serbia	−1.1	1.0	−1.9	−4.5
Average	*−1.5*	*0.4*	*0.3*	*−4.7*

Source: EBRD, *Transition Report 2009*, London, 2009; source of data for 2009 is the IMF.

highest public expenditures, averaging 44.7 per cent of GDP, or 18 per cent above the regional average (see Table 10.2).

In analysing total public spending and particularly social transfers in the former Yugoslav republics of the Western Balkans, one must bear in mind that, after the war, many people in Bosnia and Herzegovina, Croatia, and Serbia were affected in terms of diminished working ability (disabled civilians and war veterans, children left without one or both parents). The number is particularly high in Bosnia and Herzegovina, where social welfare beneficiary lists of civilian and military victims of war include about 269,000 people. This is one of the main reasons (the second is the country's complicated administrative structure) that public spending in Bosnia and Herzegovina is above the regional average. In 2003–2005, average public spending in Bosnia and Herzegovina was, however, approximately equivalent to that of Serbia and Montenegro and lower than in Croatia. A major increase in public spending in Bosnia and Herzegovina was caused by unrealistic projections of budget revenues for the 2007–2008 period.

One cannot explain the increase in fiscal discipline in 2003–2007, measured by public revenues and budget surpluses generated in Bosnia and Herzegovina, without looking into key factors that led to an increase in the tax base (fiscal capacity) in Bosnia and Herzegovina. Unfortunately, those key factors did not include the rapid creation of new jobs. Although the effective unemployment

Table 10.2 Total budget expenditures of Western Balkan countries (in per cent of GDP)

Country	2003	2005	2007	2008
Albania	24.1	25.1	25.7	27.4
Bosnia and Herzegovina	41.5	42.1	47.4	47.9
Croatia	43.1	42.1	42.0	40.7
FYR Macedonia	33.4	35.2	33.8	34.2
Montenegro	43.5	41.2	45.4	44.4
Serbia	41.7	42.9	42.4	40.5
Average	*36.8*	*37.3*	*38.9*	*38.9*

Source: EBRD, *Transition Report 2009*, London, 2009.

rate was down in the pre-crisis period, this growth in fiscal capacity was not down to lower unemployment, higher employment, or higher average wages. There were two leading factors. One was the introduction of VAT in 2006, with a flat tax rate of 17 per cent, which caused an increase in the fiscal burden on consumers, since the weighted average tax rate of sales taxes from May 2001 through to the end of 2005 had been 13.5 per cent. The other, more important reason related to the 2006–2008 period and was the credit expansion in both business and personal lending. From 2004 to 2008, additional purchasing power of KM 4.1 billion (€2.2 billion) was generated in Bosnia and Herzegovina based on new lending to households. In the same period, lending to enterprises grew by KM 4.2 billion (€2.3 billion). The aggregate increase in purchasing power in that period, based on credit expansion, amounted to €4.5 billion, the equivalent of 40 per cent of GDP in 2008. Credit expansion, higher purchasing power, and the resulting increase in the tax base, coupled with the introduction of VAT (in 2006) at a flat rate of 17 per cent, which, in turn, increased the fiscal burden on consumption by approximately one quarter, were the grounds for unrealistic budget projections during 2007 and the first half of 2008. A sudden drop in lending during 2009 and 2010 (see Figure 10.1) meant significantly reduced fiscal revenues, which resulted in a budget deficit of 4.0 per cent against projected spending in 2009.

According to the IMF report, the total public debt of Bosnia and Herzegovina is projected to increase from 39.1 per cent of GDP in 2010 to 43 per cent in 2011, while the fiscal deficit will reduce from 4.5 per cent to 3 per cent of GDP on a consolidated basis (see Table 10.3).[14] The consolidated balance of public revenues and expenditures (the fiscal balance of general government) includes all revenues and expenditures of the budgets of all administrative levels in Bosnia and Herzegovina (budget of Bosnia and Herzegovina, the two entity budgets, the cantonal budgets, and the budgets of all municipalities), as well as the revenues and expenditures of all public social insurance funds (pension funds, health insurance funds, and unemployment insurance).

Problems of fiscal instability in both entities (FBiH and RS) and a lack of public revenues to finance spending in the recession year (2009) resulted in signing a Stand-By Arrangement (SBA) with the IMF for 1,014.6 million SDR

Table 10.3 Fiscal balance of general government in Bosnia and Herzegovina (in per cent of GDP)

	2006	2007	2008	2009	2010	2011
Fiscal revenues	47.2	46.7	45.9	44.6	45.9	45.8
Fiscal expenditures	46.1	47.1	49.5	50.2	50.4	48.8
Fiscal balance	1.1	–0.3	–3.6	–5.7	–4.5	–3.0
External public debt	21.1	18.2	17.2	21.7	26.2	29.4
Total public debt	21.4	32.9	30.8	35.4	39.1	43.0

Source: International Monetary Fund, Public Information Notice No. 10/154, 3 December 2010 (www.imf.org). Data for 2010 and 2011 are the IMF estimates.

Table 10.4 Projected payments to the IMF based on existing use of resources and present holdings of SDRs (millions of SDR)

	2011	2012	2013	2014	2015
Principal	0	22.83	136.97	146.27	32.13
Charges and interest	5.05	5.00	4.09	2.10	0.76
Total	**5.05**	**27.83**	**141.06**	**148.37**	**32.89**

Source: www.imf.org/external/np/fin/tad/exfin2.aspx?memberKey1=75&date1key=2011-02-02

(special drawing rights). That amount is equivalent to 600 per cent of the Bosnian quota at the IMF. By the end of 2011, some 338.2 million SDR had been withdrawn (equivalent to 200 per cent of the country's quota). Bosnia and Herzegovina's liabilities to service this debt amounted to 355.3 million SDR, of which interest was 17 million SDR and the principal was 338.2 million SDR (see Table 10.4). Bosnia and Herzegovina's total public debt was well below the average level for Euro-zone countries in 2011 (55 per cent of the level of public debt in Euro-zone countries).[15]

State-owned capital as the basis for fiscal sustainability and potential source of funds for development projects

The creditworthiness and liquidity of Bosnia and Herzegovina in the future will depend on its fiscal capacity and ability to generate income from assets owned by the entity governments. In this context, the quality of assets owned by the entities determines Bosnia's borrowing capacity and its ability to service public debt on a regular basis (solvency and liquidity). The most valuable assets owned by the government of FBiH have been its majority stakes in the following companies:

- Elektroprivreda BiH dd Sarajevo – electricity production (90 per cent ownership);
- BH Telecom dd Sarajevo – telecommunications (90 per cent ownership);
- Elektroprivreda HZ HB dd Mostar – electricity production (90 per cent ownership);
- HT Mostar dd Mostar – telecommunications (50.1 per cent ownership).

The net book value of these companies' assets (the book value of the equity) and the book value of the stakes owned by the government of FBiH at the end of 2010 were €2.69 billion and €2.36 billion, respectively (see Table 10.5).[16] According to the Ministry of Finance of the FBiH, the entity's total public debt (internal plus external) was €2.69 billion.

The company with the highest book value of equity in the RS is the Mixed Holding Elektroprivreda RS ad Trebinje. Its book value was €607 million[17] as of 31 December 2010 and the book value of the stake owned by the RS government

Table 10.5 State-owned capital in the four largest companies in the Federation of Bosnia and Herzegovina

Company	Book value of the equity as of 31 December 2010 (€ millions)	Stake owned by the government of FBiH (€ millions)
JP Elektroprivreda BiH dd Sarajevo	1,489	1,340
JP BH Telecom dd Sarajevo	558	502
JP Elektroprivreda HZ HB dd Mostar	479	431
HT Mostar dd Mostar	165	83
Total	**2,691**	**2,356**

Sources: the annual reports for 2010 cited in endnote 16.

was €395 million. The RS government sold its 67 per cent stake in Telekom Srpske (telecommunications) for €646 million to Telekom Srbije (a Serbian-based telecom operator owned by the government of Serbia) in 2007. The financial resources from the transaction have been used to finance development projects and projects at municipality level through loans extended by the Investment Development Bank of the Republic of Srpska (the bank is owned by the RS government). Additional sources for servicing the public debt obligations of the RS will be predominantly based on the entity's fiscal capacity and, to a much lesser extent, on the possibility of selling state-owned capital, since the most liquid stake in RS government ownership has been already sold. According to the RS Ministry of Finance, the total public debt of the entity in 2010 was €1.79 billion.

Based on the above analysis, the public debt servicing and additional borrowing capacity of the FBiH is quite high, given the FBiH government's ownership. It still owns the book value of capital in the four major infrastructure companies totalling €2.35 billion. The market value of these companies is higher than the book value, as the four companies have been able to earn substantial profits. Over the last five years, the average (yearly) net profit of BH Telecom has been approximately €75 million. During the recession of 2009, special attention was focused on the FBiH and its alleged financial collapse. From the above data, it is obvious that the net public debt of the FBiH is not large (net public debt as the difference between the public debt and assets owned by a government). For Bosnia and Herzegovina (and its two entities), the major feature is that state-owned capital is worth more than the total value of public debt. The ownership of capital affects solvency, but does not mean an ability to pay due obligations (liquidity), however, unless there are regular inflows of money coming from dividends and/or one-time large inflows of money based on privatization.

In this sense, the successful conduct of future economic policy and implementation of major capital projects at entity, inter-entity, and cross-border levels require the entity governments to determine the timing of investment activities and financial resources to finance capital projects. For Bosnia and Herzegovina and its entities to ensure sufficient funds in the medium term for regular funding of liabilities arising from the repayment of foreign debt and to fund capital projects, without which it is impossible to encourage the development cycle, assets owned by the government of Bosnia and Herzegovina and its entities will have to be deployed to provide additional financial resources and avoid constant pressure of default. In this sense, the entities, and particularly the FBiH, which still owns major stakes in the most attractive companies in the FBiH, could use any of the following three options:

1   Decide to privatize the capital available in the four major infrastructure companies (sell off minority or majority shares depending on the time schedule of privatization). Part of the privatization revenues could be deposited in special accounts opened at banks for servicing the foreign debt on a regular basis.
2   Use some of the privatization revenues to establish an investment fund to invest in the securities of countries in Western Europe as a guarantee for future regular servicing of foreign debt and to finance capital projects on the basis of public–private partnership.
3   A less conventional option would be to issue government bonds denominated in KM and 'covered' by a guarantee of an EU Guarantee Fund for Bosnia and Herzegovina (or preferably for the Western Balkans). In other words, the Fund would guarantee bond issues in local currency. Such government bonds with a guarantee from the Fund would be a safer source of financing for capital projects in Bosnia and Herzegovina and such financial assets would contribute to the development of domestic capital markets, which would allow for more successful structuring of commercial bank and investment fund portfolios. The Guarantee Fund would be a guarantee for fiscal stability and would have the right of semi-annual audit of public finances at the state and entity levels in Bosnia and Herzegovina. It could also be provided with 'a guarantee for equity swap option' – compensation for activation of the warranty (in case Bosnia and Herzegovina or its entities cannot meet their obligations) with equity in the major infrastructural companies. Another possibility is to provide the Fund with ownership of the 'golden share' in the five infrastructural companies. By using the 'golden shares', the Fund would be able to control and improve business operations in large public companies and, if necessary, use their profits for regular settlement of liabilities arising from the foreign public debt.

Development potential of the Bosnian economy

Bosnia and Herzegovina has significant potential for development of automotive, wood processing, and metal processing industries. Development of agribusinesses combined with tourism is another possibility. The population of Bosnia and Herzegovina is 3.8 million and its area is 51,129 square kilometres. In the north, west, and south of the country, there are very good natural potentials for agribusinesses. Experience in the production of metals, cars, furniture, joinery, and prefabricated houses existed before the war (Bosnia and Herzegovina had a trade surplus in the last five years before the breakup of Yugoslavia, of which 40 per cent was exported to Western Europe). Bosnia and Herzegovina's potential for tourism is considerable. The United States Agency for International Development (USAID) has financially supported development of clusters in wood processing, agribusiness, and tourism in an effort to link the economic potential of both entities. The capital of Bosnia and Herzegovina – Sarajevo – was host to the XIVth Olympic Winter Games (in 1984). The mountains of Bjelašnica, Igman, and Jahorina have excellent natural terrain for skiing and for the rapid expansion of winter tourism. The Una, Neretva, Vrbas, and Drina rivers are already well known for rafting. The Una river is one of the cleanest rivers in the Western Balkans and is known for its beauty. The Sarajevo Film Festival has become a top-ranking film festival in Southeastern Europe and thanks to it and to MESS Theatre Festival and the Sarajevo Jazz Festival, Sarajevo has become one of the cultural centres of the Balkans. The development of religious tourism began over 30 years ago. Medjugorje in the south of Bosnia and Herzegovina (western Herzegovina) is a centre of pilgrimage for Catholic believers. In the last 20 years, the place has been visited by more than two million tourists.

Doing business in Bosnia and Herzegovina has not been easy since the end of the war, but some foreign direct investors have succeeded in tripling or quadrupling total turnover, exports, and income in only five years (2003–2008). Good examples are Arcelor Mittal Zenica, CIMOS TMD Gradacac, and Alloy Wheels Jajce. Although Bosnia and Herzegovina suffered huge human capital losses during the 1992–1995 war, it is still ranked as a country with a high human development index (United Nations Development Programme – Human Development Report 2010). The skills and knowledge inherited from the pre-war period make it less costly to train workers here than in certain other countries in which car, metal processing, and wood processing industries have not been developed. In June 2008, the Bosnia and Herzegovina authorities signed the Stabilization and Association Agreement (SAA) with the EU. Bosnia and Herzegovina is also a member of CEFTA – a regional free trade agreement for the Western Balkans. Bosnia and Herzegovina's geographical position in the heart of Southeastern Europe makes it potentially attractive for foreign direct investment because of its proximity to the EU and location advantages as a platform for relatively low-cost production, as well as free access to EU and regional markets.

Bosnia and Herzegovina and the Western Balkans

Prospects for the development of Bosnia and Herzegovina will depend largely on the prospects for economic growth in Western Europe and the Western Balkans – the regions with which Bosnia and Herzegovina has had the most intensive economic cooperation, both in foreign trade and with regard to foreign direct investment. In this context, one of the key challenges for Bosnia and

Herzegovina, the Western Balkans, and the European Union in the coming period will be how to enhance economic cooperation and link up the Western Balkan economies through cross-border projects that benefit all involved.[18] Joint financing of such cross-border projects could solve some of the problems and so contribute to increasing public and private business investment and employment, improving cooperation in the Western Balkans, reducing the gap in GDP per capita between the region and the EU, and linking up financial markets in the region so as to reduce transaction costs.

Notes

1. This text was published under the same title on the webpage of SEESOX, St Antony's College, Oxford, as an opinion piece in March 2012. It was written during my stay as an Alpha Bank Visiting Fellow with SEESOX, St Antony's College in 2011/2012. It is reproduced in this collection with the kind permission of SEESOX, St Antony's College, University of Oxford.
2. The author's calculation based on the World Bank data (http://data.worldbank.org/country/bosnia-and-herzegovina).
3. The author's calculation based on the World Bank data.
4. The seminal papers for the development of IS-LM-BP model were Robert A. Mundell, 'Capital Mobility and Stabilization Policy under Fixed and Flexible Exchange Rates', *Canadian Journal of Economic and Political Science* 29 (4): 475–485, 1963; and J. Marcus Fleming, 'Domestic Financial Policies under Fixed and Floating Exchange Rates', *IMF Staff Papers* 9: 369–379, 1962.
5. Changes in the money supply in an economy with a currency board regime are determined by changes in the current account balance. See more in S. Hanke, L. Jonung, and K. Schuler, *Russian Currency and Finance: A Currency Board Approach to Reform*, Routledge, London, pp. 62–70, 1993.
6. On the impossible trinity and quadrilemma, see: http://economics.ucsc.edu/research/downloads/quadrilemma-aizenman-11.pdf.
7. The Economist, *The Pocket World in Figures 2010*, Profile Books, London, 2009, p. 32.
8. Sources: the Federal Banking Agency and the Banking Agency of the Republika Srpska.
9. Sources: Agency for Statistics of Bosnia and Herzegovina (www.bhas.ba); the International Monetary Fund.
10. Source: Central Bank of Bosnia and Herzegovina (www.cbbh.ba).
11. Data from the Central Bank of Bosnia and Herzegovina (www.cbbh.ba/index.php?id=33&lang=en&sub=mon&table=konsolidovani_bilans_komercijalnih_banaka_bihh).
12. Central Bank of Bosnia and Herzegovina, *Financial Stability Report 2010*, Sarajevo, 2011.
13. Sources of data for Bosnia and Herzegovina's foreign trade are: the Central Bank of Bosnia and Herzegovina and the Statistics Agency of Bosnia and Herzegovina.
14. Source: International Monetary Fund, *IMF Executive Board Concludes 2010 Article IV Consultation with Bosnia and Herzegovina – Public Information Notice (PIN) No. 10/154*, 3 December 2010. This document is available at: www.imf.org/external/np/sec/pn/2010/pn10154.htm.
15. Based on data published by the IMF, the EBRD, the Ministry of Finance, the Treasury of Bosnia and Herzegovina, and the Central Bank of Bosnia and Herzegovina.
16. Sources: JP Elektroprivreda BiH dd Sarajevo, Annual Report 2010, available at: www.elektroprivreda.ba/upload/documents/izvjestaji/annual_report_2010.pdf; JP Elektroprivreda HZ HB, Annual Report 2010, Mostar, available at: www.ephzhb.ba/wp-

content/uploads/Izvjesca/GI_2010_eng_final.pdf; Hrvatske telekomunikacije d.d. Mostar, *Annual Report 2010*, Mostar, 2011, available at: www.hteronet.ba/upload/natjecaji/prilog_br_2_124959.pdf; JP BH Telecom dd Sarajevo, *Annual Report for 2010*, Sarajevo, 2011, available at: www.bhtelecom.ba/1229.html.
17 Source: Elektroprivreda Republike Srpske, *Annual Report 2010*, Trebinje 2011, available at: www.ers.ba/index.php?option=com_content&view=article&id=118&Itemid=113&lang=ba.
18 One of the possible ways of financing was presented by the author of this paper. See Fikret Čaušević, 'What Type of Fiscal Policy Is Needed to Foster the Economic Development of the Balkans?', paper presented at a workshop organized by the Association Bourgogne Balkan Express and Science Po Paris, 'Accession of the Western Balkans to the EU: Evaluating a Process', Dijon, France, 11 May 2010.

References

The data for this paper were drawn from the various institutional webpages cited in the endnotes.

Čaušević, Fikret, 'What Type of Fiscal Policy Is Needed to Foster the Economic Development of the Balkans?', presented at a workshop organized by the Association Bourgogne Balkan Express, and Sciences Po Paris, 'Accession of the Western Balkans to the EU: Evaluating a Process', Dijon, France, 11 May 2010.

Central Bank of Bosnia and Herzegovina, *Financial Stability Report 2010*, Sarajevo, 2011.

Elektroprivreda Republike Srpske, *Annual Report 2010*, Trebinje, 2011.

Fleming, J. Marcus, 'Domestic Financial Policies under Fixed and Floating Exchange Rates', *IMF Staff Papers* 9: 369–379, 1962.

Hanke, S., L. Jonung, and K. Schuler, *Russian Currency and Finance: A Currency Board Approach to Reform*, Routledge, London, 1993.

Hrvatske telekomunikacije d.d. Mostar, *Annual Report 2010*, Mostar, 2011.

International Monetary Fund, *IMF Executive Board Concludes 2010 Article IV Consultation with Bosnia and Herzegovina – Public Information Notice (PIN) No. 10/154*, Washington, 3 December 2010.

JP BH Telecom dd Sarajevo, *Annual Report for 2010*, Sarajevo, 2011.

JP Elektroprivreda BiH dd Sarajevo, *Annual Report 2010*, Sarajevo, 2011.

JP Elektroprivreda HZ HB, *Annual Report 2010*, Mostar, 2011.

Mundell, Robert A., 'Capital Mobility and Stabilization Policy under Fixed and Flexible Exchange Rates', *Canadian Journal of Economic and Political Science* 29 (4): 475–485, 1963.

The Economist, *The Pocket World in Figures 2010*, Profile Books, London, 2009.

Index

Page numbers in *italics* denote tables, those in **bold** denote figures.

9/11 terrorist attacks 35, 80, 92
agency, theory of 75
aggregate demand 66, 85–6, 123
agribusinesses, Bosnia and Herzegovina 176, 177
agriculture, Bosnia and Herzegovina 136, 138, 148
AIG 65
Albania: budget deficit 96; business environment *102*, *104–5*, *107*, *108*, *112*; competitiveness 110, *111*, 159; consolidated budget balances *172*; credit activity 116, *118*, 119, *120*, 122; current account balance *37*, *120*, *152*; current account deficit 119; economic growth 35, 38, 39; exchange rate regime 87, 93; exports 87; external debt *37*, *123*, *124*, *152*, *153*; financing, access to 110–11; foreign direct investment *126*; foreign exchange reserves 37; GDP 95–6, *120*, *153*; GNI per capita **108**; government spending *172*; imports 87; public debt 86, 95, 96; trade balance *152*; trade with EU 87
Algeria 37
Argentina 40; external debt 40; inflation 61
Armenia: economic growth 39; wealth coefficient 39
Asian financial crisis (1997–98) 5
Australia: economic growth 36; financial markets 33; market capitalization *34*
auto industry 8; Bosnia and Herzegovina 69, 136, 176

balance of trade, G-7 *52*
Bank of England 63; interest rates 63
Bank for International Settlements 23, 25
banking sector: assets 26; Canada 60; capital to assets ratios 20; China 6; Euro-zone 20–3; excess reserves 97; France 22, 60; Germany 22, 60, 61; Ireland 6; Italy 22, 60, 61; Japan *25*, 60; lending 9, 23, 25, 61, 93; *see also* credit activity; non-performing loans (NPLs) 96, 116, 169; privatization of 9; problems of regulation 23–6; United Kingdom (UK) 60; United States (US) 17, *25*, 60; Western Balkans 93, 96; *see also* Bosnia Herzegovina, banking sector; central banks
Barro, Robert 78
Barroso, José Manuel 30
Basle (II) 23, 24
Basle (III) 25
Belgium, public debt 91, 92
BH Telecom dd Sarajevo 174, *175*
Big Bang reforms (1986), United Kingdom (UK) 2–3
bonds/bond issues 9, 10–11, 59; *see also* Euro-Balkan bonds; government bonds
Bosnia and Herzegovina 8, 87, 119; agribusinesses 176, 177; agriculture 136, 138, 143; auto industry 69, 136, 176; banking sector 22, 67, 140, 143, 146, *147*, 154, 166, 167–8 (excess mandatory reserves 97; foreign assets and liabilities 169–70; lending 26–7, 28, 29, 30, 67, 168–9; non-performing loans (NPLs) 169); budget deficit 173; budget surplus 171; business environment *102*, 105–6, *108*, *112*, 157, 160–1; competitiveness 110, *111*, 157–64; consolidated budget balances *172*; construction industry 69, 70, 122, 145,

148; corporate income tax 157, 160, 161, 162, 163; credit activity 117, 118, 119, *120*, 122, 168–9, 173; current account balance *120*, *152*; current account deficit 119, 151, 157, 158, 159; customs policy 158, 162, 163, 164; debt (private sector 118; to IMF 12, 27, 123, *124*, 173–4; *see also* external debt; public debt); deposits *31*; and ECB monetary policy 21–2; economic growth 26, 39, 158, 167–8, 169; economic position in Southeastern Europe 151–4; electricity generation/distribution 69, 136, 140, 148; employment 69–70, 136, 148–51, 167; ethnic structure 12; and EU Stabilization and Association Agreement (SAA) 158, 162, 177; exchange rate regime 87, 93, 166; excise policy 162–3; export industries 68–70, 136, *142*; exports *68*, 70, 88, 151, 158, 159, 161, 171; external debt 11, 88, *123*, *124*, 151, *152*, *153*, 154, 157; financial (in)stability 26–31; financial liberalization 67; financial markets 28; financial sector 137, 138, 143, 146, 148, 167; financing, access to 28, 110–11; fiscal discipline and sustainability 171–4; fiscal policy 157, 160–1, 162–3, 166–7; food industry 136, 145; foreign direct investment *126*, 137, 140, 145–6, 157, 162, 163, 167, 177; GDP 68, 70, *120*, 135, 136–8, 151, 152, *153*, 154, 157, 158, 166, *168* (ratio of external debt to 151–2; sectoral distribution of 138, *139*, 140, *141*); and global financial/economic crisis 67–71; GNI per capita **108**, 109; goods markets 28; government bond issues 167, 176; government spending 70, 87, 171–2; household consumption 70; human development index (HDI) 159–60, 177; imports *68*, 70, 151, 158, 161, 163, 171; infrastructure reconstruction 135, 145, 155; interest rates 67; labour market efficiency 28; Law on the Central Bank 93; manufacturing industry 136, 138, 143, 145, 148, 167; metal sector 69–70, 136, 145, 155, 176; military industry 136; mining industry 138, 140, 143, 148; monetary policy 166; personal income tax 70, 150, 151, 160; pharmaceutical industry 145; population reduction 27, 136–7; post-conflict economy 135–6; post-conflict reconstruction 135, 137, 145, 167; private sector indebtedness 118; privatization 136, 137, 154, 167, 176; production and output 136–8; public debt 11, *31*, 70, 86, 95, 167, 173–4, 175, 176; purchasing power 68, 173; Quick Start Package (1997) 158; real estate 146; retail and wholesale trade 145–6, 148; service sector 138, 148, 149; as small open economy 166–7; social security contributions 150–1, 161; social security spending 87; state-owned capital 174–6; taxation 26, 27, 146, 150–1, 160–1, 16*4* (corporate income tax 157, 160, 161, 162; indirect 26, 27, 146, 150, 154, 163; personal income tax 70, 150, 151, 160; VAT 30, 68, 163, 173); tourism industry 136, 138, 140, 146–7, 148, 176, 177; trade 138, 140, 143, 148, 158, 162, 177; trade balance *68*, 151, *152*, *171*; trade deficit 68, 151, 157, 158–9, 170–1; trade with EU 87; trade policy 157–64; trade volume 68, **171**; transport and communications 138, 140; unemployment 12, 148–9, *150*, 172–3; war in, impact of 11, 135, 136–7; wealth coefficient 39, 138; wood processing industry 69, 136, 154, 176, 177

Brazil 1, 40, 49; capacity utilization 62; employment rate 62; financial crisis (1999) 5; food prices 62; GDP **51**, *52*; inflation 61; interest rates 61; wealth coefficient **51**

Brenner, Reuven 74

Bretton Woods 17, 58

BRIC countries 19, 20, 57; share in world GDP 1, 49, **51**, *52*

Brown, Martin 122

budget deficit 9; Albania 96; Bosnia and Herzegovina 173; Euro-zone 91–2; France 92; Germany 92; Greece 91; Italy 92; Russia 39; transition countries 171; United States (US) 35, 64, 66; Western Balkans 86, 171

budget surplus: Bosnia and Herzegovina 171; United States (US) 35, 92; Western Balkans 171

Bulgaria: business environment *102*, 106, 107; competitiveness 110, *111*, 159; corruption 111; credit activity 118, 119, *120*; current account balance *120*, *152*; current account deficit 119; economic

Bulgaria *continued*
  growth 39; external debt 123–4, 125,
    151, *152*, *153*; financing, access to 111,
    116; foreign direct investment 125, *126*;
    GDP 108, *120*, *153*; private sector
    indebtedness 118; wealth coefficient 39
bureaucratic inefficiency 111, *112*, *113*,
    114, *115*, 128
business cycles 6–7, 46; real 4–5
business environment 102–10; barriers to
    business 110–17; *see also individual
    countries*

Canada: balance of trade *52*; commercial
    banks 60; current account balance *52*;
    economic growth 36; financial markets
    33; financial system 59, 60; institutional
    investors 43; market capitalization *34*,
    60; share in world GDP *42*, 49, *52*;
    wealth coefficient *50*
capacity utilization, fast-growing
    developing countries (FGDC) 62
capital 11
capital account liberalization 40
capital flows 46, 50–1, 73; China 5–6
capital markets 60; development of 44, 45,
    125, 127–8
capital to assets ratios 20
capitalism, global 77
car industry *see* auto industry
CEFTA (Central European Free Trade
    Agreement) 158, 162, 177
Central Bank of Bosnia and Herzegovina
    97, 146, 154
central banks 93; regional 45; Western
    Balkans 93; *see also* Bank of England;
    Central Bank of Bosnia and
    Herzegovina; European Central Bank
    (ECB); Federal Reserve System (the
    Fed)
Chicago Board Options Exchange (CBOE)
    3
Chile: current account balance *37*; external
    debt *37*; foreign exchange reserves *37*;
    inflation 61
China 1, 5, 73; banking sector 6; capital
    flows 5–6; current account balance *37*,
    53; current account surplus 36; economic
    growth 35, 54, 74; exports 54; external
    debt 36, *37*; financial markets 33; food
    prices 62; foreign direct investment 6,
    42; foreign exchange reserves 36, *37*, *53*;
    imports 54; inflation 61, 63; interest rates
    61, 62; market capitalization *34*; savings
  37; share in world GDP 49, **51**, *52*, 74;
    trade surplus 36; and US trade 55;
    wealth coefficient *51*
Christian fundamentalism 79
Cline, William 4
closed economy 100n6
commercial banks *see* banking sector
competitiveness 110–25; Bosnia and
    Herzegovina 110, *111*, 157–64
construction industry, Bosnia and
    Herzegovina 69, 70, 122, 145, 148
consumer price index 62
consumption: household, Bosnia and
    Herzegovina 70; tax levied on 41, 66
corporate income tax, Bosnia and
    Herzegovina 157, 160, 162, 163
corporate securities 59
corruption, as barrier to business 111, *112*,
    113, *114*, *115*, 128
CPFF (commercial paper funding facility),
    Federal Reserve System (the Fed) 63
credit activity 116–19, *120*, 121–3, 128;
    see also individual countries
credit default swaps (CDS) 65
Croatia 8, 9, 87, 107, 111, 119, 158, 159;
    business environment *102*, 104, 107,
    108, *112*; competitiveness 110, *111*,
    159; consolidated budget balances *172*;
    credit activity 118, *120*, 122; current
    account balance *120*, *152*; current
    account deficit 119; exchange rate
    regime 87, 93; exports 87; external debt
    11, 88, *123*, *124*, 125, 151, *152*, *153*;
    foreign direct investment 125, *126*; GDP
    119, *120*, *153*; GNI per capita **108**;
    government spending 87, *172*; imports
    87; private sector indebtedness 118;
    public debt 12, 86, 95; social security
    spending 87; trade balance *152*; trade
    with EU 87
current account balances **110**, *152*; fastest
    growing economies (1990–2004) *37*;
    G-7 *52*; *see also individual countries*
current account deficits 37, 123, 152;
    Albania 119; Bosnia and Herzegovina
    119, 151, 157, 158, 159; Bulgaria 119;
    Croatia 119; and expansionary fiscal
    policy 85; G-7 countries 50, 51;
    Montenegro 109, 118, 119; Romania
    119; Serbia 119; Spain 51; transition
    countries 39; United States (US) 35, 54,
    55, 56, 64; Western Balkans 109
current account surplus: China 36; Russia
    51

customs policy, Bosnia and Herzegovina 158, 162, 163, 164
Czech Republic 37; current account balance *37*; economic growth 35; external debt *37*; foreign direct investment 38; foreign exchange reserves *37*; interest rates 38

deflation 63
democracy, and economic growth 78
deregulation *see* financial deregulation and liberalization
derivatives markets 2, 3, 33, 63, 64, 65; problems of regulation 23–6
developing countries: external debt *45*; and financial globalization 4; food prices 62; foreign direct investment 41, 43; foreign exchange reserves 1, 19; governments, role of 81; institutional investors in 43; labour costs 41; share in world GDP 42; social insurance systems 43; tax competition between 41; *see also* fast-growing developing countries (FGDC)
development financing 43–5
dollar 17, 54, 63; share in world foreign exchange reserves 18
dotcom bubble 5, 33, 92
Draghi, Mario 20

economic globalization 7–8, 73, 74, 76–7
economic growth 9, 26, 35–40, 128; and business environment 108–10; and democracy 78; and financial globalization 4; and financial integration 122; transition countries 38–9; twenty fastest growing economies 1990–1998–200*4 38*; Western Balkans 26, 108–10; *see also individual countries*
economic policy: United States (US) 65–6; *see also* fiscal policy; monetary policy
economic rights 78
Ecuador 40
Ekelund, Robert B. Jr. 75
electricity generation/distribution, Bosnia and Herzegovina 69, 136, 140, 148
Elektroprivreda BiH dd Sarajevo 174, *175*
Elektroprivreda HZ HB dd Mostar 174, *175*
Elektroprivreda RS ad Trebinje 174–5
employment: Bosnia and Herzegovina 69–70, 136, 148–51, 167; Brazil 62; full 2, 5; informal, Bosnia and Herzegovina 148, 149; United States (US) 2

Estonia: economic growth 39; external debt 151; interest rates 40
ethnic structure, Bosnia and Herzegovina 12
euro 17, 18, 20–3, 35, 63, 91; role of in Western Balkans 87–8
Euro-Balkan bonds 10, 89, 90, 97–100, 127–8
Euro-zone 7; banking sector 20–3; budget deficit 91–2; public debt 91–2; sovereign debt crisis 18, 20–3; and Western Balkans trade 87–8
European Bank for Reconstruction and Development (EBRD) 95, 127, 140, 154–5
European Central Bank (ECB) 63, 91; government bond purchases 21; interest rates 35; monetary policy 18, 20–3
European Financial Stability Facility (EFSF) 7
European Monetary Cooperation Fund 91
European Monetary Institute 91
European Stabilization Mechanism (ESM) 7
European Union (EU) 7, 12; and Bosnia Herzegovina trade 158, 162, 177; fiscal policy 91–2
European Union Guarantee Fund for the Western Balkans 10–11, 89, 98, 99, 127, 128, 176
exchange rate regimes 17, 94; Western Balkans 87, 93; *see also individual countries*
exchange rates 44, 46; fast-growing developing countries (FGDC) 62; fixed 62, 85, 94, 166; flexible 62, 94–5
excise policy, Bosnia and Herzegovina 162–3
export industries, Bosnia and Herzegovina 68–70, 136, *142*
exports 53–4, 123; Bosnia and Herzegovina *68*, 70, 88, 151, 158, 159, 161, 171; Western Balkans 87–8
external debt 9, 11, 121, *152*, *153*; developing countries *45*; and expansionary fiscal policy 85; fastest growing economies (1990–2004) *37*; transition countries 151; Western Balkans 88; *see also individual countries*

Fannie Mae 64
fast-growing developing countries (FGDC): capacity utilization 62; exchange rates 62; inflation 61, 62, 63; interest rates 61–2

Federal Reserve System (the Fed) 17; balance sheet *20*; CPFF (commercial paper funding facility) 63; federal funds rate 18; interest rates 33, 35, 63, 64; monetary policy 17–18, 19, 35; TAF (temporary adjustment facility) 63

financial crisis: Asian (1997–98) 5; Brazil (1999) 5; global (2008–09) 2, 4, 6–7, 17–18, 23, 64–5, 67–71; Mexico (1994) 5; Russia (1998) 5

financial deregulation and liberalization 2–4, 5, 6, 9, 23–4, 33–47, 67, 75, 93

financial globalization 4; and developing countries 4; and economic growth 4

financial innovation 3, 56, 60

financial integration 122

financial markets 33–5, 60, 61; Australia 33; Bosnia and Herzegovina 28; Canada 33; China 33; Japan 33; liberalization of *see* financial deregulation and liberalization; Russia 33; United Kingdom (UK) 33, 60; United States (US) 33, 60, 61, 74, 92

financial sector, Bosnia and Herzegovina 137, 138, 143, 146, 148, 167

financial systems: G-7 59–61; Western Balkans 93

financial trilemma 24

financing, access to 28, 110–11, *112*, *113*, *114*, *115*, 116, 118, 121, 128

Finland, market capitalization *34*

fiscal policy 10, 94–5; Bosnia and Herzegovina 157, 160–1, 162–3, 166–7; European Union (EU) 91–2; expansionary 66, 67, 85, 87, 94; United States (US) 65–6, 92; Western Balkans 85–90, 95–7

Fligstein, Neil 7–8, 80–1

food industry, Bosnia and Herzegovina 136, 145

food prices, and inflation 62

foreign debt *see* external debt

foreign direct investment 9, 125, *126*; Albania *126*; attractiveness of countries for 42; Bosnia and Herzegovina *126*, 137, 140, 145–6, 157, 162, 163, 167, 177; Bulgaria 125, *126*; Central European countries 37, 38; China 6, 42; Croatia 125, *126*; developing countries 41, 43; euro share in 18; export-oriented 128; Macedonia *126*; Romania 125, *126*; Serbia *126*; tax incentives for 41, 128, 163

foreign exchange reserves 1, 18–19; BRIC countries 20; developing countries 19; dollar share in 18; euro share in 18; fastest growing economies (1990–2004) *37*; Southeast Asian countries 20; *see also individual countries*

France: balance of trade *52*; bank assets 22; budget deficit 92; capital markets 60; commercial banks 60; current account balance *52*; economic growth 36; exports 53; financial system 60; imports 53; market capitalization *34*, 60; share in world GDP *42*, 49, *52*; wealth coefficient *50*

Freddie Mac 64

free markets 75

Friedrich, Christian 122

full employment 2, 5

futures 3

G-4 *see* BRIC countries

G-7 57; balance of trade *52*; consumer price index 62; current account balance *52*; current account deficit 50, 51; financial systems 59–61; share in world GDP 1, *42*, 49–50, *52*, 74; wealth coefficients *50*

Gambia 159

gas-producing countries 50

GDP *109*, *153*; Albania 95–6, *120*, *153*; Bosnia and Herzegovina *see* Bosnia; Bulgaria 108, *120*, *153*; Croatia 119, *120*, *153*; Greece 108; India **51**, *52*; Macedonia *120*, *153*; Montenegro 109, *120*, *153*; Poland 96; Romania 108, 119, *120*, *153*; Serbia *120*; Slovenia *153*; Turkey 108; Western Balkans 88

GDP, world *52*, 64, 65; BRIC countries share in 1, 49, **51**, *52*; by region *44*; China share in 49, **51**, *52*, 74; developing countries share in 42; G-7 share in 1, *42*, 49–50, *52*, 74; Japan share in 1, *42*, 49, **50**; over-the-counter markets (OTC) and 23; US share in 1, *42*, 49, **50**; Western Balkans share of 93

Germany: balance of trade *52*; bank assets 22; bank lending 61; and Bosnia and Herzegovina trade 158, 159; budget deficit 92; capital markets 60; commercial banks 60; current account balance *52*; economic growth 36; exports 53; financial system 60, 61; imports 53, 54; market capitalization *34*,

Index 185

60; share in world GDP *42*, 49, *52*;
unification of 73; wealth coefficient *50*
globalization *see* economic globalization;
financial globalization; political
globalization
GNI per capita, Western Balkans **108**, 109
goods markets 45; Bosnia and
Herzegovina 28
government bonds 88, 94, 95, 98, 127;
Bosnia and Herzegovina 167, 176; ECB
purchase of 21; *see also* Euro-Balkan
bonds
government debt *see* external debt; public
debt
government securities 45; US 19–20
government spending 94, 95; Albania *172*;
Bosnia and Herzegovina 70, 87, 171–2;
Croatia 87, *172*; Macedonia *172*;
Montenegro *172*; Serbia 87, *172*;
Western Balkans 171
governments, role of 81
Great Britain *see* United Kingdom (UK)
Greece: budget deficit 91; business
environment 107, *115*; competitiveness
111; current account balance *37*; debt to
IMF 27; external debt *37*; financing,
access to 111; foreign exchange reserves
37; GDP 108; public debt 12, 91
Greenspan, Alan 80
Guatemala: current account balance *37*;
economic growth 35; external debt *37*;
foreign exchange reserves *37*

Hayek, Friedrich 77
Hayes, Donald 11
Hebert, Robert F. 75
hedge funds 5
Hinduism 79
Hong Kong 57; current account balance
53; economic growth 36; foreign
exchange reserves *53*; market
capitalization *34*
households: credit to 116, 117, 122, 123,
168, 169; securities investment 61
HT Mostar dd Mostar 174, *175*
human capital 8, 99, 135
human development index (HDI) 159;
Bosnia and Herzegovina 159–60, 177
Hungary 37, 122; current account balance
37; economic growth 35, 38, 39;
external debt *37*; foreign direct
investment 37; foreign exchange
reserves *37*; interest rates 38
Hypo-Alpe-Adria Group 167

Iceland, economic growth 36
imperfect competition 47
imperfect markets 74
imports 53, 54; Bosnia and Herzegovina
68, 70, 151, 158, 161, 163, 171; Western
Balkans 87
income tax 66; *see also* corporate income
tax; personal income tax
India 1, 49, 73; capacity utilization 62;
current account balance 53; economic
growth 74; food prices 62; foreign
exchange reserves *53*; GDP **51**, *52*;
inflation 61; poverty 74; wealth
coefficient *51*
Indonesia 57; food prices 62
inequality, social 73
inflation 17, 61–3, 73; and food prices 62
infrastructure projects: Bosnia and
Herzegovina 135, 145, 155; Western
Balkans 88, 89, 98, 99
Institute of International Finance (IIF)
121
institutional investors 43, 59, 60, 127, 128
insurance companies 59
interest rates 2, 37, 41, 56, 93, 94; Bank of
England 63; Bosnia and Herzegovina
67; European Central Bank (ECB) 35,
63; and fast-growing developing
countries (FGDC) 61–2, 63; short-term
46; transition countries 38, 39, 40;
United Kingdom (UK) 3; United States
(US) 3, 33, 35, 63, 66
International Financial Corporation (IFC)
145
International Monetary Fund (IMF) 1, 7,
17, 37, 43, 66, 95, 124, 125; Bosnia and
Herzegovina debt to 12, 27, 123, *124*,
173–4; country quotas 57–9; country
voting rights 59; Ireland debt to 12, *27*;
Kosovo debt to 125; Macedonia debt to
27, 123, 125; Romania debt to *27*, 123,
124; Serbia debt to *27*, 123, 124
international trade *see* trade
Intesa Sanpaolo Sarajevo 168
Investment Development Bank of the
Republic of Srpska 175
Iraq, US-led invasion of 80
Ireland 5; banking sector 6; current
account balance *37*; debt to IMF 12, *27*;
economic growth 35, 36, 38; external
debt *37*; foreign exchange reserves *37*;
interest rates 37; public debt 6, 12
Islamic fundamentalism 79, 80
Israel 80

Italy: balance of trade *52*; bank assets 22; bank lending 61; budget deficit 92; capital markets 60; commercial banks 60; current account balance *52*; economic growth 36; financial system 60; GDP *42*; market capitalization *34*, 60; public debt 91, 92; wealth coefficient *50*

Japan 73; balance of trade *52*; banking sector *25*, 60; capital markets 60; current account balance *52*; economic growth 36; exports 53; financial markets 33; financial system 60; GDP *42*; imports 53, 54; market capitalization *34*, 60; property prices 5; share prices 5; share in world GDP 1, 49, **50**, *52*; wealth coefficient *50*
Judaism 79

Kalemli-Ozcan, Sebnem 119, 121
Kamil, Herman 119, 121
Kazakhstan 151
Keynes, J.M. 6, 7, 9, 46, 65–7, 92
Kose, A.M. 4
Kosovo 87, 119; business environment *102*; debt to IMF 125; exchange rate regime 87, 93; external debt 11; monetary policy 93; public debt 12
Kuwait: current account balance *37*; external debt *37*; foreign exchange reserves *37*; savings 37
Kyrghyz Republic 151

labour 11
labour costs, developing countries 41
labour market efficiency, Bosnia and Herzegovina 28
Latvia: economic growth 39; external debt 151; interest rates 40; wealth coefficient 39
Lebanon: current account balance *37*; economic growth 35; external debt *37*; foreign exchange reserves *37*
Lehman Brothers 17, 65
Lintner, John 9, 125
Lipset, Seymour Martin 78
liquidity risk 40, 41
Lithuania: economic growth 39; interest rates 40
Long Term Capital Management (LTCM) hedge fund 5
long-term refinancing operations 21
Luxembourg, economic growth 36

Maastricht Treaty 35, 86, 91
Macedonia 27, 87, 119; business environment 102–3, 107, 108, *113*; competitiveness *111*, 159; consolidated budget balances *172*; credit activity 116, 117, *118*, 120, 122; current account balance *120*, *152*; debt to IMF *27*, 123, 125; economic growth 39; exchange rate regime 87, 93; exports 87; external debt 11, *123*, *124*, *152*, *153*; financing, access to 111; foreign direct investment *126*; GDP *120*, *153*; GNI per capita **108**, 109; government spending *172*; imports 87; public debt 12, 86, 95; trade balance *152*; trade with EU 87; wealth coefficient 39
McKinnon, Ronald 2, 3, 37, 54
main refinancing operations (MRO) 21
Malaysia 57
manufacturing industry, Bosnia and Herzegovina 136, 138, 143, 145, 148, 167
market capitalization 33, 60, 61; major world capital markets *34*
market economies, political-cultural approach to 80–1
market fundamentalism 7, 74–7
Markowitz, Harry 9, 125
'me first rule' 75, 76, 77
metal sector 8; Bosnia and Herzegovina 69–70, 136, 145, 155, 176
Mexico 57; financial crisis (1994) 5; interest rates 61
military industry, Bosnia and Herzegovina 136
mining industry, Bosnia and Herzegovina 138, 140, 143, 148
MJP Elektroprivreda a.d. RS 30
Moldova 151
monetary policy 10; Bosnia and Herzegovina 166; European Central Bank (ECB) 18, 20–3; US/Federal Reserve 17–18, 19, 35, 65–6, 92; Western Balkans 93
monetary targeting 17
money supply 93
Montenegro 9, 119; business environment 102, 107, 108, *113*; competitiveness 110, *111*, 159; consolidated budget balances *172*; credit activity 117–18, 119, *120*, 122; current account balance *120*, *152*; current account deficit 109, 118, 119; economic growth 109; exchange rate regime 87, 93; external

Index   187

debt 11, 88, 118, *123*, 124, 151, *152, 153*; financing, access to 111; GDP *120, 153*; GNI per capita **108**, 109; government spending *172*; monetary policy 93; private sector indebtedness 118; public debt 12, 86, 95; trade balance *152*
Mundell–Fleming model 10, 85, 93–5, 166–7
Mussa, Michael 3–4, 55
mutual funds 59, 60

Namibia 159
National Bank of China 63
national debt *see* external debt; public debt
NATO 12
neo-Marxism 8
neoliberalism 8
Netherlands, market capitalization *34*
Nicaragua: current account balance *37*; economic growth 35; external debt *37*; foreign exchange reserves *37*
Nixon, Richard 17
NLB Group 168
non-performing loans (NPLs) 96, 116, 169
Norway, economic growth 36
Nova Banka Banja Luka 168

Obama, Barack 23, 66, 67
Obstfeld, Maurice 4
O'Connor, Stephen 24
oil, and Iraq war 80
oil prices 63
oil-producing countries 50
Ongena, Steven 122
open economy 85, 93, 95, 100n6
open society 7, 77
options 3
outright market purchase (OMP) 21
over-the-counter (OTC) markets 2, 23–4, 64, 65

Palestine 80
Paraguay 40
pension funds 43, 59
pension insurance systems 43
People's Bank of China 18
perfect capital mobility 94, 95
personal income tax, Bosnia and Herzegovina 70, 150, 151, 160
pharmaceutical industry 8; Bosnia and Herzegovina 145
Philippines 57
Poland 37; current account balance *37*; economic growth 35; external debt *37*; foreign direct investment 37; foreign exchange reserves *37*; GDP growth 96; interest rates 38
policy instability, as barrier to business *112*, *113*, *114*, *115*
political globalization 7, 73, 76–7
political rights 78
political sovereignty, theory of limited 73
Popov, Alexander 122
Popper, Karl 77
portfolio investment 43, 125, 127–8
Portugal, debt to IMF *27*
poverty 6, 46; Africa 74; India 74
Prasad, E. 4
private sector 46; credit to 118, 119
privatization: banking sector 9; Bosnia and Herzegovina 136, 137, 154, 167, 176
Prodi, Romano 92
production multiplier 94, 95
profit maximization 77
property prices, Japan 5
Protestantism 78–9
public debt 7, 9, 11–12, 20, 45, 46, 66–7, 94, 95; Albania 86, 95, 96; Belgium 91, 92; Bosnia and Herzegovina 11, *31*, 70, 86, 95, 167, 173–4, 175, 176; Croatia 12, 86, 95; Euro-zone 91–2; Greece 12, 91; Ireland 6, 12; Italy 91, 92; Kosovo 12; Macedonia 12, 86, 95; Montenegro 12, 86, 95; Russia 39; Serbia 12, 86, 95; Slovenia 12; United States (US) 7, 18, 92; Western Balkans 86, 95; *see also* external debt
public spending *see* government spending
public–private partnerships 98
purchasing power, Bosnia and Herzegovina 68, 173

Qatar 37
quantitative easing 19

Raiffeisen Bank 167
rational expectations hypothesis 4–5, 76
real business cycles 4–5
real estate 123, 125; Bosnia and Herzegovina 146
recession, world (2001–2002) 35
reflexivity 76
regional central banks 45
Regional Cooperation Council, Memorandum of Understanding (March 2012) 125
regional financing 43–5

religious fundamentalism 7, 78–80
Republika Srpska (RS) 30–1, 174–5; debt and deposits *31*; social welfare contributions 150–1; tax burden 150; unemployment 149
retail and wholesale trade, Bosnia and Herzegovina 145–6, 148
Robinson, Joan 47
Rogof, K. 4
Romania: business environment *102*, 106–7; competitiveness 110, *111*, 159; corruption 111; credit activity *118*, 118, 119, *120*; current account balance *120*, *152*; current account deficit 119; debt to IMF 27, 123, 124; external debt *123*, *124*, *152*, *153*; financing, access to 111, 116; foreign direct investment 125, *126*; GDP 108, 119, *120*, *153*; trade balance *152*
Russia 1, 39–40, 49; budget deficit 39; current account balance *53*; current account surplus 51; economic growth 39; exchange rate regime 39; external debt 39; financial crisis (1998) 5; financial markets 33; food prices 62; foreign exchange reserves 39, 52, *53*; inflation 61; interest rates 39, 40, 61–2; public debt 39; savings rate 40; share in world GDP **51**, *52*; wealth coefficient 39, *51*

Sanchez-Villegas, Carolina 119, 121
Saudi Arabia 62
savings 2, 3, 37, 40; United States 3, 54, 55
Schnabel, Isabel 122
Scholes, Myron 5
securities markets 59–60; household investment in 61; *see also* corporate securities; government securities
Serbia 27, 87, 119, 158, 159; business environment *102*, 105, 108, *113*; competitiveness 110, *111*, 159; consolidated budget balances *172*; credit activity 118, *120*; current account balance *120*, *152*; current account deficit 119; debt to IMF 27, 123, 124; exchange rate regime 87, 93; external debt 11, *123*, *124*, 151, *152*, *153*; financing, access to 111, 116; foreign direct investment *126*; GDP *120*, *153*; GNI per capita **108**, 109; government spending 87, *172*; public debt 12, 86, 95; social security spending 87; trade balance *152*; trade with EU 87

service sector 45, 123; Bosnia and Herzegovina 138, 148, 149
share prices 5; Japan 5
shareholder yield 75
shares 59
Sharpe, William F. 9, 125
Shaw, Edward 2, 3, 37, 54
Singapore 57; current account balance *53*; economic growth 36; foreign exchange reserves *53*; savings 37
Slovak Republic 37; current account balance *37*; economic growth 38, 39; external debt *37*; foreign exchange reserves *37*; interest rates 38
Slovenia 40; credit activity 122; current account balance *37*, *152*; exports 88; external debt 11, 37, 88, *152*, *153*; foreign exchange reserves *37*; GDP *153*; public debt 12; trade balance *152*
Smith, Adam 41, 75
social inequality 73
social insurance systems, transition countries 43
social security contributions, Bosnia and Herzegovina 150–1, 161
social security spending 87
social transfers, Western Balkans 172
solvency risk 40
Soros, George 7, 64, 75, 76, 77
South Korea 5; current account balance *37*, 39, *53*; economic growth 38, 39; exchange rate regime 39; external debt *37*; foreign exchange reserves *37*, 39, *53*; interest rates 61; wealth coefficient 39
Southeast Asia 20, 57; exports 53; imports 53
sovereignty, limited 73
Spain: current account deficit 51; economic growth 36; market capitalization *34*
Stability and Growth Pact 20, 23, 92
Stabilization and Association Agreement (SAA), EU–Bosnia Herzegovina 158, 162, 177
Stiglitz, Joseph 3, 7, 76–7
stock exchanges, integration of 11, 89–90
Strauss-Kahn, Dominique 66, 85
swap contracts 3, 23
Sweden, market capitalization *34*
systemic risk 41

T-bills 19–20
TAF (temporary adjustment facility) 63

Index 189

Taiwan: current account balance *52*;
foreign exchange reserves *53*
Tajikistan 151
tax: as barrier to business 111, *112*, *114*,
115, 128; Bosnia and Herzegovina 26,
27, 146, 150–1, 160–1; on consumption
41, 66; incentives for FDI 41, 128, 163;
increases in 94, 95; indirect, Bosnia and
Herzegovina 26, 27, 146, 150, 154;
profit 150; *see also* corporate income
tax; income tax; personal income tax;
value added tax (VAT)
Taylor, Alan 4
telecommunications, media, and
technology (TMT) sector 33, 35
Telekom Srbije 175
Telekom Srpske 175
temporary adjustment facility (TAF) 63
Thailand 57
Thatcher, Margaret 2
Thurow, Lester 79
tourism industry, Bosnia and Herzegovina
136, 138, 140, 146–7, 148, 176, 177
trade: Bosnia and Herzegovina 138, 140,
143, 148, 158, 162, 177; Euro-zone–
Western Balkans 87–8; trends in 53–5
trade balance *152*; Bosnia and
Herzegovina *68*, 151, *152*, **171**
trade deficit 39, 123; Bosnia and
Herzegovina 68, 151, 157, 158–9,
170–1; and expansionary fiscal policy
85; transition countries 39; United States
(US) 3, 35, 54, 55–7, 64
trade liberalization 85, 93, 118–19
trade policy, Bosnia and Herzegovina 157–64
trade surplus, China 36
trade volume 123; Bosnia and Herzegovina
68, **171**
transition countries: budget deficit 171;
current account deficit 39; economic
growth 38–9; governments, role of 81;
indebtedness 151; interest rates 38, 39,
40; social insurance systems 43; trade
deficit 39; vulnerability indicators 40
transport and communications, Bosnia and
Herzegovina 138, 140
Treynor, Jack 9, 125
Turkey 57, 111, 158; business environment
107–8, *115*; competitiveness *111*; GDP
108

unemployment 6, 9, 46; Bosnia and
Herzegovina 12, 148–9, *150*, 172–3; US
2

UniCredit Mostar 167
United Kingdom (UK): balance of trade
52; Big Bang reforms (1986) 2–3;
commercial banks 60; current account
balance 52; economic growth 36;
financial markets 33, 60; financial
system 59, 60; foreign direct investment
42; institutional investors 43, 60;
interest rates 3; market capitalization *34*,
60; share in world GDP *42*, 49, *52*;
wealth coefficient *50*
United States Agency for International
Development (USAID) 147, 177
United States (US) *42*; balance of trade *52*;
bank lending *25*, 61; budget deficit 35,
64, 66, 92; budget surplus 35; Bush
(George W.) administration 2, 64, 65–6,
80, 92; and China trade 55; Christian
fundamentalism 79; Clinton
administration 2, 92; commercial banks
60; Commodity Futures Modernization
Act (2000) 2, 23–4; current account
balance *52*; current account deficit 35,
54, 55, 56, 64;
Dodd–Frank Act (2010) 3, 23, 24;
economic growth 2;economic policy
65–6; employment growth 2; exports 53,
54; external debt 3, 55, 56; Federal
Open Market Committee (FOMC) 66;
and financial crisis (2008–09) 64–5;
financial innovations 3, 56, 60; financial
markets 33, 60, 61, 74, 92; financial
system 59; fiscal policy 65–6, 92;
foreign direct investment 42; Glass–
Steagall Act (1999) 2; imports 53, 54;
inflation 63, 73; institutional investors
43, 60; interest rates 2, 33, 35, 64, 66;
market capitalization 33, *34*, 60;
monetary policy 17–18, 19, 35, 65–6,
92; 9/11 terrorist attacks on 35, 80, 92;
public debt 7, 18, 92; Reagan
administration 2; savings 3, 54, *55*;
Securities and Exchange Commission
(SEC) 2, 23; securities 19–20; share in
world GDP 1, 49, **50**, *52*;
telecommunications, media, and
technology (TMT) sector 33, 35; trade
deficit 3, 35, 54, 55–7, 64;
unemployment 2; war on terror 35;
wealth coefficient *50*
Uruguay 40

value added tax (VAT), Bosnia and
Herzegovina 30, 68, 163, 173

Venezuela, inflation 61
Vietnam: current account balance *37*; economic growth 35; external debt *37*; foreign exchange reserves *37*
Volcker, Paul 17
vulnerability indicators, transition countries 40

war in Western Balkans (1992–1995) 8, 11, 86–7, 135
war on terror 35
Washington Consensus 118
wealth, (re)distribution of 73, 80
wealth coefficients 33, 35–6, 38, 39, 138; BRIC countries *51*; G-7 countries *50*
Wei, S.J. 4
Western Balkans 8–12; banking sector 93, 96; budget deficits 86, 171; budget surplus 171; business environment 102–10; central banks 93; consolidated budget balances *172*; current account deficits 109; economic growth 26, 108–10; economic strength of 92–3; euro, role of in 87–8; exchange rate regimes 87, 93; external debt 88; financial liberalization 93, 118–19; financial systems 93; fiscal policy 85–90, 95–7; GDP 88; GNI per capita **108**, 109; government bond issues 88; government spending 171; human capital 8, 99; infrastructure projects 88, 89, 98, 99; monetary policy 93; public debt 86, 95; share of world GDP 93; social transfers 172; trade with Eurozone 87–8; trade liberalization 93, 118–19; wartime devastation 8, 11, 86–7, 135
Western Balkans Stock Exchange (WBSE) 11, 89–90
Western European Union 12
wholesale trade *see* retail and wholesale trade
Wolfensohn, James 42–3
wood processing industry 8; Bosnia and Herzegovina 69, 136, 154, 176, 177
Woodruff, Judy 64
World Bank 1, 3, 37, 42, 95, 137, 140
World Economic Forum, *Global Competitiveness Report* 110

Yesin, Pinar 122
Yoshitomi, Masaru 3–4, 55
Yugoslavia 8, 73, 86–7

Zettelmeyer, Jeromin 122